THE DIARY OF A
BOOKSELLER

THE DIARY OF A
BOOKSELLER

SHAUN BYTHELL

P

PROFILE BOOKS

First published in Great Britain in 2017 by
PROFILE BOOKS LTD
3 Holford Yard
Bevin Way
London
WC1X 9HD
www.profilebooks.com

10 9 8 7 6 5 4 3 2 1

Typeset in Granjon by MacGuru Ltd
Printed and bound in Great Britain by Clays, St Ives plc

A CIP catalogue record for this book is available from the British Library.

ISBN 978 1 78125 862 0
eISBN 978 1 78283 363 5

FEBRUARY

Would I like to be a bookseller *de métier*? On the whole – in spite of my employer's kindness to me, and some happy days I spent in the shop – no.

George Orwell, 'Bookshop Memories', London, November 1936

Orwell's reluctance to commit to bookselling is understandable. There is a stereotype of the impatient, intolerant, antisocial proprietor – played so perfectly by Dylan Moran in *Black Books* – and it seems (on the whole) to be true. There are exceptions of course, and many booksellers do not conform to this type. Sadly, I do. It was not always thus, though, and before buying the shop I recall being quite amenable and friendly. The constant barrage of dull questions, the parlous finances of the business, the incessant arguments with staff and the unending, exhausting, haggling customers have reduced me to this. Would I change any of it? No.

When I first saw The Book Shop in Wigtown I was eighteen years old, back in my home town and about to leave for university. I clearly remember walking past it with a friend and commenting that I was quite certain that it would be closed within the year. Twelve years later, while visiting my parents at Christmas time, I called in to see if they had a copy of *Three Fevers* in stock, by Leo Walmsley, and while I was talking to the owner, admitted to him that I was struggling to find a job I enjoyed. He suggested that I buy his shop since he was keen to retire. When I told him that I didn't have any money, he replied, 'You don't need money – what do you think banks are for?' Less than a year later, on 1 November 2001, a month (to the day) after my thirty-first birthday, the place became mine. Before I took over, I ought perhaps to have read a piece of George Orwell's writing published in 1936. 'Bookshop Memories' rings as true today as it did then, and sounds a salutary warning to anyone as naive as I was that the world of selling second-hand books is not quite an idyll of sitting in an armchair by a roaring fire with your slipper-clad feet up, smoking a pipe and reading Gibbon's *Decline and Fall* while a stream of charming customers engages you in intelligent conversation, before parting with fistfuls of cash. In fact, the truth could scarcely be more different. Of all his observations in that essay, Orwell's comment that 'many of the people who came to us were of the kind who would be a nuisance anywhere but have special opportunities in a bookshop' is perhaps the most apposite.

Orwell worked part-time in Booklover's Corner in Hampstead while he was working on *Keep the Aspidistra Flying*, between 1934 and 1936. His friend Jon Kimche described him as appearing to resent selling anything to anyone – a sentiment with which many booksellers will doubtless be familiar. By way of illustration of the similarities – and often the differences – between bookshop life today and in Orwell's time, each month here begins with an extract from 'Bookshop Memories'.

The Wigtown of my childhood was a busy place. My two younger sisters and I grew up on a small farm about a mile from the town, and it seemed to us like a thriving metropolis when compared with the farm's flat, sheep-spotted, salt-marsh fields. It is home to just under a thousand people and is in Galloway, the forgotten south-west corner of Scotland. Wigtown is set into a landscape of rolling drumlins on a peninsula known as the Machars (from the Gaelic word *machair*, meaning fertile, low-lying grassland) and is contained by forty miles of coastline which incorporates everything from sandy beaches to high cliffs and caves. To the north lie the Galloway Hills, a beautiful, near-empty wilderness through which winds the Southern Upland Way. The town is dominated by the County Buildings, an imposing hôtel-de-ville-style town hall which was once the municipal headquarters of what is known locally as 'the Shire'. The economy of Wigtown was for many years sustained by a Co-operative Society creamery and Scotland's most southerly whisky distillery, Bladnoch, which between them accounted for a large number of the working population. Back then, agriculture provided far more opportunities for the farm worker than it does today, so there was employment in and about the town. The creamery closed in 1989 with the loss of 143 jobs; the distillery – founded in 1817 – closed in 1993. The impact on the town was transformative. Where there had been an ironmonger, a greengrocer, a gift shop, a shoe shop, a sweet shop and a hotel, instead there were now closed doors and boarded-up windows.

Now, though, a degree of prosperity has returned, and with it a sense of optimism. The vacant buildings of the creamery have slowly been taken over by small businesses: a blacksmith, a recording studio and a stovemaker now occupy much of it. The distillery re-opened for production on a small scale in 2000 under the enthusiastic custody of Raymond Armstrong, a businessman from Northern Ireland. Wigtown too has seen a favourable change in its fortunes, and is now home to a community of bookshops and booksellers. The once boarded-up windows and doors are open again, and behind them small businesses thrive.

Everyone who has worked in the shop has commented that customer interactions throw up more than enough material to write a book – Jen Campbell's *Weird Things Customers Say in Bookshops* is evidence enough of this – so, afflicted with a dreadful memory, I began to write things down as they happened in the shop as an *aide-mémoire* to help me possibly write something in the future. If the start date seems arbitrary, that's because it is. It just happened to occur to me to begin doing this on 5 February, and the *aide-mémoire* became a diary.

WEDNESDAY, 5 FEBRUARY

Online orders: 5
Books found: 5

Telephone call at 9.25 a.m. from a man in the south of England who is considering buying a bookshop in Scotland. He was curious to know how to value the stock of a bookshop with 20,000 books. Avoiding the obvious answer of 'ARE YOU INSANE?', I asked him what the current owner had suggested. She had told him that the average price of a book in her shop was £6 and that she suggested dividing that total of £120,000 by three. I told him that he should divide it by ten at the very least, and probably by thirty. Shifting bulk quantities these days is near impossible as so few people are prepared to take on large numbers of books, and the few that do pay an absolute pittance. Bookshops are now scarce, and stock is plentiful. It is a buyer's market. Even when things were good back in 2001 – the year I bought the shop – the previous owner valued the stock of 100,000 books at £30,000.

Perhaps I ought to have advised the man on the telephone to read (along with Orwell's 'Bookshop Memories') William Y. Darling's extraordinary *The Bankrupt Bookseller Speaks Again* before he committed to buying the shop. Both are works that aspirant booksellers would be well advised to read. Darling was not in fact *The Bankrupt Bookseller* but an Edinburgh draper who perpetrated the utterly convincing hoax that such a person did indeed exist. The detail is uncannily precise. Darling's fictitious bookseller – 'untidy, unhealthy, to the casual, an uninteresting human figure but still, when roused, one who can mouth things about books as eloquently as any' – is as accurate a portrait of a second-hand bookseller as any.

Nicky was working in the shop today. The business can no longer afford to support any full-time staff, particularly in the long, cold winters, and I am reliant on Nicky – who is as capable as she is eccentric – to cover the shop two days a week so that I can go out buying or do other work. She is in her late forties, and has two grown-up sons. She lives in a croft overlooking Luce Bay, about fifteen miles from Wigtown, and is one of Jehovah's Witnesses, and that – along with her hobby of making strangely useless 'craft' objects – defines her. She makes many of her own clothes and is as frugal as a miser, although extremely generous with what little she has. Every Friday she brings me a treat that she has found in the skip behind Morrisons supermarket in Stranraer the previous night, after her meeting at Kingdom Hall. She calls this 'Foodie Friday'. Her sons describe her as a 'slovenly gypsy', but she is as much part of the fabric of the shop as the books, and the place would lose a large part of its charm without her. Although it wasn't a Friday today, she brought in some revolting food which she had pillaged from the Morrisons skip: a packet of samosas that had become so soggy that they were barely identifiable as such. Rushing in from the driving rain, she thrust it in my face and said 'Eh, look at that – samosas. Lovely', then proceeded to eat one of them, dropping sludgy bits of it over the floor and the counter.

During the summers I take on students – one or two. It allows me the freedom to indulge in some of the activities that make living in Galloway so idyllic. The writer Ian Niall once wrote that as a child at Sunday school he was convinced that the 'land of milk and honey' to which the teacher referred was Galloway – in part because there was always an abundance of both in the pantry of the farmhouse in which he grew up, but also because, for him, it was a kind of paradise. I share his love of the place. These girls who work in the shop afford me the luxury of being able to pick my moment to go fishing or hill-walking or swimming. Nicky refers to them as my 'wee pets'.

The first customer (at 10.30 a.m.) was one of our few regulars: Mr Deacon. He is a well-spoken man in his mid-fifties with the customary waistline that accompanies inactive middle-aged men; his dark, thinning hair is combed over his pate in the unconvincing way that some balding men try to persuade others that they still retain a luxuriant mane. He is smartly enough dressed inasmuch as his clothes are clearly well cut, but he does not wear them well: there is little attention to detail such as shirt tails, buttons or flies. It appears as though someone has loaded his clothes into a cannon and fired them at him, and however they have landed upon him they have stuck. In many ways he is the ideal customer; he never browses and only ever comes in when he knows exactly what he wants. His request is usually accompanied by a cut-out review of the book from *The Times*, which he presents to whichever of us happens to be at the counter. His language is curt and precise, and he never engages in small talk but is never rude and always pays for his books on collection. Beyond this, I know nothing about him, not even his first name. In fact, I often wonder why he orders books through me when he could so easily do so on Amazon. Perhaps he does not own a computer. Perhaps he does not want one. Or perhaps he is one of the dying breed who understand that, if they want bookshops to survive, they have to support them.

At noon a woman in combat trousers and a beret came to the counter with six books, including two nearly new, expensive art books in pristine condition. The total for the books came to £38; she asked for a discount, and when I told her that she could have them for £35, she replied, 'Can't you do them for £30?' It weighs heavily upon my faith in human decency when customers – offered a discount on products that are already a fraction of their original cover price – feel entitled to demand almost 30 per cent further off, so I refused to discount them any further. She paid the £35. Janet Street-Porter's suggestion that anyone wearing combat trousers should be forcibly parachuted into a demilitarised zone now has my full support.

Till total £274.09*
27 customers

---

* This figure does not take into account our online sales, the money for which Amazon deposits into the shop's bank account every fortnight. Online turnover is considerably less than that of the shop, averaging £42 per day. Since 2001, when I bought the shop, there have been tectonic shifts in the book trade, to which we have had no choice but to adapt. Back then online selling was in its relative infancy, and AbeBooks was the only real player for second-hand books; Amazon at that point sold only new books. Because AbeBooks was set up by booksellers, the costs were kept as low as possible. It was a very good means of selling more expensive books – the sort that might have otherwise been hard to sell in the shop – and because there were relatively few of us selling through it back then, we could realise pretty decent prices. Now, of course, Amazon is consuming everything in its path. It has even consumed AbeBooks, taking it over in 2008, and the online market-place is now saturated with books, both real and electronic. Yet we have no real alternative but to use Amazon and AbeBooks through which to sell our stock online, so reluctantly we do. Competition has driven prices to a point at which online bookselling is reduced to either a hobby or a big industry dominated by a few huge players with vast warehouses and heavily discounted postal contracts. The economies of scale make it impossible for the small or medium-sized business to compete. At the heart of it all is Amazon, and while it would be unfair to lay all the woes of the industry at Amazon's feet, there can be no doubt that it has changed things for everyone. Jeff Bezos did not register the domain name 'relentless.com' without reason. The total for the number of customers may also be misleading – it is not representative of footfall, merely of the number of customers who buy books. Normally, the footfall is around five times the figure for the number who buy.

THURSDAY, 6 FEBRUARY

Online orders: 6
Books found: 5

Our online stock consists of 10,000 books from our total stock of 100,000. We list it on a database called Monsoon, which uploads to Amazon and ABEBooks. Today an Amazon customer emailed about a book called *Why Is There Something Rather Than Nothing?* His complaint: 'I have not received my book yet. Please resolve this matter. So far I did not write any review about your service.' This thinly veiled threat is increasingly common, thanks to Amazon feedback, and unscrupulous customers have been known to use it to negotiate partial and even full refunds when they have received the book they ordered. This book was posted out last Tuesday and should have arrived by now, so either this customer is fishing for a refund or there has been a problem with Royal Mail, which happens extremely rarely. I replied, asking them to wait until Monday, after which, if it still has not arrived, we will refund them.

After lunch I sorted through some boxes of theological books that a retired Church of Scotland minister had brought in last week. Collections that focus on a single subject are usually desirable, as buried among them will almost certainly be a few scarce items of interest to collectors, and usually valuable. Theology is probably the only exception to this rule, and this proved to be the case today: there was nothing of any consequence.

After the shop closed at 5 p.m. I went to the co-op to buy food for supper. A hole has recently worn through the left pocket of my trousers, and I keep putting my change there, forgetting about it. At bedtime, when I undressed, I found £1.22 in my left boot.

Till total £95.50
6 customers

FRIDAY, 7 FEBRUARY

Online orders: 2
Books found: 2

Today was a beautiful sunny day. Nicky arrived at 9.13 a.m., wearing the black Canadian ski suit that she bought in the charity shop in Port William for £5. This is her standard uniform between the months of November and April. It is a padded onesie, designed for skiing, and it makes her look like the lost Teletubby. During this period she emits a constant whine about the temperature of the shop, which is, admittedly, on the chilly side. She drives a blue minibus, which suits her hoarder lifestyle ideally. All the seats have been removed, and in their place can be found anything from sacks of manure to broken office chairs. She calls the van Bluebell but I have taken to calling it Bluebottle, as that is largely what it contains.

Norrie (former employee, now working as a self-employed joiner) came in at 9 a.m. to repair a leak on the roof of the Fox's Den, the summerhouse in the garden.

Over these past fifteen years members of staff have come and they have gone, but – until recently – there has always been at least one full-time employee. Some have been splendid, some diabolical; nearly all remain friends. In the early years I took on students to help in the shop on Saturdays, which the full-time staff did not like to work, and between 2001 and 2008 turnover increased steadily and strongly, despite the obvious trend towards buying online. Then – after Lehman Brothers went to the wall in September of that year – things nose-dived and turnover was back where we started in 2001, but with overheads that had risen considerably during the good times.

Norrie and I built the Fox's Den a few years ago, and during Wigtown's annual book festival we use it as a venue for very small and unusual events. Last year the most tattooed man in Scotland gave a twenty-minute talk about the history of tattooing, and stripped down to his underpants to illustrate various elements of it as the talk progressed. An elderly woman, mistaking the building for a toilet, inadvertently wandered in towards the end of the talk to find him standing there, almost naked. I'm not sure that she has recovered.

As he was leaving, Norrie and Nicky had a heated discussion about something that I caught the tail end of. It appeared to be about evolution. This is a favourite topic of Nicky's, and it's not uncommon to find copies of *On the Origin of Species* in the fiction section, put there by her. I retaliate by putting copies of the Bible (which she considers history) in among the novels.

Found a book called *Gay Agony*, by the unlikely-sounding author H. A. Manhood, as I was going through the theology books brought in by the retired minister. Apparently Manhood lived in a converted railway carriage in Sussex.

Till total £67
4 customers

SATURDAY, 8 FEBRUARY

Online orders: 4
Books found: 4

Today Nicky covered the shop so that I could travel to Leeds to look at a private library of 600 books on aviation. Anna and I left the shop at 10 a.m., and as we were leaving, Nicky advised, 'Look at the books, think of a figure, then halve it.' She also told me that when the apocalypse comes and only the Jehovah's Witnesses are left on earth (or whatever her version of the apocalypse is – I do not pay much attention when she starts on religion), she intends to come round to my house and take my stuff. She keeps eyeing up various pieces of my furniture with this clearly in mind.

Anna is my partner, and is an American writer twelve years my junior. We share the four-bedroom flat above the shop with a black cat called Captain, named after the blind sea captain in *Under Milk Wood*. Anna worked for NASA in Los Angeles and came to Wigtown for a working holiday in 2008 to fulfil an ambition to work in a bookshop in Scotland, near the sea. There was an immediate attraction between us, and following a brief return to California, she decided to come back. In 2012 her story piqued the interest of Anna Pasternak, a journalist who was visiting Wigtown during the book festival that year, and she wrote a piece for the *Daily Mail* about it. Soon afterwards Anna was approached by a publisher who wanted her to write a memoir, and in 2013 her first book, *Three Things You Need to Know About Rockets*, was duly published by Short Books. Despite her literary success, she is a self-confessed 'linguistic impressionist', with a tendency to re-invent language when she speaks that is both endearing and frustrating. Her method of interpreting the words she hears through half-closed ears and repeating them in a version that bears some proximity to the original, but with blurred lines, results in an occasionally incomprehensible stew of words, seasoned with a handful of Yiddish words that she picked up from her grandmother.

The woman selling the aviation books had telephoned last week with a degree of urgency. They had belonged to her late husband, who died a year ago. She has sold the house and is moving out in March. We arrived at her house at 3 p.m. I was instantly distracted by her obvious wig, not to mention horse chestnuts scattered on the floor near the doors and windows. She explained that her husband had died from cancer and that she was now undergoing treatment for the same thing. The books were in a converted loft at the top of a narrow staircase. It took some time to negotiate a price, but we finally agreed on £750 for about 300 books. She was quite happy for me to leave the remainder behind. If only this was always the case. More often than not people want to dispose of the entire collection, particularly when it is a deceased estate. Anna and I loaded fourteen boxes into the van and left for home. The woman seemed relieved to have managed to say goodbye to what was clearly her husband's passion, which she obviously knew she was going to find difficult to part with, despite having no interest in the subject herself. As we were leaving, Anna asked the woman about all the chestnuts around the doors and windows. It transpired that she and Anna both have a fear of spiders, and apparently horse chestnuts release a chemical that repels them.

I bought the van (a red Renault Trafic) two years ago and have almost run it into the ground. Even on the shortest of journeys I am met with enthusiastic waves from people in the oncoming traffic who have clearly mistaken me for their postman.

This aviation collection contained twenty-two Putnam Aeronautical Histories. This is a series about aircraft manufacturers, or even types of aircraft – Fokker, Hawker, Supermarine, Rocket Aircraft, and in the past they have consistently sold well both online and in the shop for between £20 and £40 per volume. So I based my price on the assumption that I could sell the Putnams fairly quickly and recover my costs.

Many book deals begin with a complete stranger calling and explaining that someone close to them has recently died, and that they have been charged with the job of disposing of their books. Understandably, they are often still grieving, and it is almost impossible not to be sucked into their grief, even in the smallest of ways. Going through the books of the person who has died affords an insight into who that person was, their interests and, to a degree, their personality. Now, even when I visit friends, I am drawn to bookcases wherever I see them, and particularly to any incongruity on the shelves which might reveal something I didn't know about them. My own bookcase is as guilty of this as any – among the modern fiction and books about Scottish art and history that populate the shelves can be found a copy of *Talk Dirty Yiddish*, and *Collectable Spoons of the Third Reich* – the former a gift from Anna, and the latter from my friend Mike.

Anna and I drove back from Leeds over Ilkley Moor through the driving winter rain, and returned home at about 7 p.m. I unlocked the door to find piles of books on the floor, boxes everywhere and dozens of emails awaiting me. Nicky appears to gain some sort of sadistic gratification from leaving mountains of books and boxes all over the shop, probably because she knows how fastidious I am about keeping surfaces clear, particularly the floor. Perhaps because she is by nature an untidy person, she is convinced that my desire for order and organisation is highly unusual and entertaining, so she deliberately creates chaos in the shop then accuses me of having OCD when I berate her for it.

Till total £77.50
7 customers

MONDAY, 10 FEBRUARY

Online orders: 8
Books found: 7

Among the orders was one for the *Pebble Mill Good Meat Guide*.

Because we put through a reasonable volume of mail we have a contract with Royal Mail, and rather than take the parcels to the counter in the post office for Wilma, the postmaster, to deal with, we process them online, and every day either Nicky or I will take the sack of franked packages over to the post office's back room, where they are picked up and taken to the sorting office.

The post office in Wigtown, like so many rural post offices, is part of another shop, and ours is a newsagent/toyshop owned by a Northern Irishman called William. Whatever the opposite of a sunny disposition is, William has it. In spades. He never smiles, and complains about absolutely everything. If he is in the shop when I drop the mail bags off, I always make a point of saying good morning to him. On the rare occasions that he bothers to make any sort of response, it is inevitably a muttered 'What's good about it?' or 'It might be a good morning if I wasn't stuck in this awful place.' Generally, the breezier the greeting you salute him with, the more hostile his response will be. As a measure of the depth of his personal well of human misery, he tapes all the magazines in the display stand with three pieces of sellotape so that it is impossible for customers to flick through them. Wilma, in marked contrast, is witty, bright and friendly. The post office is really the hub of Wigtown's community – everyone goes there at some point during the week, and it is where gossip is exchanged and funeral notices are posted.

After lunch the till roll ran out, so I went to look for more and it appears that we have completely run out, so I ordered another twenty rolls, which should see the machine through for two or three years. Hopefully fewer, if business picks up.

Two new subscribers to the Random Book Club today. The Random Book Club is an offshoot of the shop which I set up a few years ago when business was sore and the future looked bleak. For £59 a year subscribers receive a book a month, but they have no say over what genre of book they receive, and quality control is entirely down to me. I am extremely judicious in what I choose to put in the box from which the RBC books are parcelled and sent. Since subscribers are clearly inveterate readers, I always take care to pick books that I think anyone who loves reading for its own sake would enjoy. There is nothing that would require too much technical expertise to understand: a mix of fiction and non-fiction, with the weight slightly towards non-fiction, and some poetry. Among the books going out later this month are a copy of Clive James's *Other Passports*, Lawrence Durrell's *Prospero's Cell*, Iris Murdoch's biography of Sartre, Neville Shute's *A Town Like Alice*, and a book called *100+ Principles of Genetics*. All the books are in good condition, none is ex-library, and some – several of them each year – are hundreds of years old. I estimate that if the members decided to sell the books on eBay, they would more than make their money back. There is a forum on the web site, but nobody uses it, which gives me an insight into the type of person who is attracted to the idea – they don't like clubs where they have to interact with other people. Perhaps that is why I came up with the idea in the first place – it is a sort of Groucho Marx approach to clubs. There are about 150 members and, apart from a minimal amount of advertising in the *Literary Review*, the only marketing I do is to have a web site and Facebook page, neither of which I have updated for some time. Word of mouth seems to have been the best way of marketing it. It has saved me from financial embarrassment during a very difficult time in the book trade.

Till total £119.99
11 customers

TUESDAY, 11 FEBRUARY

Online orders: 7
Books found: 5

Norrie covered the shop so that I could go to the auction in Dumfries, about fifty miles away. This is a general sale, and it is impossible to predict what you're going to find; the saleroom has everything from *chaises-longues* to washing machines, chandeliers, rugs, china, jewellery and sometimes even cars. Initially I began going to buy books, but quickly realised that the cheapest way to furnish the flat above the shop (which was empty when I bought it) was to buy furniture from the sale, so when I had full-time staff in the shop I would religiously drive there every second Tuesday and pick up bargains: pieces of antique furniture far more beautiful and infinitely cheaper than their modern equivalents from IKEA. Very occasionally I will come home with a box of books, but far more likely a Georgian bureau, a stuffed squirrel, a standard lamp or a leather armchair. Among the regulars is a charming retired submariner called Angus. He and I tend to huddle together and discuss the other buyers at the sale. He has nicknames for all of the regulars – Dave the Hat, The Bishop and others – none of them cruel, but all perfectly fitting. Today I returned with a pair of wooden Lillywhites skis, which will be used for a window display, then sold in the shop. Nowadays, because I can no longer afford full-time staff, I rarely have the opportunity to attend the auction.

When Anna is around, we always try to make the effort to go to the auction, and I will find cover for the shop. She adores it but has a £3 maximum bid, which means she always returns with a lot of rubbish, and today was no exception – a job lot that included a brass corgi, five thimbles, an old set of keys and a broken toast rack. On one occasion though, she stretched to £15 for a box of costume jewellery in which she found a ring that she thought looked interesting. She took it to a Bonhams' free valuation day; they suggested that she consign it to a sale. It made £850.

For a few years I have given over the formal drawing room above the shop to an art class for one afternoon a week. It is taught by local artist Davy Brown and takes place every Tuesday. A dozen or so retired ladies make up the group. At this time of year the house is bitterly cold, so I left Norrie instructions to light the fire and put the space heater on for an hour before they were due to arrive, but he forgot. One of them almost needed to be resuscitated. I would happily let them use the space for free, but they kindly pay me enough to cover the heating costs and a bit more beside.

When Anna and I returned to the shop after the auction, I

noticed that the left-hand window display was completely flooded (there is a large window on each side of the door to the shop which we use for themed displays). It has always been a bit leaky, but nothing like as bad as this. I removed all the soaked books and disposed of them. Now, in their place, the window display consists of six mugs, a towel and a saucepan catching the drips. Every year there is something in the house or the shop that demands the attention of a builder, and invariably it comes in the winter, when the weather is battering relentlessly and the coffers are at their emptiest. I try to budget on about £7,000 a year for keeping the roof over my head and the walls standing, and so far this has been pretty much what it has cost.

Eliot – Wigtown Book Festival director – arrived at 7 p.m. In the last weekend of September, and through to the first weekend in October, Wigtown plays host to a literary festival. In the time I have been running the shop this has grown from a handful of events with tiny audiences largely made up of locals to a huge affair with 300-seat marquees and over 200 events, which include cultural luminaries from all quarters. It is an extraordinary festival, and now – from its humble beginnings with a few volunteers running it – it has an office with five paid staff and an audience of several thousand, drawn from all over the world. Eliot was a journalist, and an extremely good one. He moved to Wigtown a few years ago, and it became quickly apparent that he was ideally suited to run the festival, so money was found to pay him and a salaried position created. He has become a good friend, and I am godfather to his second child. Now, sadly, he lives in London and I see less of him than I would wish, but when he attends Festival Company board meetings in Wigtown, he stays with me. As always, shortly after his arrival he removed his shoes and threw them on the floor. Within ten minutes I had tripped over them.

Till total £5
1 customer

WEDNESDAY, 12 FEBRUARY

Online orders: 15
Books found: 14

Cold, dark and miserable day today; driving rain all day. Eliot was in the bath between 8.15 a.m. and 9 a.m., so I missed the opportunity to brush my teeth or wash prior to opening the shop.

In contrast to the weather, Nicky was irksomely bright and cheery all day. We discussed listing books for Fulfilled By Amazon, a service offered by Amazon whereby we list and label books on our database then send them up to their Dunfermline warehouse, where they are stored until ordered by a customer. Amazon's staff will then pick and pack the titles as the orders come in. It solves the problem of lack of space in the shop and is particularly useful when a collection on a subject that might not be a good seller in the shop comes in. Nicky steadfastly refuses to list on FBA, based on a series of questionable judgements that stray into areas of morality and other irrelevant fields of philosophy. I do not fully understand, or even partly understand, why Nicky objects so strongly to FBA, other than that it is a transaction involving Amazon, through whom we already sell some of our shop stock. Very few booksellers think anything positive about Amazon, but it is, sadly, the only shop in town when it comes to online selling. I've given up on trying to reason with her: she nods helpfully at my suggestions and requests, then ploughs on doing exactly as she did before with no regard whatsoever to anything I've said.

We spent part of the morning setting up a Winter Olympics window display in the non-leaking window using the pair of 1920s Lillywhites wooden skis that I bought at the auction yesterday. The other window is still full of pans and mugs collecting water from the leaks.

At lunchtime Anna and I drove to Newton Stewart, from where she caught the bus to Dumfries, then the train back to London.

At 2 p.m. a man with a Mugabe-style moustache brought in two boxes of books on art and the cinema. He had his eye on a few books in the shop, so we agreed on £30 credit for the books he brought in. This is an almost daily occurrence and is one of the ways we acquire stock, other than house clearances. Most days at least one person will come in to sell books, and about 100 books a day come into the shop this way. Normally, we reject about 70 per cent of them, but more often than not the person bringing them in will want to leave the entire lot. This creates a problem with the shop filling up with boxes of books that we don't want. Usually we pay cash for books brought into the shop, as the quantities do not require recourse to the chequebook. For these transactions we have a handsome Victorian ledger in which the seller has to enter their name, address and the amount, so that we can keep the books balanced.

Once, not long after I had bought the shop, a young man who was emigrating to Canada brought in several boxes of books to sell. When I asked him to sign the cashbook, he wrote 'Tom Jones'. I laughed and pointed out a few other names that were clearly made up but that he was the first to use Tom Jones, to which he replied 'It's not unusual' and left. When I started to price up his books, I noticed that there, on the endpaper of every book, written in biro, was the name Tom Jones. His taste in books was very similar to mine, although there were a few that I hadn't yet read. Assuming that I would like those too, I fished out half a dozen and put them aside to read later. One of them was *The Ascent of Rum Doodle,* W. E. Bowman's classic spoof of climbing literature.

Till total £104.90
8 customers

THURSDAY, 13 FEBRUARY

Online orders: 4
Books found: 4

Eliot left for London at 2 p.m.

A young woman and her mother spent most of the afternoon in the shop. The mother seemed well prepared for the temperature, but the daughter appeared to be oblivious to the near-freezing conditions. She chatted breezily away as she was paying, and told me that her name was Lauren McQuistin, and she was training to be an opera singer. She seemed vaguely familiar; must have been in before. She bought an impressive pile of fairly highbrow material and suggested that I read *Any Human Heart*. Possibly the most recommended book I have been advised to read is William Boyd's *Any Human Heart*. I tend to avoid anything that is recommended to me, preferring naively to imagine that I will dig my own literary goldmine, but so compelling was her enthusiasm that after supper I lit the wood-burning stove and began to read it. By bedtime I was completely hooked.

Till total £13
2 customers

FRIDAY, 14 FEBRUARY

Online orders: 4
Books found: 4

If anyone can be said to be a Wigtown institution, it is Vincent. He has been here as long as anyone can remember, although he spent his childhood on the Clyde. He is universally liked, and is interesting and mischievous. There is a rumour that he was educated at Cambridge, but as far as I am aware, nobody has been able to substantiate this. He must be in his eighties, but he still works long hours – longer than any of his mechanics. Vincent's garage was once a Renault dealership, from which he sold new cars. Indeed, the old showroom is still there, with all the faded and cracked Renault branding on it, but now, instead of shiny new cars, his fleet consists of vehicles that, to put it politely, have seen better days. Once, when a botanist friend was visiting, we went there to fill the van with diesel. My friend leapt excitedly out of the van and headed towards one of Vincent's fleet, which had been parked outside the showroom with four flat tyres since I have been back in

Wigtown. He pointed at a fern that was growing inside the wheel arch and identified it as something quite rare.

After lunch I drove to a farm near Stranraer to give a probate valuation on some books. I was met by a damp, taciturn farmer in a tweed cap who instructed me to follow him on his quad bike, complete with a miserable collie perched precariously on the back, barking at the van all the way. We soon arrived at a desolate-looking farmhouse in the hollow of a muddy hillside, made all the more awful by the incessant, horizontal rain.

Inside, he explained that the house had belonged to his uncle and aunt. She had died five years previously and the uncle two years ago. It was clear that nothing had been touched since then, or in fact probably in the five years since his aunt had died. A lonely-looking cat lay on a blanket on a radiator by the window and stared out across the flooded fields. The farmer went up every day to empty the litter tray and feed it. Everything was covered in dust and cat hair. There were about two thousand books, crammed into every nook and cranny, including a pile on every step of the stairs. The aunt was the reader. L. M. Montgomery, Star Trek, Agatha Christie, Folio Society and a lot of children's books, including many complete runs. Most were paperbacks and not in particularly good condition, thanks in part to the cat. I valued the lot at £300, and he asked if I would consider buying them once he had discussed it with his family. I told him that I would, but that a lot of it was rubbish. He replied that if he decided to sell them to me, it would be conditional on the entire lot being taken away.

When I returned to the shop at 3 p.m., I was immediately accosted by a customer who marched up to the counter without the slightest of pleasantries and barked, 'Gold markings.' I sighed inside and explained where the jewellery section was.

Till total £307.50
4 customers

SATURDAY, 15 FEBRUARY

Online orders: 6
Books found: 6

Yet another miserable day, which did not improve at 9.10 a.m., when the telephone rang: 'It's a bloody disgrace. I don't know how you have the nerve to call yourself a bookseller, sending out this sort of rubbish', etc. He continued in this vein for several minutes. On further questioning, it transpired that he had ordered a book from a shop with a similar name (not unusual, as Tom Jones so wisely said), and he was not happy with the condition it was in. When it became clear that he'd telephoned the wrong bookshop and that the whole affair was nothing to do with us, he told me that he would be 'taking the matter further', then hung up.

A woman wearing what appeared to be a sleeping bag with a hole cut in the top for her head and the bottom for her feet complained about the icy temperature in the shop. The shop is old, cold and rambling. It is a large, granite-fronted building on the broad main street of Wigtown. In the early nineteenth century it was the home of a man called George McHaffie. He was the town's provost, and he rebuilt the property in the Georgian style, which it retains to this day. The entire ground floor is now devoted to books, and at the last count there were about 100,000 of them. In the past fifteen years we have replaced every shelf and done considerable work, both structural and cosmetic. Customers often refer to it as 'an Aladdin's cave' or 'a 'labyrinth'. I removed the internal doors in the shop to encourage customers to explore more, but this, and the fact that it is a huge, old house with inadequate heating, often lead to unflattering comments about the temperature from customers.

Till total £336.01
8 customers

MONDAY, 17 FEBRUARY

Online orders: 9
Books found: 8

More torrential rain. An elderly customer complimented the window display, mistaking the pots, pans and mugs (which are there to catch the drips from the leak) for a cookery-themed display.

I haven't seen the cat since Saturday. Anna thinks he is being bullied by a rival cat that is coming in during the night and stealing his food. Admittedly, he does seem to be going through a lot of food and there is a smell of cat piss about the place, and Captain never does that in the house.

This morning, as I was going through boxes from our old warehouse, I found a book signed by Sir Walter Scott. It came from a book collection that I'd bought from a castle in Ayrshire. I had boxed the books and forgotten all about them for a few months. It's always a thrilling moment to know that you're handling a book that someone whose literary genius has endured for over two hundred years once held in their hands. The best market for this sort of thing is not the shop, and they usually end up on eBay or being sent to Lyon & Turnbull, a saleroom in Edinburgh that usually realises good prices for the lots I consign. I'll try this on eBay with a reserve of £200, and if it fails to sell, then it can go to L&T.

Our warehouse is a building in the garden that was shelved out for books and had a small office with a loo. It still serves as a warehouse, but we now use it to store boxes of books for which there's no space in the shop. We built it (in 2006) to expand our online stock and sales. That side of the business had one full-time employee, initially Norrie, then a friend from the nearby village of Bladnoch, whose days were occupied with listing fresh stock and dealing with orders and inquiries. For a while it seemed to make a bit of money, but as more competition crept into the online market-place, prices came down, and by 2012 it was obvious that it wasn't even making enough money to cover wages, so with considerable reluctance I had to make the only remaining full-time member of staff redundant and ship the stock to a friend in Grimsby who had a more efficient operation. Before doing that, though, I trawled through it for material I thought might improve the quality of the stock in the shop, boxed this up and moved it over to the shop. This Sir Walter Scott inscription was among those boxes of books. Nowadays everything we buy (with the exception of FBA stock) ends up in the shop, and if a book is worth listing online, either Nicky or I will list it. The only drawback with this system is that customers are inclined to move books, and occasionally we are unable to find them and fulfil orders.

Although Scott was well known when he inscribed this book (to Mary Stewart), it was six years before *Waverley* was published and his name became a household one. Dedications and presentation copies also throw up the question of the identity of the person to whom the book was inscribed: perhaps Stuart Kelly, a good friend and author of *Scott-land: The Man Who Invented a Nation*, might have an idea.

At 11 a.m. the telephone rang. It was a Welsh woman who calls every few months. She has the most depressed voice I have ever heard and always asks for eighteenth-century theology. When I read her the list of titles we have in stock, she invariably responds, 'Oh, that's very, very disappointing.' She has been calling for several years now, and while initially I would read titles to her and try to see if we had anything in stock that she might want, after years of consistently being on the receiving end of her disappointment, I have given up and just invent titles now.

The farmer from Stranraer called back and offered the book collection on the condition that we take the whole lot. This is a difficult decision as there is a considerable amount of worthless material, the house is in a revolting state and a lot of the books are in very inaccessible places. Not only does that take more time to clear, but my back is creaking and weak. Twisting awkwardly into tiny corners is becoming increasingly problematic, but I told him that I'd take them and agreed to collect them next Tuesday.

Till total £282.90
21 customers

TUESDAY, 18 FEBRUARY

Online orders: 5
Books found: 3

One of today's online orders was about a nature reserve in Zimbabwe called *Wankie*.

This morning I received a message from Amazon informing me that our online performance had dropped from Good to Fair and that if it doesn't improve they'll suspend my account. One of the principal pleasures of self-employment is that you don't have to do what the boss tells you. As Amazon marches on with its 'everything shop' crusade, it is slowly but certainly becoming the boss of the self-employed in retail. I'll have to recruit more members to the Random Book Club so that I can break free from the increasingly constraining shackles of Amazon. Performance ratings are based on several factors, including order defect rate, cancellation rate, late dispatch rate, policy violations and contact response time. These are not the easiest of metrics to follow, so I tend to ignore it until they email me to tell me that I am in trouble.

A family of four came in at 12.30 p.m. Each of them bought a book; each gave a different response to the question 'Would you like a bag?'

Mother – 'Oh, go on then.'
Father – 'No.'
Son 1 – 'Yes.'
Son 2 – 'Only if you've got one.'

At 1 p.m. Carol Crawford appeared. I like to stock a few new books, probably around 150 titles that we buy from Booksource, a distributor of predominantly Scottish books. Carol is one of their sales reps. She is a charming woman, and we always chat about a variety of things before tackling the book business. Her son, who was just a small boy when she first started to come to the shop, is now at university. Until last year she would come armed with briefcases containing folders of book covers in plastic sheets, and order forms. Now she just has an iPad. She comes about four times a year, and deciding what to buy is a tricky business, particularly since customers no longer see the cover price of a new book as what they should be expected to pay. Amazon and Waterstones put paid to that, so once again I am in the position that – should I decide to – I could probably buy the stock I buy from Booksource cheaper on Amazon than I can from the distributor. I ordered two or three copies of about forty new titles on her list, mainly of local relevance, or written by people I know.

Back in 1899 the most powerful UK publishing houses agreed that they would only supply bookshops on the condition that the books were sold at the cover price and not discounted. Any breach of this, they agreed, would result in all of them ceasing to supply any books to the culprit. This was known as the Net Book Agreement (NBA). The system worked well for everyone until 1991, when chain stores Dillons and Waterstones emerged, dwarfing the small independents. They quickly realised that they could circumvent the NBA under a clause that exempted damaged books. Using a marker pen, they scored a cross onto the edges of the books they wished to discount. Occasionally I will still come across one of these when I am buying. Bitter fighting between the publishers and the big chains ensued, culminating in a ruling by the Office of Fair Trading that declared the NBA illegal in 1997.

One of the benefits of the NBA was that the financial stability of the market it created allowed publishers to publish books that perhaps had more cultural but probably less financial value. Without it, publishers are no longer in a position to take such risks, and consequently, although the number of books printed in the UK each year has increased, the number of titles has diminished: more copies of fewer books. The book market is now controlled not by publishers but by the buyers for Waterstones and Tesco and other 'combines', as Orwell would have called them.

Smell of cat piss is getting stronger.

Till total £111.50
12 customers

WEDNESDAY, 19 FEBRUARY

Online orders: 8
Books found: 5

Finally, a day without rain. Most of the day was spent packing the books for the Random Book Club and dealing with the Royal Mail's neolithic mailing system. As the post office in Wigtown is closed on Wednesday afternoon I'll have to go and see Wilma tomorrow morning and ask her if she can send the postman over in the afternoon to pick up the six sacks of parcels.

This morning I listed the book signed by Sir Walter Scott on eBay. There's little point in listing it on Amazon or AbeBooks. Although AbeBooks has a 'Signed Books' section, this is not a copy of one of Scott's own titles, so it would never be found on a search.

Four elderly ladies came in at 10.30 a.m. I was working at the computer with my back to them but could hear them speculating about where the craft books might be. After some discussion, one of them spotted me in the corner and said to the others, 'Why don't we just ask the lady?'

Norrie thinks he knows where the water is getting in and flooding the window display, and has offered to fix it.

I have reached the part in *Any Human Heart* where Logan's son decides to name his band Dead Souls and Logan responds with laughter, telling him that Nikolai Gogol wrote a book of the same name. I had no idea, and felt as stupid as Logan's son. It will be the next book I read.

Till total £24
4 customers

THURSDAY, 20 FEBRUARY

Online orders: 6
Books found: 6

Nicky strolled in at 9.15 a.m. (fifteen minutes late), looked at the clock and said, 'Oh, is that the time?' before throwing her bag, hat and coat on the floor in the middle of the shop and going upstairs to use the loo and make herself a cup of tea.

Till total £88
7 customers

FRIDAY, 21 FEBRUARY

Online orders: 5
Books found: 5

Today's online orders include one of the most boring titles I have seen for a while: *British Transport Film Library Catalogue since 1966*. It includes such riveting films as 'AC electric locomotive drivers' procedures', 'Service for Southend' and 'Snowdrift at Bleath Gill'. Despite the popular perception that books about trains are extremely dull (the reputation of trainspotters as banana-sandwich-eating, anorak-wearing bores is probably in part responsible for this), they are among the best-selling books in the shop. Invariably it is men who buy them, and more often than not they sport beards. They are generally among the most good-natured of the shop's customers, possibly because they're delighted when they see the size of the railway section, which normally comprises about two thousand books.

A customer wearing yellow Crocs asked where the parking meters were in Wigtown. When I explained that there were none and that there are no parking restrictions, she looked completely flabbergasted and commented, 'My God, this is wonderful. It's like this place is trapped in a time warp of fifty years ago.'

I locked the cat flap last night when Captain came in. No smell of cat piss this morning. Anna may well be correct about the unwelcome visiting cat.

Till total £24.50
1 customer

SATURDAY, 22 FEBRUARY

Online orders: 4
Books found: 4

The first telephone call of the day was from Mrs Phillips, near Dumfries: 'I am ninety-three years old and blind, you know.'

I went to value her books about two years ago – interesting collection in a very nice house. When I arrived, I discovered that she'd cooked lunch for me and her grandson, who was visiting. I had already eaten – a dry sandwich with an unidentifiable filling bought from the petrol station in Newton Stewart – but didn't want to decline since she'd gone to the trouble. It was prawns in aspic. Today she was calling to order a book, *Babar*, for her great-granddaughter. She's one of the few customers who still order books through the shop, rather than directly online from Amazon.

One of the shop's Facebook followers came in to buy books today. She and her boyfriend want to move here and I overheard her whispering 'Don't say anything stupid or he'll post it on Facebook.' I will write something mean about her later. When I set up the Facebook account for the shop four years ago, I had a look at other bookshops that had done the same. The content seemed almost universally bland and didn't really convey the full horror or the exquisite joy of working in a bookshop, so I took a calculated risk and decided to focus on customer behaviour, particularly the stupid questions and the rude comments. It appears to have paid off, and those who follow the shop seem to become more delighted the more offensive I am about customers. I recently checked to see who is following me, and a significant number of bookshops are on the list.

Till total £227.45
14 customers

MONDAY, 24 FEBRUARY

Online orders: 3
Books found: 3

It was a depressingly wet day when I awoke, but by 9.30 a.m. the sun was blazing. The Polish builders arrived to remove the leylandii hedge and replace it with a new stone wall. After they had cut down the hedge they decided to set fire to it, blanketing most of the town in thick, acrid smoke. For much of the day I could see people staggering past the door of the shop, coughing and swearing.

Till total £277
16 customers

TUESDAY, 25 FEBRUARY

Online orders: 4
Books found: 4

Sandy, the most tattooed man in Scotland, brought in some walking sticks he'd made. We have an arrangement whereby he gets £6 credit in the shop for each one he brings me. I then sell the sticks for £10 each. They sell well – probably one or two a week – and he adds a label with the name of the wood and some local lore about it. His taste in reading is mainly for Scottish folklore and ancient history. He is a pagan and lives near Stranraer, but comes over once every couple of weeks with a friend and makes a day out of his trip to Wigtown, going for lunch or coffee and browsing in the shops. He is incredibly affable, always good-natured and invariably has something interesting to say. Best of all, he loves winding up Nicky.

At noon I made a sandwich, and Anna and I headed off in the van with fifty or so cardboard boxes to the old farmhouse near Stranraer. The grizzled farmer in his damp tweed cap met us again and took us back up to the house where the old couple had lived. It was even more filthy than I remembered. Anna and I started boxing the books and ferrying them to the van. The lonely cat gasped a cracked 'meow' every time we passed it, then resumed its wistful stare out across the flooded fields full of cattle with their backs to the driving rain.

As is often the way with clearing books that have been in the same place for a long time, by the time we were finished we were comprehensively covered in dirt and cat hair – a facet of the genteel art of bookselling that people rarely imagine. I paid the farmer and creaked off down the potholed driveway, the van grinding slowly under the weight of the load.

The experience of clearing a deceased estate is one familiar to most people in the second-hand book trade and it is one to which you slowly become desensitised, except in situations like this, in which the dead couple is childless. For some reason the photographs on the wall – the husband in his smart RAF uniform, the wife as a young woman visiting Paris – evoke a kind of melancholy that is not there in deals where couples are survived by their children. Dismantling such a book collection seems to be the ultimate act of destruction of their character – you are responsible for erasing the last piece of evidence of who they were. This woman's book collection was a record of her character: her interests, as close as anything she left to some kind of genetic inheritance. Perhaps that's why her nephew waited so long before asking us to look at the books, in the same way that people who lose a child often can't bear to remove anything from their bedroom for years.

Till total £124
9 customers

Online orders: 4
Books found: 4

This morning a customer asked for books by Nigel Tranter, clearly confident that we wouldn't have any. I directed him to the Scottish room, where we have most of Tranter's work, including his architectural material, with a couple of exceptions. A few minutes later he scuttled out of the shop, trying not to be noticed. Some people just want you to know what their reading habits are and have no intention of buying anything.

An incredibly haughty woman telephoned demanding the festival bed for the entire festival. The festival bed is a mezzanine bed that we built last year in the shop, partly as a homage to Shakespeare & Co. in Paris, partly as a publicity stunt and partly as an occasionally necessary extra bed. When I told her that it was unlikely that we were going to do it this year, she didn't seem to want to understand and kept insisting that she needed it for the night of 29 September at the very least. It wasn't long before the conversation took an ominous turn with the alarming words 'I have an ulterior motive – I want to speak to you and Anna.'

It transpired that she's written an autobiography. It is called *No, I Am Not Going on the Seesaw.* The conversation was littered with references to the people she knows in publishing ('I am not thinking about self-publishing, you know'), her insistence on finding her own proofreader ('I have it on good authority that most proofreaders are incompetent') and pregnant pauses to which she clearly attached weighty significance.

She talked – again at considerable length – about how she felt she should be part of the programme for the 2015 festival. She will never, ever be part of the festival.

Finished *Any Human Heart.* Absolutely adored it. Started reading Gogol's *Dead Souls.* We had a copy in the Black Penguin Classics section.

Till total £66
7 customers

Online orders: 4
Books found: 1

On my sister's advice, I checked TripAdvisor to see whether anyone had reviewed the shop. There were nine reviews, two of which made references to the quality of the food. We do not serve food. We have never served food. Two more complained that the shop 'wasn't as big' as they had expected it to be.

Inspired, I wrote a ridiculous review praising the owner's magnificent good looks, convivial charm, captivatingly beautiful scent, the wonderful stock, the electric atmosphere and a litany of other unlikely superlatives. In no time at all it had been removed and TripAdvisor had sent a threatening email warning me not to do it again. I went straight back onto their site and wrote another one, and encouraged the shop's Facebook followers to do the same.

After lunch I checked eBay to find that the book signed by Sir Walter Scott sold for £250, so I emailed the winning bidder and sent them an invoice. It's easy to miss things like important signatures or inscriptions in books when you're buying, but equally so when you're selling. Once, shortly after I bought the shop, I bought ten boxes of books unseen from another dealer, a man called David McNaughton, who had been in the trade for nearly forty years. He wanted £10 a box and assured me that it was reasonable stock. From previous dealings with him I had no reason to doubt this. What I didn't expect, though, was to find a book signed by Florence Nightingale, dedicated to one of her nurses. It was a Charles Kingsley title – I forget which. Florence Nightingale was fond of inscribing books and giving them to her friends, and consequently there are quite a few of these about, but it still made £300 on eBay. A nurse in Missouri bought it. I sent David a case of wine and told him what had happened. Sadly, he died a few years ago. He was among the last of a generation of what can now be seen as traditional book dealers. Before the days of Amazon and AbeBooks – web sites to which one may quickly refer to check prices – booksellers would have to acquire and carry about all of that information, and David was a mine of biographical, bibliographical and literary information. Now this knowledge – accumulated over almost a lifetime, once so valued and from which a good living could be earned – is all but useless. Those dealers who could tell you the date, publisher, author and value of a book just by looking at it are few and far between, and their ranks are shrinking daily. I still know one or two of them, and they are among the people I admire most in the trade. Without exception, all of those I encountered and had dealings with – from what now feels like a bygone era of bookselling – were honest and decent.

There was a stray cat in the Scottish room as I was closing up. It hissed and leapt through the cat flap as I chased it out.

Till total £11
3 customers

FRIDAY, 28 FEBRUARY

Online orders: 6
Books found: 6

Sara Maitland brought in three boxes of books to sell from her personal library. We discussed one of her best-known books, *A Book of Silence*, and the possibility of her doing an event at Hogmanay: possibly a silent walk followed by a talk on the importance of silence. Sara lives nearby, up in the hills behind New Luce, and is an occasional visitor to the shop. It's always a pleasure to see her.

This morning I went to Callum's to collect thirty boxes I'd been storing in his garage. This largely consists of a collection of 500 books on golf which I have been trying to get rid of for over a year. Callum is a close friend; I've known him for about twelve years, and we often go hill-walking, sailing and mountain-biking together. He lives in an old farmhouse near Kirkinner, about four miles from Wigtown, with his three sons, aged between ten and fifteen. He is from Northern Ireland, and is a couple of years older than I am. He has had an extraordinarily interesting range of jobs over his working life, from geological exploration in Venezuela to picking Scots pine cones in the Highlands, to being a financial adviser. Currently, he's cutting and selling firewood, among other things. I suspect that one of the reasons we get along so well is that neither of us has ever seen ourselves as suited to having any kind of career, and although there are some things on which we disagree, there seem to be far more on which we are in agreement.

The books in his garage were from a collection that I bought from a house in Manchester last year. I didn't have space on the shelves to put it out, and the warehouse was full, so when Callum offered his garage as a temporary store, I gratefully accepted. Now he needs the space back, so I'll have to find an alternative solution.

Dumfries and Galloway Life magazine came for a photo shoot in the shop in the afternoon. I'm not sure what it was for, but they needed a lot of books as a backdrop. They took an hour and were gone by 4 p.m.

Till total £51
3 customers

MARCH

When I worked in a second-hand bookshop – so easily pictured, if you do not work in one, as a kind of paradise where charming old gentlemen browse eternally among calf-bound folios – the thing that chiefly struck me was the rarity of really bookish people.

George Orwell, 'Bookshop Memories'

Really bookish people are a rarity, although there are vast numbers of those who consider themselves to be such. The latter are particularly easy to identify – often they will introduce themselves when they enter the shop as 'book people' and insist on telling you that 'we love books'. They'll wear T-shirts or carry bags with slogans explaining exactly how much they think they adore books, but the surest means of identifying them is that they never, ever buy books.

These days it is so rare that I find the time to read that, when I do, it feels like the purest form of indulgence – more so than any other sensory experience. When an important relationship in my thirties came to an end, the only thing I could do was read, and I amassed a pile of books into which I sank and escaped from the world around me and inside me. The landscapes of Jonathan Meades, William Boyd, José Saramago, John Buchan, Alastair Reid, John Kennedy Toole and others protected me from my own thoughts, which were pushed into the background, where they could silently process without bothering me. I created a physical wall on my desk, made from the books, and as I read them the wall slowly came down until it was gone.

In a more real sense, books are the commodity in which I trade, and the enormous numbers of them out there in the world excite a different part of my mind. When I go to a house to buy books, there is an anticipation unlike anything else. It is like casting a net and never knowing what you will find when you gather it in. I think that book dealers and antique dealers probably have the same sense of excitement when following up a call. As Gogol put it in *Dead Souls*: 'Once, long ago, in the years of my youth, in the years of my childhood, which have flashed irretrievably by, it was a joy for me to drive for the very first time to a place unknown.'

SATURDAY, I MARCH

Online orders: 5
Books found: 5

Beautiful sunny day.

Our Amazon Seller Rating has dropped to Poor.

Kate, the postie, delivered the mail this morning at 10 a.m. as always. Among the usual bills and pleas from charities was a letter from Royal Mail informing me that – as part of an efficiency drive – they are increasing their rates. Apparently we're all going to be saving money because their price increase is less than inflation. I did a few calculations and worked out that my average parcel will go from £1.69 to £1.87. This is a rise of 10 per cent. Last time I checked, inflation was about 2 per cent. Will Amazon increase the amount of postage they charge customers in line with the Royal Mail increase? Almost certainly not. At the moment, the £2.80 postal charge for a book bears no resemblance to the actual cost of posting individual books, so on some heavier books we lose money on postage, which is irritating, and on smaller books we make money on the postage, which irritates the customer. The only winner is Amazon, which takes 49p of the postage charged to the customer, leaving us with £2.31 postage per book.

At lunchtime a customer asked if we ever lose books to thieves. It's not something I've ever really considered much, despite the labyrinthine layout of the shop affording potential thieves with a wealth of opportunity. Occasionally in the past I have been unable to find books and assumed that perhaps theft had been their fate, but they've nearly all turned up eventually in different places. There seems to be something somehow less morally culpable about stealing a book than stealing, say, a watch. Perhaps it is that books are generally perceived as being edifying, and so acquiring the knowledge contained within them is of a greater social and personal value than the impact of the crime. Or, at least if it doesn't outweigh the crime, then it certainly mitigates it. Irvine Welsh explored this idea in *Trainspotting*, when Renton and Spud are caught shoplifting from Waterstones. In court Spud admits that he stole the books to sell on, while Renton claims that he stole the copy of Kierkegaard with which he was found because he wanted to read it. When the sceptical magistrate challenges him on his knowledge of the existentialist philosopher, Renton replies:

> I am interested in his concepts of subjectivity and truth, and particularly his ideas concerning choice; the notion that the genuine choice is made out of doubt and uncertainty, and without recourse to the experience of others. It could be argued, with some justification, that it's primarily a bourgeois, existential philosophy and would therefore seek to undermine collective social wisdom. However, it's also a liberating philosophy, because when such societal wisdom is negated, the basis for social control over the individual becomes weakened and … but I am rabbiting a bit here. Ah cut myself short. They hate a smart cunt. It's easy to talk yourself into a bigger fine, or fuck sake, a higher sentence. Think deference, Renton, think deference.

The magistrate acquits Renton, but convicts Spud.

In any case, I deeply dislike security cameras and would rather lose the occasional book than have that sort of intrusive monitoring in the shop. This is not *Nineteen Eighty-Four*.

The smell of cat piss is back.

Till total £236
14 customers

MONDAY, 3 MARCH

Online orders: 9
Books found: 8

Another beautiful day, marred at an early stage by a customer wearing shorts and knee-length woollen socks who knocked over a pile of books and left them lying on the floor. Shortly afterwards, a whistling customer with a ponytail and what I can only assume was a hat he'd borrowed from a clown bought a copy of Paulo

Coelho's *The Alchemist,* I suspect deliberately to undermine my faith in humanity and dampen my spirits further.

A book we had sold on Amazon called *Orient-Express: A Personal Journey*, and which we had sent out three weeks ago, was returned today with a note from the customer that reads: 'Unfortunately not as expected. Require a more pictorial version. Please exchange or refund.' I suspect that the customer was treating us like an online library and had read the book.

Eliot arrived at 5 p.m. for a visit of as yet unknown duration. I'm fairly sure he has a Festival board meeting some time during the week, but he hasn't told me yet.

Till total £90
4 customers

TUESDAY, 4 MARCH

Online orders: 6
Books found: 6

The shop has a regular visitor who goes by the name of William, or Agnes, depending on whichever takes his or her fancy when he or she wakes up. As usual, he/she turned up with a bag of books to sell. William or Agnes is an octogenarian transgender man/woman from Irvine who drives a Reliant Robin. I'm not sure from which gender into which he/she has transitioned, hence the he/she thing here. He/she had massive hooped ear-rings on and was quite excited about the books he/she had brought in, which were, as always, rubbish. Gave him/her £4 for them. He/she spent some time complaining about the complexities of the benefits system, ending his/her rant with 'I am a very busy man-stroke-woman.'

Since being awarded the Book Town status, Wigtown has attracted increasing numbers of people who come here to sell books as well as to buy them. The concept of a Book Town originated with Richard Booth in the 1970s. He convinced booksellers to move to the Welsh Marches town of Hay-on-Wye, testing the theory that a town full of bookshops would encourage people to visit, and the economy could be re-invigorated. It worked, and the concept eventually arrived in Scotland. Wigtown's Book Town project was launched in 1998. Although it was initially met with suspicion by many locals, it has changed the place for the better, and the town, in line with its motto, is flourishing once again. When I moved back here from Bristol in 2001, I recall reading a letter in the *Galloway Gazette* in which the correspondent – complaining that she could no longer buy a pair of socks in Wigtown – blamed the bookshops for this travesty. That resentment is all but gone now, and it would take a brave person to argue that the Book Town project hasn't improved the lot of the town immeasurably. It's not even possible to buy socks in the nearby market town of Newton Stewart these days. That woman must be incandescent by now.

Bev dropped off a box of the mugs onto which she's printed the cover of *Gay Agony*.

Till total £57
5 customers

WEDNESDAY, 5 MARCH

Online orders: 3
Books found: 3

An Australian customer paid for a £1.50 book in small change but clearly had no idea what each coin was and took about five minutes to work it out. At one point he asked, 'What do you use these 1p and 2p coins for?'

Anna telephoned at 3 p.m. and we reminisced about a famous instance of her linguistic impressionism: the time her friend Sarah was visiting from America and we went to Glentrool in the Galloway Hills. Glentrool, apart from being a beautiful mountainous region, cut through by tumbling burns and dotted with lochs, was the site of an important battle in 1307 that marked the start of Robert the Bruce's campaign against the English dominion of Scotland, culminating in the Battle of Bannockburn in 1314. When we were walking to a waterfall there with Sarah, Anna explained to her that 'Glentrool was where Robert the Burns took his last stand.' And thus, in one short sentence, managed to confuse Robert the Bruce, Robert Burns and General Custer, and to rewrite the outcome of a critical battle in Scottish history.

Till total £70.49
11 customers

THURSDAY, 6 MARCH

Online orders: 7
Books found: 7

In the morning I unloaded the boxes of books about golf that I picked up from Callum's on Saturday. I've tried to sell them on eBay as a job lot twice, but with no luck, so I will probably put them into the auction in Dumfries once I have checked whether there's anything in there that's worth listing online. Nicky can check that this weekend. The warehouse is starting to look a bit messy.

A customer wearing a huge chunky gold cross on a chain asked, 'Do you have a section for old Bibles and church things?' I wasn't entirely sure what he meant by 'church things', so I pointed him at the theology section. We do have some beautiful and very cheap old Bibles, but the people who ask for them never, ever buy them. He managed to find an unpriced miniature Bible from 1870 and asked me what the price would be. I told him £4. He didn't buy it. There must be some kind of psychological effect created by finding an unpriced book. Whatever price you suggest when asked, however low, seems to be more than the customer is prepared to pay. I have lost count of the number of times people have brought books to the counter that we have yet to price up and said, 'This one's got no price on it. It must be free.' It wasn't funny the first time, and fourteen years later it has completely lost the sheen it never had in the first place.

Just before closing time a woman with a strong Yorkshire accent bought a cookbook and told me, 'You're not from round here.' I replied that I was brought up here. Again, I have heard this so often that it is slowly driving me insane. She told me that my accent has a 'strange twang'.

Till total £47
3 customers

FRIDAY, 7 MARCH

Online orders: 4
Books found: 4

When I came downstairs from breakfast to open the shop, I discovered that Nicky had already arrived and switched everything on. She greeted me with her usual melodic 'Helloooo!' before scampering upstairs to put whatever horrors she had raided from the Morrisons skip last night into the fridge.

Eliot left at 2 p.m., leaving a pair of shoes behind, each shoe in a different room.

This morning, as I was working my way through a couple of bags of books, I found a shopping list in one of them. The handwriting looked very like Nicky's. Among the things on the list were 'Hair Gunk', 'Leg Razors' and 'Witch Face Wash'. When I asked Nicky about the shopping list, she denied all knowledge, telling me that she doesn't shave her legs during winter and offering to show me as evidence.

At 2 p.m. I left the shop and drove to Dumfries to catch the London train and visit Anna in Hampstead for the weekend. I left Nicky with the thirty boxes of books about golf to check and list on Fulfilled By Amazon. She complained bitterly about it again, but reluctantly agreed to do it.

Read Hogg's *Confessions of a Justified Sinner* on the journey south, an extraordinarily modern book considering it was written in 1824.

Till total £90.50
6 customers

SATURDAY, 8 MARCH

In London.

Till total £305.48
28 customers

MONDAY, 10 MARCH

Online orders: 7
Books found: 4

Today was a beautiful sunny day. Callum called to see if I wanted to climb a hill, but I was alone in the shop so couldn't.

At about noon a young family came into the shop: parents with a boy of about seven and a girl of about nine. The boy went straight to the children's section and immersed himself there for an hour, until his parents told him that it was time to go for lunch, at which point he reluctantly dragged himself away from the chair near the children's books and pleaded with his mother to buy him a copy of *The House at Pooh Corner*. She came to the counter and paid the £2.50 for a paperback copy with a look of exasperation, saying 'I've never come across a child who reads as much – all he does is read. He spends every penny of his pocket money on books.'

Nicky didn't manage to list a single book over the weekend because, as her note says: 'The printer wilnae work.' I checked: she hadn't switched it on.

Local news today is that Bladnoch distillery has gone into liquidation.

Till total £47
3 customers

TUESDAY, II MARCH

Online orders: 6
Books found: 6

Today was another beautiful day, and quite warm too. Nicky came in wisely wrapped up in scarf, hat and coat. Even on a cold day it is often warmer outside than it is in the shop.

Much of today was spent going through boxes of books I've had in storage for a year. They came from a large Victorian house near Castle Douglas. It was snowing heavily when I picked them up a year ago. The van struggled to haul the load up the slippery hill back onto the main road as I was leaving, and I thought I might have to spend the night in the house with the strange man from whom I had bought them, but it managed to get away. As I had no storage space at the time, I put the boxes in storage at Callum's along with the golf books. Among the books I sorted through today was a rare pamphlet signed by Seamus Heaney. Harrington in London is offering the only other copy online for £225, so I put mine up at £140.

Old ladies' art class upstairs – nobody died of exposure.

When I was closing up, I decided to open the cat flap again in the hope that the intruder has become bored with bashing his head against it and found someone else's house to piss in.

Till total £49
6 customers

WEDNESDAY, 12 MARCH

Online orders: 4
Books found: 3

Very quiet day.

Just before closing, Mr Deacon appeared, looking flushed and flustered, and asked if I could order a book about James I for his aunt, whose ninetieth birthday is next Friday. As always, he produced a review from *The Times* and left it with me to order. It should be here next week.

As I was locking up the back of the shop, I could hear the sound of geese honking on the salt-marsh at the bottom of the hill, the bleating of new-born lambs in the fields and the croaking of frogs in the pond in the garden. No people. No traffic. Growing up in rural Scotland, sounds like these are the familiar indicators of seasonal change, and for me the onset of spring is the highlight of the year. Once you've lived in a city for a few years, I suppose there's a detachment from these signals of seasonal shift to which the frogs, the lambs and the geese – spring's harbingers from the water, the land and the sky – alert you.

Till total £28.49
4 customers

THURSDAY, 13 MARCH

Online orders: 4
Books found: 4

Nicky was in today as she's taking tomorrow off (Friday and Saturday are her usual two days). She began the day by complaining about the smell of cat pee again. I told her that it's a stray, and that Mike in the co-op has borrowed a trap from Cats Protection and is trying to catch it. She still blamed Captain. Mike's garden backs onto mine and Captain is as frequent a visitor in his kitchen as his cats are in mine. The stray has been spraying in his house too.

Eliot has asked me to help write a business plan for The Open Book idea so that we can work out if it can stand on its own financially. If it can, then it will operate under the umbrella of the Festival Company. The Open Book is a plan that Anna, Finn and Eliot have come up with: they want to take an empty shop in the town that has accommodation above it and give people the opportunity to come and run it for a fortnight so that they know what it is like be a bookseller. Finn is a friend from childhood who lives nearby. He's an organic dairy farmer, and one of the wittiest people I know. About ten years ago he was co-opted to be the chairman of what was then the Wigtown Festival volunteer group. Within a year he had turned it into the Wigtown Festival Company, a charity (which meant it could access new funds), and transformed it from a few inexperienced but enthusiastic volunteers into a slick, professional organisation with full-time, paid staff. After a few years off, he is now back on the board of trustees. I thought I'd do some research for the business plan, so I googled 'Run a Bookshop'. Ironically, top of the list is a book for sale on Amazon called *The Complete Guide to Starting and Running a Bookshop*.

In the early afternoon I received a phone call from a woman at Yell.com regarding my Yellow Pages advert and online listing. She asked me if my business was 'located in Wigwamshire', which she referred to as a 'locality area', and continued that she would give me 'an example, for example'. She also described my Yell.com web site as having a 'completely different look, but very similar'. To what, I have no idea.

Seven people brought boxes of books to the shop to sell today. As is often the way at this time of year, I bought more than I sold.

Till total £120
9 customers

FRIDAY, 14 MARCH

Online orders: 3
Books found: 2

No Nicky today. She is de-cluttering, apparently. One of today's online orders was for a book about instruments measuring radio-activity, for a customer in Iran. At 11.30 a.m. the telephone rang. It was Nicky: 'Do you want my fridge? I am getting rid of everything that runs on electricity.' The moment she opens her mouth a gem of some sort will emerge, fully formed.

Mother appeared at 2 p.m. with four hanging baskets for the front of the shop, all planted up. She does this every year, despite my protestations that I am quite capable of doing it myself.

Till total £42
3 customers

SATURDAY, 15 MARCH

Online orders: 3
Books found: 2

Today's first customer was a short man with a wispy beard who suddenly appeared at the counter, startling me. He grinned and said, 'You've got some stuff here, haven't you? Some stuff. Some stuff.' He bought a copy of *The Hobbit*. I am putting a mental jigsaw together of what a hobbit looks like, based on a composite of every customer I have ever sold a copy to.

After lunch a customer asked if we had a copy of *To Kill a Mockingbird*. We didn't, but a few moments after he had left, a woman brought in two boxes of books to sell, one of which contained a copy. It's much more rewarding when this happens the other way around.

Till total £78.98
13 customers

Online orders: 7
Books found: 6

One of today's orders was for a book called *Sexing Day-Old Chicks*.

The first customer of the day was an unusually smartly dressed Maltese woman who told me that there are no second-hand bookshops in Malta. I'm not quite sure what she was doing in Wigtown, but she seemed pleasant, even if she didn't buy anything. Just as she was leaving, the telephone rang. It was the librarian from Samye Ling Buddhist centre in Eskdalemuir, about sixty miles away. They have been clearing old stock and want to sell some of it. I have arranged to visit them next week.

My mother came into the shop when it was fairly busy and started to share her less than flattering opinions about the SNP at considerable volume. She comes from the west of Ireland, and despite having lived in Scotland for nearly fifty years, retains the lilt of the country of her childhood. Or so I am assured by my friends – it is undetectable to my ear. She has a capacity for talking that I am quite convinced is unparalleled in the world, and she abhors a silence the way that nature abhors a vacuum. On several occasions I have witnessed her say the same thing (normally a description of what she had for lunch that afternoon, or where she went that morning) in over a dozen different ways in a single breath. My father, by contrast, is a quiet man. This he attributes to the lack of opportunity to speak afforded by my mother's incessant babble. He is a tall man, 6 foot 3, and trained as an engineer, but he turned to farming in his late twenties. Between them, they have managed to build several businesses and send my two sisters and me to boarding school.

Unannounced visits from family and friends are not uncommon and are certainly not the exclusive preserve of my mother. Familiar visitors often openly talk about things I would not deem fit for strangers' ears. It often strikes me that perhaps bookshops primarily play a recreational role for most people, being peaceful, quiet places from which to escape the relentless rigours and digital demands of modern life, so that my friends and family will quite happily turn up unannounced and uninvited to interrupt whatever I happen to be doing with little or no regard for the fact that it is my workplace. If I was working in the co-op or the library, I doubt whether they'd take such a cavalier approach to casual social visits. Nor, I suspect, would they speak quite so freely in the company of complete strangers in any other workplace.

After I had closed the shop I called Mr Deacon to let him know that the biography of James I he ordered has arrived.

Till total £41
4 customers

TUESDAY, 18 MARCH

Online orders: 2
Books found: 2

The morning was cold and damp, so I lit the fire. By 11 a.m. there had been five customers through the door; not one of them bought anything. Then a tall, emaciated man in a hoodie came in and asked if we had any books on pharmacology because 'they've just put me on this new heroin substitute and I want to find out more about it'.

Mr Deacon appeared at lunchtime and paid for the book he'd ordered. His aunt's birthday is on Saturday, so he should have time to send it to her.

Till total £82.99
9 customers

WEDNESDAY, 19 MARCH

Online orders: 2
Books found: 2

At 10.30 a.m. I went upstairs to make a cup of tea. When I came back downstairs, I was met with a familiar, earthy smell. No sooner had I sat down and started listing books than a short, very scruffy, bearded Irishman shot out from behind a shelf. His appearance (and smell) disguise a man whose knowledge of books is remarkable. He brings me a load of good material about twice a year, delivered in his van, in which he clearly lives. This time he brought four boxes of books on railways and two boxes of books about Napoleon, for which I gave him £170.

At 2 p.m. the telephone rang. It was a woman at the council whose job it is to find work for people with learning difficulties:

> Woman: 'We have a young man looking for work in a bookshop. He has Asperger's syndrome. Have you heard of Asperger's syndrome?'
>
> Me: 'Yes.'
>
> Woman: 'Well, you know how some people with Asperger's are really good at one specific thing, like maths or drawing?'
>
> Me: 'Yes.'
>
> Woman: 'Well, he's not like that.'

So I agreed to take him on for a trial period. He starts on Tuesday.

Before the shop closed I stamped and bagged all the books for the Random Book Club, and (hopefully) charmed Wilma into sending the postman over in his van tomorrow to pick them up.

After years of buying, pricing, listing and selling books, certain publishers become very familiar to you: the significant quantities of books published by Macmillan in the early twentieth century; Blackie and Son with their distinctive Talwin Morris cover illustrations; A. & C. Black, with their famous Scottish travel guides; Fullarton and Cassell, two short-lived publishers who along with Newnes and Gresham embraced the technological revolution that enabled paper to be made from wood pulp in the mid-nineteenth century, and all of whose publications are distinctive for their waxy pages; Ward Lock, with their series of red travel guides to the UK; David & Charles, of Newton Abbot, whose books on regional railways are second to none; Hodder and Stoughton, who published the once desirable *King's England* series, now no longer sought after; and Nelson, whose red cloth editions of John Buchan's works still sell in healthy numbers.

Others stand out less for their design or style, and more for their content. Take Hooper and Wigstead, the publisher of Francis Grose's *Antiquities of Scotland*, whose pages contain the very first version to appear in a book of Burns's *Tam o'Shanter*; William Creech, who published Sir John Sinclair's first *Statistical Account of Scotland* – and introduced the word 'statistic' to the English language; John Wilson, who produced the Kilmarnock edition of Burns's *Poems, Chiefly in the Scottish Dialect*; John Murray, the publisher of *On the Origin of Species by Means of Natural Selection*; William Strahan, who brought Adam Smith's *Inquiry into the Nature and Causes of the Wealth of Nations* to the world.

More recent publishers have had a similar impact: Penguin, whose unexpurgated British edition of *Lady Chatterley's Lover* saw them end up in court; Shakespeare & Company, who dared to publish *Ulysses*; small presses such as William Morris's short-lived Kelmscott Press; and the Golden Cockerel Press, for whom the artist Eric Gill (the typeface designer behind Gill Sans, Perpetua and others) designed a typeface which he named after the press. The list goes on, but these publishers – these individuals – took risks and brought new ideas to the world, each with their own distinctive style, from their subject matter to their design, typography and production values.

Till total £131.33
10 customers

THURSDAY, 20 MARCH

Online orders: 4
Books found: 4

Bum Bag Dave came in shortly after the shop opened and bought three books from the aviation section. He is a knowledgeable character, scruffy and bushily bearded, and slightly paranoid that a firm of local solicitors has got it in for him, for some reason. His nickname derives from the fact that he is always adorned with at least two bum bags, one of which hangs around his neck, while the other is around his waist. On special occasions he has several more, and nearly always has a suitcase or rucksack too. He lives in nearby Sorbie and travels around all day on the bus, making use of whatever free facilities are available – the library and such. As he was leaving today, he asked me what time the bus to Whithorn leaves. When I told him that I had no idea, he replied, 'You ought to know that sort of thing. You're supposed to be providing a public service.' This is news to me. He also has a digital watch that beeps every few minutes and at least one mobile phone that seems to be constantly emitting various irritating noises.

In the early afternoon an elderly man telephoned. He had found a book we are selling online for £3 and wanted to buy it directly. Due to his bad hearing and a lot of confusion, the whole process took half an hour. While he was on the telephone the postman appeared and removed the five bags of random books.

Bum Bag Dave was still shuffling about with his various beeping devices at 5.15 p.m. and asked if we have a section on pets. I told him, yes, but we were closed. At 5.25 p.m. he was still wandering about the shop, muttering about lawyers ripping him off.

Till total £107.49
14 customers

FRIDAY, 21 MARCH

Online orders: 5
Books found: 4

Nicky was back in working today. We had the usual argument about her making a mess and putting books on the wrong shelves. She threatened to quit, which she usually does about once a month.

At lunchtime I left for Samye Ling, the Tibetan Buddhist retreat in Eskdalemuir. *En route* I picked up Anna from Dumfries railway station for a break from her London life.

Samye Ling has been considerably enlarged since I last visited twenty years ago, and is a spectacular incongruity in the bleak Scottish moorland, speckled with golden Buddhas, pagodas and colourful temples and buildings, as well as a smattering of semi-derelict Portakabins and other relics of the centre's infancy. We found the library, and met Maggy, the librarian – a woman in her sixties in a wheelchair.

The library is new and is a massive unshelved room with piles of books on the floor. I went through the stock they want to dispose of and offered her £150. She clearly expected more, but when I told her that I was quite happy to leave them so that they could ask someone else in to look at them, there was a chorus of 'No!' from the other volunteers working there, so I had to take all the rubbish too, but there was some reasonable stock among it – a general mix of fiction and non-fiction, the sort of thing you'd normally find in someone's house rather than what you might expect from the library of a Tibetan monastery. No doubt they have taken out all the material that would be appropriate for them to keep in their collection.

Anna was completely smitten with Samye Ling – the contrast between the landscape and the architecture, even between different parts of the place, some of which looked genuinely oriental while others looked as though they might have been built by the council shortly after the end of the Second World War.

We drove back to Wigtown and Anna's demeanour relaxed as we grew closer to the shop. Her first instinct when she enters the shop is to find Captain, the cat, and within moments they were happily reunited.

The transformer on one of the lights in the Scottish room has blown. I am sick of changing light bulbs on those strings of lights, so bought three used French brass chandeliers from eBay.

Isabel came in to do the accounts. She and her husband have a farm near Newton Stewart, and Isabel is proficient in the accounting package SAGE. She has agreed to organise my accounts for me, thus relieving me of the most dreaded task of the week. She normally comes on Wednesday, but one of her daughters was performing in a concert this week, so she postponed. Her parting words today were 'You've got lots of money in your account.' Nobody has ever used those words in that order when speaking to me before.

Till total £122
11 customers

SATURDAY, 22 MARCH

Online orders: 3
Books found: 3

The sun shone all day, and it was warm enough to open the front door. Nicky arrived at her customary hour (fifteen minutes late), and we started to unload the boxes of books from Samye Ling. Nicky has found a company called Cash for Clothes, which pays £50 a ton for used books. She booked them to collect from the shop on Wednesday so we should be able to dispose of much of the rubbish from the Samye Ling deal.

A few weeks ago a woman bought a copy of *Where No Man Cries*, by Emma Blair. She told me, to my surprise, that Blair was not in fact a woman, but was a 6-foot 3-inch beer-drinking, chain-smoking Glaswegian man called Iain Blair who had only achieved success with his romantic novels when he gave himself a female *nom de plume*. Blair's books have been among the most borrowed books from Scottish libraries in the past twenty years. Before becoming a writer, Blair had been an actor. Apparently his career ended abruptly when, after being called to audition for a part in *Raiders of the Lost Ark*, he was kept waiting for so long that when Steven Spielberg eventually came into the room and said 'Can you come back tomorrow?' he replied, 'No, I fucking cannot.' He died in 2011.

The chandeliers arrived just as Norrie was in the shop to collect some paint that had been delivered here by mistake. He offered to take them away and get them working again, as they have seen better days.

Till total £160.38
17 customers

MONDAY, 24 MARCH

Online orders: 8
Books found: 5

Just as I was returning from the kitchen with my cup of tea, a customer with polyester trousers about six inches too short and a donkey jacket almost knocked it out of my hand and asked, 'Have you ever had a death in here? Has anyone ever died falling off a stepladder in the shop?' I told him, 'Not yet, but I was hoping today might be my lucky day.'

In the emails today was one from a former employee, Sara, who worked for me during school holidays a few years ago: 'Yo Bitch-tits, I need a reference. Here's the form attached. Make it good, you bastard or I will come and get you.' So I wrote this and emailed it to her.

Tel. 01988 402499 www.the-bookshop.com

17 North Main Street, Wigtown DG8 9HL

Monday, March 24, 2014

TO WHOM IT MAY CONCERN

REFERENCE FOR SARA PEARCE

Sara worked Saturdays at The Book Shop, 17 North Main Street, Wigtown, for three years while she was at the Douglas Ewart High School. When I say 'worked', I use the word in its loosest possible terms. She spent the entire day either standing outside the shop, smoking and snarling at people trying to enter the building, or watching repeats of Hollyoaks on 4OD. Although she was generally punctual, she often arrived either drunk or severely hungover. She was usually rude and aggressive. She rarely did as she was told, and never, in the entire three years of her time here, did anything constructive without having to be told to do so. She invariably left a trail of rubbish behind her, usually consisting of Irn-Bru bottles, crisp packets, chocolate wrappers and cigarette packets. She consistently stole lighters and matches from the business, and was offensive and frequently violent towards me.

She was a valued member of staff and I have no hesitation in recommending her.

Till total £109.39

12 customers

TUESDAY, 25 MARCH

Online orders: 3
Books found: 3

Two of today's orders were for 1960s bus timetables for the north of England.

Andrew, the volunteer with Asperger's, turned up at 11 a.m. He was accompanied by the woman from the council, who came with him to make sure that he arrived safely and everything was in order. She suggested that I put him in charge of arranging the crime section into alphabetical order. By noon he had reached the Bs; then he went home.

Shortly after Andrew had left, an extremely rude old woman demanded a copy of Simon Sebag Montefiore's biography of Stalin. We had one in the Russia section, which she brought to the counter. It was an unusually pristine copy in a mint jacket, clearly unread – original price £25. She asked how much it was; I pointed to the sticker that says £6.50. She pushed it away from her and turned, walking out muttering, 'Too expensive.' I'm pretty sure she'll be back, so I re-priced it at £8.50.

Anna's friend Lucy arrived for a visit. She's staying until Monday.

Till total £34.50
7 customers

WEDNESDAY, 26 MARCH

Online orders: 5
Books found: 4

Beautiful sunny morning. Continued sorting through the boxes of books from Samye Ling.

Isabel was in today to do the accounts. The happy 'You've got loads of money' comment after her last visit was long gone, and a measured warning about the state of the shop's parlous financial affairs was her parting comment this time. I suppose that after she told me that I had loads of money I decided it was time to pay off some overdue bills.

No sign of Cash for Clothes, who were supposed to collect the books we can't sell and rotated stock.

Carol-Ann arrived at 5 p.m. She stayed the night because she has to work in Stranraer tomorrow morning, and it is much closer for her from here than from Dalbeattie, where she lives. When Carol-Ann was in her teens, she worked in the shop on Saturdays; she is now in her mid-twenties and has become a good friend. She and Anna get on extremely well, and are forever hatching plans for unlikely businesses which mercifully never reach fruition.

Nicky is working tomorrow and decided to sleep over in the festival bed. The house seemed full and noisy with her, Carol-Ann, Anna and Lucy, all of whom talk a great deal.

Till total £95.75
8 customers

THURSDAY, 27 MARCH

Online orders: 5
Books found: 5

Lucy, Carol-Ann and Nicky demanded a breakfast of bacon rolls, so I spent the first part of the morning chained to the frying pan. When I asked Nicky why Cash for Clothes hadn't turned up, she told me that she hadn't got back to them to confirm the collection because 'you were in a grumpy mood, so I decided not to bother'. She's now booked them, so hopefully they will be here soon and we can clear some space in the shop. There are roughly forty boxes of books to go, around about half a ton.

Top priority of the day was clearing the books off the table and onto shelves so that we can process more boxes of fresh stock, which seem to be piled everywhere, including in friends' sheds. After lunch I went to the bank in Newton Stewart to lodge the takings, and came back to discover that Nicky had opened nearly every box (in flagrant defiance of my 'one box at a time' rule) and had only cleared about half of the table – the one job that I asked her to do before I left. A loud argument ensued and Lucy looked embarrassed, made an excuse and went upstairs. Carol-Ann, on the other hand, laughed like a hyena and goaded us into further conflict.

Someone posted a link on Facebook to a web site of Hungarian librarians being photographed holding books with photos of faces on the cover concealing their own faces. I spent the evening trying to persuade Lucy and Anna to do this but using the 1980s porn mags I bought about a year ago. It is not going well so far.

Till total £128
15 customers

FRIDAY, 28 MARCH

Online orders: 4
Books found: 4

The old woman who complained about the price of the Stalin biography came back. When she found that I had put the price up, she told me that I couldn't do that. I told her that I could. She was furious, but she bought it, muttering that she would never set foot in the place again.

Nicky arrived at 9.15 a.m., as usual, and after a brief repeat of yesterday's row, a new argument followed concerning what she ought to be working on in the shop. We agreed to make a list every morning of what needs to be done so that there is no confusion. Later in the day I found she had made a few additions, including 'Remind Shaun several times to call people back', 'Take Shaun seriously', 'Do not waste valuable time poncing about in front of the camera for Facebook', 'Offer the customer at least three times the value of the books he's selling'. To my delight she has recently acquired a half-hearted suitor. Every time he sees her van (Blue-bottle) parked near the shop, he drops in to say hello and chat to her. He is invariably intoxicated, regardless of the time of day, and he attempts to conceal the smell with overpowering quantities of Brut 33. Nicky makes little, if any, effort to disguise her dislike for him, but this seems only to fuel his ardour.

After lunch I went to the co-op to buy milk. Mike told me that he had caught the stray tom-cat which has been spraying in his house and my shop. Captain will be relieved. He has been jumpy for weeks, and the place has reeked of cat piss.

Anna, Lucy and I went to Galloway House Gardens in the afternoon and picked wild garlic, then spent the evening making wild garlic pesto, using olive oil, parmesan and walnuts. This is one of Anna's highlights of the year.

Nicky found a book in the Samye Ling collection called *Vamping Made Easy*. Disappointingly, it is about piano scales.

Mr Deacon dropped in to order a book shortly before closing, and confirmed that his aunt had received and was delighted with the biography of James I.

Till total £97
10 customers

SATURDAY, 29 MARCH

Online orders: 6
Books found: 6

Nicky took today off, so I was alone in the shop again. Six orders today, including one on Scottish medieval poetry, which is shipping to Baghdad.

An elderly couple came in after lunch, wielding a Farmfoods bag full of books. This is never a promising start. They had been clearing an aunt's house and had come across a few old books which, it transpired, were part of an incomplete set of Dickens – in dreadful condition – from the 1920s. They wanted a valuation. As the husband produced the first book, I told him that it was worth nothing. He clearly did not believe me and continued to produce the others, one at a time, asking, 'How about that one?' I tried to explain that there was no point in showing me any more if they were all from the same set, but five minutes later he was still proffering them.

I went upstairs in the late afternoon, but by the time I got to the kitchen another voice was summoning me down. Standing in the shop was a tall hipster with a beard and tweed cap, holding a Tesco bag full of books. A Tesco bag is an improvement on a Farmfoods bag in terms of the quality of books it is likely to contain, but only a marginal one, and the books in this particular case were indeed better but still stock of which I already had an abundance, so I rejected them, primarily because he kept calling me 'Buddy'.

Till total £105
12 customers

MONDAY, 31 MARCH

Online orders: 5
Books found: 5

Half an hour late opening the shop this morning because I forgot that the clocks had gone forward.

Monsoon was playing up, so I checked the settings. By chance this led me to discover some of Nicky's 'Frequently Used' notes for describing books on our online listings:

'no ink marks'
'which looks to be unread'
'some lovely pictures!'

Normally the notes I would use for describing books would be along the lines of:

'Previous owner's name on front free endpaper'
'Blind stamped front board, five raised bands'
'Deckled edges to pages, bevelled boards'

But, as Nicky frequently points out, these are terms that are only of use when talking to other people in the trade. They are unhelpful when dealing with people who have no understanding of the jargon of books. Ian, my bookseller friend from Grimsby, often has this conversation with his wife, who believes that the language of book jargon belongs to a bygone age and that the internet has made it all but redundant, with the exception of auction catalogues. When I bought the shop in 2001, before the internet morphed into the monstrous retail machine that it has in part become, many booksellers would send out catalogues of their stock to customers on their mailing lists, and by necessity they would have to provide detailed descriptions of the titles they were selling, but the use of vocabulary such as 'gilt dentelles', 'verso' or 'recto', 'octavo', 'fleuron' and 'colophon' has since become almost irrelevant to the selling of books. To my knowledge there is nobody in the trade who still sends out catalogues, and with the swift and apparently inexorable decline in bricks-and-mortar bookshops, I fear that we may go the same way. Our times, though, are not the first transitional period in the history of publishing and bookselling. As Jen Campbell points out in *The Bookshop Book*, following Gutenberg's invention of movable type and the first 'mass market' books becoming available, 'Vespasiano da Bisticci, a famous bookseller in Florence, was so outraged that books would no longer be written out by hand that he closed his shop in a fit of rage, and became the first person in history to prophesy the death of the book industry.'

Our Amazon status has shot back up to Good again.

Since it was a pleasant day, I painted the benches in front of the shop during lunch. An elderly neighbour with whom I have a nodding acquaintance was passing (I had bought the books from her late sister's estate several years previously). She was making her way towards the co-op with her shopping trolley and stopped in front of the shop and started chatting. She told me that she had spent a good deal of money on her garden bench fifteen years ago because it was the first garden she had ever owned and she felt like treating herself. When I asked her where she'd lived before Wigtown, she listed a number of places, including Tokyo and Jerusalem, where she helped create the first Hebrew dictionary. I had no idea that she had led such an interesting life. Ah, the dangers of making assumptions about people. No doubt I do it on a daily basis with my customers, and dismiss people as key-jangling buffoons when they may well have led soldiers onto the beaches of Normandy or pioneered ground-breaking medical research.

After lunch I drove to Dumfries and dropped Anna and Lucy at the railway station to return to London (each armed with a jar of wild garlic pesto) and was back in the shop by 4 p.m.

For the last hour of the day the shop was occupied by a family of six – mum, dad and four girls aged between six and sixteen. When the time came to pay for their books, the mother told me that they had all been out for a walk in the morning and the girls had been miserable, despite the sunny weather. She had asked why they were so unhappy and they replied in unison that all they wanted to do was visit The Book Shop as they hadn't been here for two years and were really excited about returning. They spent £175 and left with six bags of books. These things happen far too rarely, but when they do they serve as a welcome reminder of why I chose to enter the world of bookselling, and of how important bookshops are to many people.

My mother came in at 4 p.m. and dropped off a box of three Creme Eggs for Easter. I'm not overly fond of chocolate, but my appetite for it is quite unsophisticated. Anna is very partial to extremely strong dark chocolate, as is Callum, and they regularly gang up to mock me for having the same taste as a small child. On the rare occasions during which I am afflicted by a craving, mine is for sugary milk chocolate and Creme Eggs are exactly what I want.

After I had locked up I went to the co-op for milk and bread. Mike was working there, and he told me that the Cats Protection League had neutered the spraying cat he had trapped. He and Emma (his partner) have decided to keep it.

Till total £288.48
14 customers

APRIL

Our shop had an exceptionally interesting stock, yet I doubt whether ten per cent of our customers knew a good book from a bad one.

George Orwell, 'Bookshop Memories'

Of course, one person's good book is another person's bad book; the matter is entirely subjective. One of my friends is a fine jewellery dealer in London. I once asked him how he decided what to buy and what not to buy when he was at auction. He explained that when he'd started out in the trade, he bought things that looked inoffensive and that – he considered – would have universal appeal. He quickly learned that these did not sell particularly well and rarely commanded a high price, so he changed his strategy – 'Now, if I see something which evokes a strong reaction in me, I'll buy it. Whether I absolutely adore it or utterly hate it, I can guarantee that I'll get a good price for it.'

Plenty of booksellers specialise. I don't. The shop has as wide a range of subjects and titles as I can cram into it. I hope that there's something for everybody, but even with 100,000 titles in stock many people still leave empty-handed. Whether someone buys a Mills and Boon for £2.50 or a bashed paperback copy of Spinoza's *Ethics* for £2.50 is irrelevant. Each will, I hope, derive equal pleasure from the experience of reading.

TUESDAY, 1 APRIL

Online orders: 2
Books found: 2

Norrie came in and replaced the strip lights with chandeliers, plunging the Scottish room into darkness for the entire morning. They look infinitely better than the hideous strip lights, which lent the place the atmosphere of a hospital corridor. Over the years I've been replacing them and only have four left to do out of the twenty-two that were here when I took over in 2001.

Andrew (the volunteer with Asperger's) came in at 11 a.m. and worked until noon. He's made it as far as the Cs in the crime section now but became very flustered when someone asked him where the railway books were, and had to have a sit down.

This morning I received an email from my mother, who had to borrow my father's iPad to send it because hers is 'constipated' – could I come down and fix it some time soon? I replied that I'd get round to it as soon as I could.

At 3 p.m. I drove to the bank in Newton Stewart, returning just before closing to discover that Cash for Clothes had been and collected the boxes of books, and paid me £25 for them. They pay by weight and took away half a ton of books.

In today's post was a letter from Mrs Phillips ('ninety-three and blind') addressed simply to 'Shaun Bythell, Book Dealer in Wigtown, Scotland', which by virtue of Galloway being so unpopulated found its way here. As always, it was a request for a book for one of her great-grandchildren: this time *Kidnapped,* by Robert Louis Stevenson.

Till total £71
10 customers

WEDNESDAY, 2 APRIL

Online orders: 1
Books found: 1

The first visitor of the day was a wild-haired woman who regularly drops off the *Green Handbook for Southwest Scotland*, a booklet full of addresses of homeopaths and crystal healers. She came round when I was on the telephone. Every time she visits I'm on the telephone, so I never have the opportunity to tell her that I don't want her to drop them off any more because nobody ever picks them up.

She was closely followed by a couple in their late sixties, clad in clinging Lycra cycling gear. They came to the counter with four Wainwright Lakeland climbing books in nearly mint condition.

The man put them on the counter and asked, 'What can you do for me on those?' so I added them up. The total came to £20, and I told him that he could have them for £17. He visibly winced, then replied, 'Can't you do them for £15?' When I pointed out that would be a 25 per cent discount, he said, 'If you don't ask, you don't get.' Finally they coughed up the £17 and left a trail of resentment in their wake.

Till total £115.94
10 customers

THURSDAY, 3 APRIL

Online orders: 6
Books found: 5

The day got off to a bad start with a telephone call from Carol-Ann at 8.50 a.m. telling me that she was outside and asking why the shop wasn't open. I told her that I open at 9 a.m., came down and let her in. I had forgotten that she had called the previous afternoon to ask if it was all right to meet with one of her business clients in the kitchen. She works for a company that helps people to start small businesses and has a vast area to cover, so she often uses the shop as a place to hold meetings. She immediately accused me of looking rough and developing a bald patch. Nicky arrived shortly afterwards and agreed about both.

Mother emailed me again to request assistance with her constipated iPad.

After lunch I drove to Glasgow to look at a collection of railway books. It turned out to be an extremely good library, all in pristine condition. The seller was an old man who was dealing with his late brother's estate. I gave him £400 for eight boxes. Books about railways are probably the best-selling subject in the shop, something I could never have imagined when I bought the business fifteen years ago.

The day ended with an Association of Wigtown Booksellers'

(AWB) meeting here at 5.30 p.m. Tea, biscuits, etc. as usual. The discussion was largely about what we are going to do for a venue during the May festival now that the distillery has closed. It's a bit embarrassing since the theme is whisky and most events were scheduled to take place in the distillery. The May festival is organised by the AWB, which comprises a handful of us who have bookshops in Wigtown. We have no budget, and the festival is run on a shoestring. Although it lacks the financial weight and big names of the September festival, it is slowly becoming part of Wigtown's cultural calendar. Anne, one of the full-time festival employees, provides invaluable help with putting the programme together, and I suspect that without her it might not happen.

The meeting went reasonably well, with the usual discussions about new signage, who is doing what, Joyce's broken shoulder etc., but the highlight came when the subject of producing an app about the Wigtown Martyrs was brought up. Most of us were either vaguely supportive or indifferent to the idea, although two of the company held fairly extreme polar opposite opinions on the subject and a row ensued during which accusations of bigotry and prejudice were levelled across the table while the rest of us looked on in awkward embarrassment.

The Wigtown Martyrs were two women who refused to wear the religious straitjacket of their day: the late seventeenth century. During that time dogma dictated that – among many other things – the king was recognised as the official head of the Church. In Scotland there was opposition to this, and the rebels were known as the Covenanters. They faced ruthless persecution by government forces in what became known as 'The Killing Times'. Margaret Wilson and Margaret McLaughlan were two women of the covenant who were executed for their beliefs. They were tied to wooden stakes on the shore at the foot of Wigtown hill as the tide came in. The elder Margaret was tied further out in the hope that the younger Margaret, watching her drown, would change her mind and conform. She did not. There is a monument on the salt-marsh marking the site of the execution – the Martyrs' Stake – and their graves are in the Church of Scotland cemetery in the town. Before they were taken to be drowned, they were imprisoned in the cell in the old tollbooth. This room is now known as the Martyrs' Cell.

It is unfortunate that Wigtown's most famous daughters came to such an unedifying end. Wigtown has put forth many significant people into the world, among them Helen Carte, who (along with her husband Richard) ran the D'Oyly Carte Opera Company; Paul Laverty (who is Ken Loach's screenwriter) was at Wigtown's now defunct Catholic school; the botanist John McConnell Black and footballer Dave Kevan are sons of Wigtown too. Indeed, the actor James Robertson Justice – a one-time resident of the town – so loved the place that on a number of occasions he falsely claimed it as his birthplace.

Till total £301
14 customers

FRIDAY, 4 APRIL

Online orders: 3
Books found: 1

Three orders, all Amazon; only found one. One of the missing books was Rory Stewart's *The Places in Between,* which Nicky had listed as being on shelf Q6 in the Scottish room, despite its being a book about Afghanistan, written by a man who was born in Hong Kong. Perhaps the Scottish-sounding name confused her. As I was taking the sacks of mail over to Wilma, I bumped into Jock, who used to work in the shop when John Carter owned it. Jock is famous for his long-winded and frankly unlikely stories. They usually involve someone trying to trick him, and then him spotting their ruse and getting the better of them. Almost all of them end up in a fight, which he inevitably wins. He is notoriously difficult to understand both because of his strong accent and dialect, and because he has no teeth. Today he told me about a woman whose garden he works in once a week. According to Jock, she's not a very good driver because of her poor vision. 'She's got carrots in her eyes.'

At 12.15 p.m. a customer telephoned to tell me that he'd bought a book from us which was the first in a 'triology'. It had cost him £7.20, including postage, and he was very happy with it. He now wants to buy volume II, but our copy of volume II is the only copy available online and is £200, which he wasn't prepared to pay. He wanted it for the same price as he had paid for volume I. I tried to explain that as ours was the only copy available online it was a much more scarce book, and the price remained at £200. He told me he was 'disgusted' and hung up.

Following a conversation with Anna, I am considering organising a Random Book Club event in London – probably a talk by an author, but the audience won't know who the author will be until the talk starts. I emailed Robert Twigger, and he is happy to help out. Rob is a regular at Wigtown Book Festival, and normally stays in my house for the full ten days. He is a writer, and has won many awards and prizes: his best-known work is probably *Angry White Pyjamas*, for which he won the William Hill Sports Book of the Year award. He is an adventurer and an explorer, an extremely entertaining man, and I count myself very lucky to know him, and to have him as a good friend. He lived with his family in Cairo until the revolution of 2011, after which they decided to move back to the UK. He now lives in Dorset. During the September book festival last year I noticed that Eliot had unplugged one of my table lamps and had plugged in his Kindle. This was an affront on so many levels that when I pointed it out to Rob, he decided that the best form of revenge was to download a book called *Two in the Bush: The Fine Art of Vaginal Fisting* onto it. I doubt whether his wife was terribly impressed.

Callum and I went for a pint after I had closed the shop, then I nipped to the co-op for some milk. Mike was working, and he looked more than a little sheepish. I asked him how the newly neutered stray cat was settling in, and he told me that he had been verbally abused by a woman yesterday who had come into the co-op and accused him of stealing her cat. Apparently she had been looking for it for weeks, since it had run away. She was not best pleased to hear it has had its balls chopped off.

Till total £103.99
12 customers

SATURDAY, 5 APRIL

Online orders: 3
Books found: 2

Nicky in, as always fifteen minutes late and armed with an excuse which, however unlikely it sounds, I know is the truth. Today's offering was that she'd dropped an éclair that she was eating (raided from the Morrisons skip) on her lap while she was driving and had to stop and clean her skirt before the chocolate melted into it. I made her a cup of tea in a different mug from her customary MacDonald tartan one. She is particularly fussy about bone china, and a common porcelain mug appeared to cause her undue confusion. Shortly after she arrived, Smelly Kelly, her Brut 33-soaked suitor appeared and tried to convince her to join him for some sort of family reunion. She was having none of it.

One of today's orders was for a book titled *A History of Orgies*.

Another new Random Book Club member signed up today.

At 11 a.m. an extremely large woman brought in six boxes of cookery books, mostly about dieting. I gave her £70 for them.

After lunch I brought in the eight boxes of railway books I picked up on Thursday in Glasgow. As I was stacking them in the front of the shop, a man (who had managed to position himself so that I had to say 'excuse me' with every single box I brought in) asked me 'Are those more boxes of books?', as if he had unearthed a dark secret. When I told him that they were, he laughed loudly for an uncomfortably long time.

When you deal with large numbers of different people every day, you start to notice behavioural patterns. One of the more curious for me is to see what people laugh at. I have no idea why that customer found it so unimaginably amusing that a bookseller was bringing boxes of books into a bookshop. Quite often it is something that isn't the slightest bit amusing that triggers laughter, and even more frequently people will laugh at one of their own banal comments or observations. Sometimes it appears to be used as a sort of punctuation mark to denote the end of a sentence. I once bought a psychology library from a house in Cumbria, among which was a book called *Laughter*, by Robert R. Provine. According to him, only primates have the capacity to laugh, and 'there are thousands of languages, hundreds of thousands of dialects, but everyone speaks laughter in pretty much the same way'. Nor is laughter particularly confined to humour; speakers tend to laugh 20 per cent more than their audiences. Despite this, and the fact that laughter is clearly social shorthand for amicability, the things at which customers laugh still baffle me.

After work I went down to my parents' house to fix Mum's 'constipated' iPad. One of their friends was there, and we had a long conversation about pets, during which he confessed that he never gives his dogs food that he would not be prepared to eat himself. On a number of occasions this has resulted in him eating tinned dog food.

Till total £345.87
23 customers

MONDAY, 7 APRIL

Online orders: 6
Books found: 6

One order was for the Penguin edition of John Steinbeck's letters, which we had listed a few weeks ago for £5. It sold online for £24. At the time of listing, ours was price-matched against the cheapest copy online, which must have sold, and ours has been re-priced against the next cheapest, which was £24. This usually works the other way round and books online become cheaper as dealers undercut one another.

Our Amazon seller status has dropped from Good to Fair again, thanks to the unfulfilled orders from Friday and Saturday.

Sold a book called *The Dieter's Guide to Weight Loss During Sex* to an American woman.

When I was sorting through the books that a man had brought in in bin-liners on Saturday, I found a woven Victorian bookmark in a book onto which were stitched the words 'I love little Pussy' with a picture of a cat beneath it.

The shop was extremely busy today, no doubt because it is school holiday time. At 5 p.m. a woman asked if her husband had left, so I told her that I had no idea who her husband was or what he looked like. She scowled and left.

Email in the inbox at closing from Crail Bookshop in Fife, which has just closed down. They have 12,000 books that they want to sell, and offered me a chance to look at them with a view to buying. I declined. Trade stock has usually been run down and the best books removed before it is sold as a single lot.

Another email from a collector in Edinburgh who has 13,000 books to sell. I replied asking for more information.

Till total £239.37
33 customers

TUESDAY, 8 APRIL

Online orders: 4
Books found: 4

At 10.15 a.m. a woman walked in and roared, 'I am in my element! Books!', then continued to shout questions at me for an hour while she waddled about the shop like a 'stately goose', as Gogol describes Sobakevich's wife in *Dead Souls*. Predictably, she didn't buy anything.

Andrew arrived at 11 a.m. and worked until noon. He managed to finish the Cs in the crime section.

Just as I came downstairs from making a cup of tea, a man came to the counter with a copper bracelet from the table of antiques in the shop and asked, 'C'est combien?' Quite why he chose to speak in French I have no idea. He wasn't even French; he was Scottish.

Eliot arrived at 4 p.m., and promptly removed his shoes. Within five minutes I had tripped on them twice.

Four customers commented on how fat Captain has become.

The shop was bustling all day, but I managed to finish *Dead Souls* despite this.

Till total £451.41
33 customers

Online orders: 1
Books found: 1

Unusually, Nicky was at work on time today; she's occasionally ten minutes early but normally fifteen minutes late. She arrived clutching her hairbrush and toothbrush and ran upstairs to smarten herself up. She looked exactly the same when she came down. When I asked her why she was in such a flap, she replied, 'Dinnae try to eat cold stir-fry when you're driving. I went over a bump and most of it ended up going up my sleeves and down my cleavage.'

She dodged off for lunch just as an American family came in. Three generations. The grandfather came to the counter with three books, slammed them down and barked, 'Here, lad' at me, then thrust his credit card at the machine and followed with, 'You people take credit cards, don't you?' while his grandchildren charged about the shop making chaos as their father shouted at them. He came to the counter with an eighteenth-century four-volume history of Scotland, priced at £100, and asked where our section on Badenoch was. When I told him that we don't have a specific section on Badenoch, he ploughed on, telling me that that was where his family was from, as though this was somehow better than being from any other place. The sense of peace when they left was practically palpable but, in their defence, they bought the £100 set. They are redeemed.

Often, even after you've told customers that you do not have a copy of the book they're looking for in stock, they will insist on telling you at great length and in tedious detail why they're looking

72

for that particular title. A few possible explanations for this have occurred to me, but the one by which I am most convinced is that it is an exercise in intellectual masturbation. They want you to know that this is a subject about which they are informed, and even if they are wrong about whatever they've chosen to pontificate on, they drone on – normally at a volume calculated to reach not only the cornered bookseller but everyone else in the vicinity too.

Finn, Anna and I were having a meeting in the kitchen when Eliot burst in, talking loudly on his phone. Rather than apologise for the intrusion, he kicked off his shoes and carried on talking. Eventually we moved into the drawing room, unable to compete with the volume of the one half of Eliot's conversation that he was sharing with us.

Nicky stayed the night. Eliot had offered to buy supper at the pub, so I grabbed Nicky and we headed over. We had a couple of pints then came back. Nicky went straight to bed in the festival bed, while Eliot and I clattered about upstairs, just a few feet above her head.

Till total £537
24 customers

THURSDAY, 10 APRIL

Online orders: 3
Books found: 3

Awoke at 7 a.m. to the symphonic chaos of Eliot stomping, stamping and crashing around having baths, cups of tea, packing etc. before he finally left at 7.30 a.m. Shortly after that I heard Nicky stirring downstairs, making a tiny fraction of the noise that Eliot had, doing exactly the same things.

Nicky suggested that we make small posters asking customers to read a passage from their favourite book to us on film in the shop, to which I reluctantly agreed, then forced Carol-Ann to do one. Nicky chose for her a book aimed at eleven-year-olds from the children's section. She looked deeply offended but read a bit anyway.

Till total £424
31 customers

Online orders: 3
Books found: 3

Foodie Friday. Today Nicky brought in two egg custard tarts that she had pillaged from the skip. She had accidentally sat on one of them in her van.

At 11 a. m., as I came downstairs from making a cup of tea, a customer in socks and sandals accosted me and said, 'I want to talk to you about the price of your copy of *The Busconductor Hines*. It says it is £65. Surely that can't be right.' So I checked online, and ours was indeed the cheapest first edition in a mint jacket available. He tutted and eventually came to the counter with a paperback edition of it priced at £2.50. Last week a similar thing happened involving a copy of Iain M. Banks's *Feersum Endjinn*.

During lunch I overheard a group of customers in their early twenties discussing the shop. One of them said it was the 'coolest shop' she'd ever been in. Presumably she was referring to the temperature.

As I was locking up the back of the shop, I noticed that there were several large rafts of frogspawn in the pond.

Till total £182.49
19 customers

SATURDAY, 12 APRIL

Online orders: 4
Books found: 2

Nicky turned up, as usual at this time of year, in her black ski suit. She looked as though she belonged in the freezer unit of an industrial butcher's rather than a bookshop. This morning she told me that she 'couldnae be bothered' to process the orders on the Royal Mail system and that I could do it on Monday. I have given up the struggle with Nicky when it comes to this sort of thing. In the past, when I've asked her to do things, she has nodded enthusiastically then completely ignored what I have said and proceeded to do whatever she feels like doing. She is reliable and industrious, though, and exceptionally entertaining. And she loves the shop and does whatever she can to improve the stock and make the business work better. It is just slightly unfortunate that we have different opinions about what those things are.

The wind today was a cold easterly, so I lit the fire at 10 a.m. Plenty of customers. As I was walking through the shop putting fresh stock on the shelves, I spotted three young boys quietly reading on the festival bed. I normally discourage customers from going onto the festival bed, largely because it is usually children who treat it as a play area and mess it up, after which I have to go up and tidy it. There's a rope across the access, but these boys must have crawled under it. It would have taken a heart of stone to tell them to move, as they sat there, quietly engrossed.

This evening I started reading the copy of *The Third Policeman* that an old girlfriend gave to me years ago and I hadn't got round to reading.

Till total £479.97
36 customers

MONDAY, 14 APRIL

Online orders: 3
Books found: 2

The last customer of the day was a young Italian woman who bought a two-volume edition of Boccaccio's *Decameron*, dated 1679, which had been on the shelves for at least ten years. It was the only decent thing to come from the contents of a flat above a near-derelict Italian café in New Cumnock, which had belonged to an old woman who had died a few months before we were asked to clear the books by one of the executors of her estate.

I drove there on a dark, sleeting Monday night back in January 2003 after I had shut the shop, and met the woman who had been charged with the thankless task of disposing of the contents of the flat. The place was in a dreadful state; the roof was leaking badly, the floral wallpaper was peeling, bare bulbs clung to cobweb-covered cables from ceilings of exposed lath and crumbling plaster. There was no evidence of anything having been cleaned for years. It had clearly been inhabited by an elderly spinster; all the bedding was pink and covered with cat hair. There were probably two thousand books, all damp and thick with cat hair too, and – with the exception of the *Decameron* – every one of them was from The Book Club, a publisher that most booksellers avoid at all costs (the market for them is almost non-existent). While I was searching for something that might have made the trip worthwhile among the damp dross, the woman who met us explained that the last occupant had been the only daughter of an Italian immigrant who had come to Scotland in the 1920s. He had met and married a Scottish woman, and they had opened a café in an empty property below the flat. It had rapidly become the busiest place in the town, bustling and thriving.

The executor found a dusty chest of drawers, pulled one of them open and extracted a yellowed photograph album which contained hundreds of black-and-white photographs of the place in its heyday – full of smiling people, every table full, people dancing. When the Italian man died, a few years after his wife in the 1970s, he had handed on the business to his only child, his daughter, but times had changed and the business declined and eventually closed. Downstairs the big glass windows were boarded up, and the place – once busy – was as silent as the grave, save for the sound of the rain coming through the roof and dripping onto the floor. The optimism of that young Italian man, with his Scottish wife, his thriving business and his young daughter, the courage it took him to move to another country, learn a new language and start a business and a new life could never have anticipated the sad end that fate dealt to his dream. I am quite sure that the two-volume *Decameron* would have been among the few possessions he brought with him from Italy, and I wonder how long it might have been passed down through his family, only to end that inheritance here in a damp flat in New Cumnock with nobody to pass it on to. But now it will have a new life in the hands of the young woman who bought it today, and who knows what the next few hundred years will have in store for it?

Till total £248.28
21 customers

TUESDAY, 15 APRIL

Online orders: 3
Books found: 2

Sandy the tattooed pagan dropped in to see if our stick supply needs to be topped up. We haven't sold one for at least a month.

Telephone call from the council telling me that Andrew won't be coming in any more as he found the experience too exhausting. I was growing to like him.

Mr Deacon dropped in at 4.20 p.m. to order a copy of Jenny Uglow's *A Gambling Man*, a copy of which I had, by chance, put on the shelves earlier in the day. He was as delighted as he allows himself to become in company.

Till total £179.99
12 customers

WEDNESDAY, 16 APRIL

Online orders: 5
Books found: 5

Two very sweet ginger-haired girls came in this morning and asked if this was Captain's shop. They must be locals, or perhaps they follow the shop on Facebook. Captain's fame has clearly spread wider than I had thought. While we were chatting about how fat Captain has become recently, a man in an extremely tight pair of shorts came to the counter and bought a book called *The Book of Successful Fireplaces*.

In the early afternoon a man who was probably about my age came in and kicked off his shoes, and left them by the door. I suppose I am not really in a position to criticise; quite often I wander about the place barefoot during the summer, but I am not sure if I would do it in anyone else's shop.

Till total £340.35
35 customers

THURSDAY, 17 APRIL

Online orders: 3
Books found: 3

Nicky arrived in her summer ensemble, her ski suit now consigned to the winter wardrobe until November. Today's outfit comprised a long skirt made from some sort of nettle fibre, and a home-made paisley shirt with a brown tunic (again home-made). She could easily pass for an extra from a low-budget adaptation of *Robin Hood*.

One of the books ordered today was for *The Female Instructor*, an early Victorian 'guide to domestic happiness'. In today's context it reads more like a guide to domestic abuse.

In the afternoon a customer asked if he could be videoed reading from his favourite book, so I set up the tripod and sat him by the fire. His reading was beautiful; he chose to read from *Cold Comfort Farm*, and read it in a lyrical Welsh accent. After he'd finished I was chatting to him and his wife and asked what they were doing in the area. She told me that they were on their way to Larne, to which I replied, 'Why? It's an awful place.' Larne, apparently, is where they live.

Till total £319.70
30 customers

FRIDAY, 18 APRIL

Online orders: 5
Books found: 5

Good Friday.

Katie was working in the shop today as Nicky was off doing Jehovah's Witness things. Katie is a medical student who has worked in the shop for several summers and lacks any respect for me whatsoever. She moved here with her mother and sister from Oxford when she was a child.

A customer came to the counter and said, 'I've looked under the W section of the fiction and I can't find anything by Rider Haggard.' I suggested that he had a look under the H section.

Till total £197.89
18 customers

SATURDAY, 19 APRIL

Online orders: 3
Books found: 3

Katie was in again today, covering for Nicky, so I asked her to package the books for the Random Book Club (which now has 163 members) and deal with the Royal Mail account for them. When I went to the post office to ask Wilma if the postman could pick them up, she told me that he could do it on Tuesday (Easter Monday = Bank Holiday).

As the shop was about to close, there was a telephone call from Mrs Phillips ('I am ninety-three and blind, you know'), who couldn't remember the title of Mrs Gaskell's first novel and wanted to know if I could tell her.

Till total £250.49
17 customers

MONDAY, 21 APRIL

Online orders: 3
Books found: 2

The first customer brought in a book covered in bubble wrap and tissue paper. It was a theological work in Latin, dated 1716. He asked for a valuation, so I suggested that about £40 would probably a reasonable price for it, at which point he told me (indignantly) that Bonhams had valued it at £50.

One of the orders today was for a book called *Liquid Gold: The Lore and Logic of Using Urine to Grow Plants*.

Till total £162.43
18 customers

TUESDAY, 22 APRIL

Online orders: 3
Books found: 3

Telephone call at 11 a.m. from someone who asked 'How do you go about doing book readings in your shop?' Further scrutiny revealed that his genre is fantasy and that he wants to read from his latest book, which is about mermaids – 'It's set in the sea.' It is hard to imagine where else it could be set.

At 2 p.m. a customer came to the counter with a beautifully illustrated book on salmon fishing from the 1920s which he had found in the Garden Room. It was unpriced. He asked how much it was, and – feeling generous – I said, 'You can have it for £2.50.' He walked out muttering, 'I'll get it for less on Amazon.' So I checked the book shortly afterwards and found that the cheapest Amazon copy is £22. It is now priced at £12 in the shop, but I doubt he will be back.

As I was about to close the shop, there was a telephone call from a woman in Moffat who has a legal library to sell. I tend to avoid these as they are not easy to sell on, but you never know what else you might find among them, so I arranged to go and view the collection on Saturday.

The postman picked up the seven sacks of parcels for the Random Book Club at 4.30 p.m.

Till total £286.49
22 customers

WEDNESDAY, 23 APRIL

Online orders: 2
Books found: 2

A man smelling of TCP was the only customer in the shop for the first hour of opening, during which time I attempted to put out fresh stock. He had an uncanny ability to be standing in front of every shelf to which I needed access, regardless of the subject or where in the shop the relevant shelves were.

Till total £233.48
19 customers

THURSDAY, 24 APRIL

Online orders: 3
Books found: 3

Nicky was in today so that she can take tomorrow off. She decided to eat her breakfast in the shop instead of her van. Normally she devours it while she is driving in to work, which inevitably results in most of it covering her hessian skirt and Robin Hood tabard.

An elderly customer told me that her book club's next book was *Dracula*, but she couldn't remember what he'd written.

I noticed that two of the three Creme Eggs my mother gave me were missing.

Till total £160.70
14 customers

FRIDAY, 25 APRIL

Online orders: 3
Books found: 3

No Nicky today, so no revolting gourmet delights from the Morrisons skip.

After lunch a customer brought in four boxes of books: 'You'll love these, they're all best-sellers.' I picked out a few books and offered him £5. He looked horrified and announced that he would rather give them to the charity shop, where – he confidently assured me – 'they appreciate quality'.

The phenomenon of the best-seller in the publishing industry does not seem to translate into the same financial cash cow in the second-hand book industry. Perhaps people who buy into the best-seller concept will always buy their books new, to be on the crest of the wave as it breaks rather than the troughs behind it. Perhaps also because the Dan Browns and Tom Clancys of this world are published in such vast quantities that there is never any scarcity value in them for the dealer or the collector. What passes for a best-seller in the new book market is precisely the sort of book that will be a dog in the second-hand trade. Customers often fail to understand this and think that their first edition of *Harry Potter and the Deathly Hallows* is worth a fortune, when in fact 12 million of them were printed. As an author's success and fame increase, so too will the size of the print runs of their successive books. Hence a first edition of *Casino Royale* (of which only 4,728 first edition hardbacks were printed) will be worth considerably more than a copy of *The Man with the Golden Gun*, which had a first-edition, first-issue print run of 82,000.

Till total £243.40
20 customers

SATURDAY, 26 APRIL

Online orders: 3
Books found: 2

Nicky was in today. I asked her if she knew what happened to the box of three Creme Eggs that my mother had given me for Easter and which had been behind the counter. She denied all knowledge of them at first, then told me that she'd had to give one to a 'crying child who had tripped over a rug in the shop'. When I asked her if she'd eaten any of them, she replied, 'Maybe just a wee nibble.' The crying child was clearly her. She eventually confessed to eating them all, telling me, 'I don't know why. I dinnae even like Creme Eggs.'

A customer appeared at the counter at 10 a.m. and asked 'Where are the children's books?' I pointed towards the children's section and replied 'They're just through that door there.' The customer turned 180 degrees from where I'd just pointed and aimed her finger towards the front door of the shop, through which she had – literally seconds earlier – entered the building, and said, 'What, that door there?'

After lunch I drove to Moffat to view the library of a firm of solicitors that had closed a few years earlier. Probably forty boxes. Most were of little interest, so I just took the Session Court volumes, roughly 150 of them, in fairly standard legal bindings. I'll sell them on eBay as a job lot. Bindings like these used to sell for about £300 a yard, so it will be interesting to see what these make. There are seven yards of them.

I returned to the shop to the unmistakable reek of Smelly Kelly's Brut 33, but fortunately I missed him by a few minutes.

Till total £269.99
24 customers

MONDAY, 28 APRIL

Online orders: 4
Books found: 4

Shortly after I opened the shop there was a telephone call about a book that a customer had ordered online. It arrived on Saturday, and she wasn't happy about it because the last five pages were torn: 'I've got a thing about books with torn pages, they give me the creeps. Can I return it?' I reluctantly agreed to let her send it back for a refund.

At 4.30 p.m. a man with a moustache and a baseball cap asked, 'You don't sell books, do you?' then laughed uproariously.

Till total £92.96
13 customers

TUESDAY, 29 APRIL

Online orders: 3
Books found: 2

The Maltese woman who had been in the shop in March (complaining that there were no second-hand bookshops in Malta) dropped in to introduce herself. Her name is Tracy, and she had been here back then for an interview in the Osprey Room with the RSPB, for the job of being their representative. There is a pair of ospreys that has returned to a nest just outside Wigtown for the past six years; the RSPB has a live video link to the nest in the County Buildings. She is here for the summer to work there, although quite what she is going to do is a subject of much speculation since there is no sign of the ospreys as yet this year.

Three customers, on entering the shop, complained that they couldn't see anything in the shop because it was so bright outside and their eyes had not adjusted. This is far from unusual and often explained in a tone suggesting that I am personally responsible for the involuntary reflex of the customer's irises.

I finished *The Third Policeman* during the afternoon, when the shop was quiet.

Till total £121.98
12 customers

WEDNESDAY, 30 APRIL

Online orders: 0
Books found: 0

Katie was in today. She spent most of the day pricing up fresh stock and putting it on the shelves.

I lit the stove in the shop for the last time until autumn sets in. From May to October it's warm enough in the shop for the fire not to be necessary. Also the swallows, swifts and house martins arrive in May, and the martins nest in the log store. I don't like to disturb them once they have started breeding.

No orders this morning, which usually means that there is a problem with Monsoon, so I emailed them and hopefully they will fix it.

A customer brought in a collection of books about Burma which he wanted to sell: probably fifty titles. He declined my offer of £85.

After lunch I drove to Dumfries to pick up Anna from the railway station – she is back for the Spring Festival and hates to miss out on anything that's going on in Wigtown. I sometimes suspect that she misses the cat as much as she misses me, from the attention she lavishes upon him.

When we returned from Dumfries, we were met by a customer who asked if we stock old volumes of *The Scots Magazine*. On hearing that we do not, for some reason he took this as the signal to tell me – at considerable length – which issues he was looking for, and why.

Just before closing I checked the inbox and found an email from Rob Twigger telling me that he is coming up to visit tomorrow.

Till total £147.50
14 customers

MAY

It is not true that men do not read novels, but it is true that there are whole branches of fiction that they avoid. Roughly speaking, what one might call the average novel – the ordinary, good-bad, Galsworthy-and-water stuff which is the norm of the English novel – seems to exist only for women. Men read either the novels it is possible to respect, or detective stories.

George Orwell, 'Bookshop Memories'

Despite the success of the television serialisation of *The Forsyte Saga*, the 'Galsworthy-and-water' type of books to which Orwell refers are entirely overlooked by today's customers, and Jeffery Farnol, Dennis Wheatley, Warwick Deeping, O. Douglas, Baroness Orczy – so rapaciously consumed in their heyday – now only serve as resting places for dust and dead bluebottles. As regards women being greater fiction readers, Orwell's gender stereotyping is still largely true today, although his assertion that only men 'read … the novels it is possible to respect' by today's standards sounds – at the very least – anachronistic. My own taste must be unusual by his reckoning in that I prefer fiction (but not detective stories). Most non-fiction, unless it's a passion (such as Galloway – I am currently reading Dane Love's book *The Galloway Highlands*), seems be pretty hard work as far as I can see, but the immersive capacity of a good novel to transport you into a different world is unique to the written word.

On the whole (in my shop at least) the majority of fiction is still bought by women, while men rarely buy anything other than non-fiction, a trend borne out in a completely unscientific experiment carried out by the author Ian McEwan a few years ago in London. He decided to give away free copies of one of his books during a busy lunchtime. Almost all of those who showed appreciation were women, and those who responded with suspicion were nearly all men. This led McEwan to conclude in *The Guardian* that 'When women stop reading, the novel will be dead' – a sentiment with which Orwell might, up to a point, have agreed. It is hard to predict what customers will buy, although the number of men who head straight to the railway section is uncanny.

During the Wigtown Book Festival (which takes place over ten days at the end of September), it is always the non-fiction events that can be relied upon to draw the largest audiences. Poetry seems to be the one thing for which there is barely any audience at all – a sad fact that is reflected in the shop. Poetry contributes very little to the daily takings. Heaney, Hughes, Auden, Eliot, MacDiarmid, Wendy Cope and a smattering of others tick over, but the Tennysons, Cowpers, Brownings and Lowells sit heavily on the shelves, only occasionally disturbed by the hand of a curious customer. They are poetic fossils that perhaps one day will be unearthed and dusted off by literary paleontologists.

THURSDAY, I MAY

Online orders: 0
Books found: 0

No orders again today and still no word from Monsoon.

Nicky arrived at the shop dressed in her medieval tabard and a pair of trousers so yellow that they had the appearance of the yolk of an egg that has been exposed to dangerous levels of radiation. She announced that she is going to supplement her income by turning her van into a mobile DIY shop. She disappeared during her lunch break and turned up later with an enormous piece of fungus that she had cut from a tree near the Martyrs' Stake, just at the bottom of Wigtown Hill, a hundred yards past the last house in the town. She has decided that it is edible and is most likely Chicken of the Woods. She spent much of the day trying to convince me to eat some. The only thing I'm convinced of is that she is trying to kill me.

Monsoon eventually replied to my email and logged on to our system remotely, and repaired whatever was blocking the orders.

In the middle of the afternoon, as Nicky and I were in the middle of an argument about evolution (we had just reached the usual 'you might be a monkey but I'm not' stage), Mr Deacon appeared. He had, apparently, lost his copy of *A Gambling Man* before he'd finished it and wanted to order another one. The evolution argument resumed as soon as he had left.

Till total £99.50
10 customers

FRIDAY, 2 MAY

Online orders: 3
Books found: 3

Nicky was in again today. I opened the door to find Twigger waiting outside with his bag. I had forgotten to leave any doors open before I had gone to bed last night. He had slept in the garden. I apologised, to which he replied, 'No problem, man. I like sleeping outside.'

Today was the first day of the Wigtown Spring Festival. This is a small series of events organised by the Association of Wigtown Booksellers. Without much of a budget for visiting speakers or for promotion, it is by necessity a small affair and barely generates a fraction of the footfall of the September festival, whose budget is now close to £400,000. Events in the Spring Festival take place in the shops and smaller venues which we can afford, and are usually attended by locals.

Nicky went back down the hill to cut more Chicken of the Woods. She fried it up in the kitchen. Twigger is running a book to see if she is still alive tomorrow.

Anna and I spent much of the day moving furniture in the drawing room in preparation for a Whisky Supper, which took place upstairs in the drawing room. Sixteen tickets sold. The catering was done by Maria, an Australian woman who moved to the area with her husband and children a few years ago. He is a teacher, and she set up a catering business. She is very enthusiastic. Everything, regardless of whether it is or is not, is 'fantastic'. The meal was superb, as was the whisky which we all drank to excess.

Nicky spent the night in the festival bed and promised to open the shop in the morning so that I could lie in.

Till total £182.49
13 customers

SATURDAY, 3 MAY

Online orders: 4
Books found: 4

There was no sound of activity from downstairs at 8.30 a.m., so I went down and opened the shop. Nicky was still fast asleep. Twigger, Nicky and I were all suffering this morning after last night's Whisky Supper.

After lunch I drove to Dumfries with Anna to pick up her friend Lola. Lola works in the film industry and, like Anna, is an American living in London. She is a slight woman with dark hair, and very witty. Anna introduced her to her friend Diana, another American expat living in London, and also in the film business. Diana and Lola have started a production company and are keen to turn Anna's book into a feature film. We stopped at Threave Castle on the way home. The castle is on an island in the middle of the River Dee, and access is via a small boat with an outboard motor. It was the seat of the 'Black' earls of Douglas and was built in the four-teenth century by a man who delighted in the name of Archibald the Grim, Lord of Galloway. It is an impressive fortification and was clearly designed as such, rather than as a luxurious home.

By the time we arrived home Alex (my brother-in-law) had arrived in preparation for his talk at 6 p.m. on building a new whisky distillery. Alex works for a company called Adelphi. When the business started, their strategy was to buy up casks of rare malts from distilleries, bottle it and sell it under their own label. His boss decided, though, that it would be worth producing their own whisky, so they've built a distillery in Ardnamurchan, the most westerly point on the British mainland. For someone who appears quite shy, Alex's talk was superb. In fact, by any standards it was extremely good, made even better by the frequent samples of whisky that he liberally handed out.

Till total £417.57
28 customers

SUNDAY, 4 MAY

Online orders: 3
Books found: 2

When I attempted to open the shop at 11 a.m. (Twigger had a talk upstairs at noon), I discovered that the lock was jammed and the door wouldn't open, so we hastily made signs directing people to the side door and I drove to Newton Stewart and bought a replacement mortice lock. Much of the afternoon was spent attempting to get the door open without breaking it, so that I could put the new lock in. Not the most professional or productive day of the Spring Festival, although Twigger's talk was excellent and well attended. Anna introduced him and thanked him.

Anna and Lola spent the sunny spring day wandering about the town, Anna clearly happy to show Lola her beloved places in and around Wigtown, like an overexcited tour guide. Anna has embraced Wigtown life and befriended far more people than I would ever have anticipated, being blessed with a complete lack of shyness. One of her favourite locals was a man who used to zoom about on a mobility scooter with a number plate bearing his name, 'Gibby'. When he died two years ago, she was distraught. She has so immersed herself in the community that – as with most people in Wigtown – crossing the street can take twenty minutes, depending on who you bump into on the way.

Started reading Twigger's book, *Angry White Pyjamas*, which, despite having known him for some years, I had never got round to reading.

Till total £128.50
13 customers

MONDAY, 5 MAY

Online orders: 2
Books found: 2

Bank holiday.

Nicky worked today so that Anna and I could entertain Lola. We had lunch at Margie's, then the three of us (Anna, Lola and me) cooked a leg of lamb for ten friends for supper. Margie is a Cambridge academic who bought a house in Wigtown a couple of years ago. She is Dutch and has two daughters, who are leaders in their respective scientific fields. She lived in Galloway when the girls were children, then moved to Cambridge. She's back – in part – because of Anna's book. Margie is one of Wigtown's biggest assets: hugely intelligent, funny, irreverent and generous to a fault.

Tracy called in at lunchtime to tell me that she had seen a few swallows during her lunch break. Spring has arrived.

Twigger left at 10 a.m. and headed back to Dorset.

Another late night, fuelled by red wine and the leftover whisky from Alex's talk on Saturday.

Till total £106.99
13 customers

TUESDAY, 6 MAY

Online orders: 3
Books found: 3

Norrie covered the shop because Nicky spends her Tuesdays door-stepping people and telling them about Jesus. I drove to Dumfries – Anna and Lola wanted to go to the auction. Anna came away with two boxes of rubbish, which is her usual haul. I had a long chat with Angus the submariner about the conspicuous absence of Dave the Hat, who never misses a sale. We speculated wildly about what might have happened to him. The three of us spent the day eating and wandering about the town, including a trip to Caerlaverock Castle, then dropped Lola at the railway station at 5 p.m. and came home.

Among the usual bills and demands for money in the mail was Mr Deacon's book.

Till total £120.50
13 customers

WEDNESDAY, 7 MAY

Online orders: 8
Books found: 7

At lunchtime I left a message on Mr Deacon's phone to say that he could collect his book any time.

Till total £140.01
18 customers

THURSDAY, 8 MAY

Online orders: 4
Books found: 4

A friendly, chatty customer told me that he has to dispose of his uncle's maritime history book collection, which is in his flat in the West End of Glasgow. I'll go up next week to look at it.

Mr Deacon arrived to collect his book at about 3 p.m. As he was leaving, I noticed that he was missing his left shoe.

Till total £180.83
19 customers

FRIDAY, 9 MAY

Online orders: 2
Books found: 2

A customer was waiting at the door with two boxes of books when I opened the shop this morning, all Penguins, and mostly green crime editions, which are by far the most sellable. Nicky appeared ten minutes after I had bought them for £60 and asked me how much I had paid for them. I asked her to guess, so she rifled through them and said £20.

Foodie Friday's treat this week was an out-of-date Mr Kipling's Battenberg cake from the Morrisons skip. We spent the day pricing up the Penguins and putting them on the shelves and arguing about what consideration we should give to Amazon prices when we are deciding how much to sell something for in the shop. Nicky is all for being cheaper than Amazon, but I believe that most customers understand that our prices can't always undercut the lowest on Amazon because of our overheads.

Till total £192
14 customers

SATURDAY, 10 MAY

Online orders: 6
Books found: 6

The frogspawn in the pond has all but disappeared, and hundreds of tiny tadpoles have taken their place.

Till total £170.70
14 customers

MONDAY, 12 MAY

Online orders: 5
Books found: 3

After lunch I was accosted by a man in a cagoule with a terrible lisp, who came over to my side of the counter, uncomfortably close, and asked 'Now, what do you specialise in?' to which I replied 'Books', which was, I admit, fatuous. Predictably, he was not impressed and replied, 'Do not be smart with me.' In a pointless continuation of my previous fatuous comment I replied, 'Why not?' Needless to say, the conversation did not end well. In fact, he became so odious that I had to pull rank and make Nicky deal with him.

Till total £84.50
14 customers

TUESDAY, 13 MAY

Online orders: 5
Books found: 5

Clearly we have a problem with AbeBooks, as all today's orders were Amazon, so I checked and our online stock with them has dropped from 10,000 to 450 books. I've emailed them to see what the problem is. I estimate lost AbeBooks sales to be about £100 a week. AbeBooks is the best place to sell more valuable books, and our average sale on the site is probably worth about £30, the equivalent to about six Amazon sales, so while we do not sell a vast quantity of books on AbeBooks, their value relative to Amazon is significant.

Two pairs of swallows have started building nests, one in the alleyway between the shop and next door, and another in the log shed.

At noon a customer tied his yapping terrier to one of the benches in front of the shop while he and his wife browsed. An hour later it was still yapping away. They didn't buy anything. Shortly after they had left, a man with what appeared to be an eggcup taped over his left eye asked for books on 'numerology'. I had to ask him what it meant.

Till total £107.99
12 customers

WEDNESDAY, 14 MAY

Online orders: 3
Books found: 2

At 11 a.m. a customer came to the counter with a pile of railway books for her husband. As she was paying, she told me, 'Never marry a railwayman', as though this might be something I had been seriously considering.

In the inbox this morning:

> Dear owner of the most prestigious book shop in Scotland,
>
> I do hope this email finds you well.
>
> I am an indie author of fantasy and paranormal stories, with three e-books currently available and a newly released novella, from my favourite of all places to write about, the ocean. Yes, I am one of those who believe in the existence of mermaids, or as I like to call them, asperini. This novella, The White Queen, is the first in the mini-series, Beyond Endless Tides, in which many asperini shawls [sic] strive for a secured future when they realise the worlds ocean creatures, large and small, are soon to die out due to the number of planktonia diminishing. Many of these shawls believe the key to their survival is to abandon the oceans entirely and live on land amongst the humans, or as they call them, nghozas. The only way to accomplish this is to mate with and become

nghozas themselves. Not all asperini believe in this move and like Morg, strive to find another way.

It is forced upon Morg to mate with an nghoza but is fortunate to have with her a friend of her father's who aids her escape. She knows where to find other asperini and soon makes her way to them, unsure of their creed with regard to the nghoza mating thing. To her delight she is accepted into a family, but when her old shawl turns up, there is nothing she can do but flee. Prior to leaving with the young male of the family, she learns of a mermaid (ligphur), the White Queen, who can see into the great ahead and may be the key to all asperini's survival. Morg and Ethos, together, make the journey south to seek out the mystical ligphur.

I will leave it there for now, but if you'd like to know more please feel free to ask.

I am emailing you today for I'd be very interested in doing a reading at your venue, and have a book tour in mind, whereby I'd be in the area on Friday 19th September 2014. Is it possible to arrange an event for this date? I understand if I have left this email too late for this date, so please advise me on when best suits you. That is of course if you cater for unknown author's [sic] like me.

I'd bring my own copies to the event for signings after the reading and of course, should you wish to purchase for your shelves, I will have some ready for you with a sale or return policy, at 35% discount of the lower list price. I am selling through Amazon's Createspace at £4.99, and feedaread at £5.99, they won't allow me to sell cheaper for number of pages.

I look forward to meeting you,
Best wishes

Sandy the tattooed pagan brought in three sticks and exchanged them for three books.

Till total £324.47
29 customers

THURSDAY, 15 MAY

Online orders: 2
Books found: 2

Today was a beautiful warm, sunny day.

The man who wrote the *Observer's Book of Observer's Books* – a bibliography of Observer's books – came in and complained that our stock of Observer's books was not as good as it used to be. After a brief count, I calculated that we have roughly 150.

Nicky came in to cover the shop today so I could drive to Dumfries for Anna to catch the train back to London. We stopped and had lunch with Carol-Ann and Ruaridh at Galloway Lodge in Gatehouse. Galloway Lodge is Ruaridh's business. It is a large restaurant, and Ruaridh is a friend I have known since childhood. He is unrelentingly rude and offensive towards me, and always has been. Home at 4.30 p.m. to find Nicky being lectured by a customer about how she'd managed to train her cat to use the toilet like a human, even as far as operating the flush. Nicky's expression was a wonderful blend of contempt and fascination.

Till total £75.50
9 customers

FRIDAY, 16 MAY

Online orders: 3
Books found: 2

Today was another gorgeous sunny day. Nicky was in again.

After lunch I drove to Glasgow to view the maritime history collection that the customer had mentioned last week. It was a warm, sunny day, and the house was on a beautiful, wide Georgian street in the West End of Glasgow. David (as he introduced himself) greeted me at the door and we went into an impressive first-floor drawing room, through the windows of which the spring sun lit up the room. The books were in twenty or so boxes on the floor, spine up. As I was going through them, David explained that his late uncle had been a naval officer during the war and had amassed the collection over his life. He also told me that he and his wife had bought the flat in Glasgow several years previously, when he had been offered a job that – in his words – 'it would have been churlish to refuse'. I picked out the best of the book collection and wrote him a cheque for £700.

After I had left, I thought I ought to take the opportunity of being in Glasgow to buy myself a new pair of shoes, so I parked the van in the Mitchell Street multi-storey car park and went to House of Fraser. The van, I noticed, was just about the maximum height for vehicles in the car park. As I left (with a new pair of brown brogues), the barrier arm lifted to let me through, but – presumably programmed for smaller vehicles – began to descend before the entire van had passed through, and a chain on the barrier caught the back door of the van, ripping the entire arm from its housing. Mercifully, it fell off half-way down Jamaica Street, before I had reached the A77.

In November 2001, the month I bought the shop, an old man was browsing in the maritime history section of the shop. He came to the counter and asked, 'When are you having the bonfire?' Puzzled, I asked him what he meant. He replied, 'For your books. I have never seen such rubbish. All they're good for is the bonfire.' This was my first encounter with a genuinely rude customer, and back then I was still racked with insecurities about the shop, the stock and what I was doing. Fortunately, another customer witnessed the incident and, sensing my discomfort, stepped in and said, 'Actually, this is the best maritime history section I have ever seen in any bookshop. If you don't like it you should probably leave.' He left.

Till total £127
11 customers

Online orders: 3
Books found: 3

Fiona, who has the shop next door, came into the shop this morning in a mild panic to tell me that they need an extra marquee for a live cooking demonstration as part of the food festival which is happening this weekend. Fortunately, I have a pop-up gazebo, which I bought for an event in the garden last summer.

Nicky and I went through the RBC list of people who subscribed last April and had not renewed their membership following the reminder last month. The club is shrinking again and is down to 137 members. Once we had sorted out who was in and who was out, we packaged up the books for this month and dealt with the postage.

Smelly Kelly appeared at the precise moment that Nicky had disappeared for her lunch break. I suspect her nose is now finely tuned to detect the advance of Brut 33 and give her enough advance warning to escape when he is approaching. Disappointed that she was not here, he reluctantly talked to me briefly instead. Apparently he is going into hospital next week for a hip operation.

A Northern Irish customer (an old man in blue tank-top) came to the counter with two books and asked, 'What can you do for me on those?' The total came to £4.50, so I told him that there was no way I could possibly give him a discount on books that were already cheaper than the postage alone on Amazon. He reluctantly conceded, muttering, 'Oh well, I hope you're still here next time I visit.' From his tone it wasn't entirely clear whether he was suggesting that my refusal to grant a discount on a £4.50 sale would mean that customers would leave in their droves, never to return and the shop would be forced to close, or whether he genuinely meant that he hoped the shop would survive through these difficult times.

One of today's orders was for a biography called *E. D. Morel: The Man and His Work*. Author is F. Seymour Cocks.

Till total £119
19 customers

MONDAY, 19 MAY

Online orders: 5
Books found: 5

A customer came in at 10 a.m. and asked if we had anything on the surnames of Scotland, so I directed him to Black's *Surnames of Scotland*. He looked at it briefly, then told me that it was 'too comprehensive'. Once he had left, the shop was empty so I went to the post office and asked Wilma if she would mind sending the postman over later. William the surly Ulsterman completely blanked my 'Good morning, William. Isn't it a lovely day?'

When I returned to the shop, there was a young couple waiting at the counter with two boxes of books, all modern fiction in mint condition. They had recently married and were moving into their first flat together, and had agreed to each halve their book collections. The situation seemed charmingly old-fashioned. I gave them £45 for the books.

A customer brought a few books to the counter, including a very tatty facsimile of Burns's Kilmarnock edition. The total came to £14.50 – no haggling. I asked him if he would like a bag, to which he replied, 'Probably.' I am quite certain that is the first time anyone has given that answer in the shop.

The postman arrived at just before 5 p.m. and collected the five sacks of random books.

Till total £110.99
15 customers

TUESDAY, 20 MAY

Online orders: 5
Books found: 5

Another warm and sunny day and Nicky was in, so I went for a bike ride with Callum in the afternoon on the mountain-bike trails in Kirroughtree Forest, about eight miles away. We both managed to complete the red circuit without mishap, unlike the first few times we rode it several years ago. For the first ten or so attempts, one or both of us would end up crashing into a tree, or misjudging a corner and ending up face down in a ditch.

Till total £217.50
16 customers

WEDNESDAY, 21 MAY

Online orders: 6
Books found: 5

All orders today were from Amazon, one of which was for a Patricia Wentworth first edition that should have been £50 but sold for £4. The discrepancy arose because of the price-matching software that comes with Monsoon, which is set to match the lowest price on Amazon. When we listed our copy it was the cheapest, but subsequently it had dropped to match another copy which had undercut ours. Occasionally, to try to steal a bargain, people put up fake listings of expensive books that they want, but with ridiculously cheap prices. They then wait for the price-matching software to kick in, and the copy of a genuine listing to drop to the price of the ghost listing that they have put up. They buy the book, then remove the ghost listing.

A customer who bought a copy of Pepys's diary read the Einstein quotation painted on the front of the counter ('Only two things are infinite, the universe and human stupidity, and I am not sure about the former') and asked, 'Is that a genuine quotation from Einstein?' Apparently it is highly contested, and many people don't think he said it.

After work I sat in the garden, watching the swallows and house martins swooping and looping.

Till total £309
15 customers

THURSDAY, 22 MAY

Online orders: 4
Books found: 4

The first customer of the day was an Australian woman whose inability to pronounce the letter T left me confused as to whether she was asking for 'Noddy books' or 'naughty books'. It turned out, after I'd shown her to the erotica section, that she was after Enid Blytons.

It is a strange phenomenon that, when customers visit the shop for the first time, they tend to walk very slowly through it, as though they are expecting someone to tell them they have entered a forbidden zone, and when they decide to stop, it is invariably in a doorway. This, of course, is incredibly frustrating for anyone behind them, and since that person is usually me, I exist in a state of perpetual frustration. Anthropologists insist that it is an instinctive human response on entering a new space to stop and look around for potential danger, although quite what sort of danger might be lurking in a bookshop – other than a frustrated bookseller whose temper has been frayed to the point of violence by the fact that somebody is blocking the doorway – is a mystery.

Two customers asked what had happened to the spirals of books. The book spirals were large columns of books that were piled in a helix and coated with fibreglass resin. They stood on each side of the door into the shop. Last year some children tried to set fire to one of them – unsuccessfully, as the resin eventually cracks and the rain gets in. I have asked Norrie to make a new pair out of concrete in time for the festival in September.

Till total £324.49
20 customers

FRIDAY, 23 MAY

Online orders: 5
Books found: 4

Today was a cold and grey day, not spring-like at all. Atmospheric conditions affect the radio in the shop, which is tuned to BBC Radio 3. If there is damp in the air, it won't pick up the signal. Today it spent most of the day completely silent, occasionally popping on for a few seconds of Mahler or Shostakovich.

There was another invasion of Lycra-clad septuagenarian cyclists this morning, most of whom bought a book or two, and who were flattering about both the shop and the stock.

After they had left, a customer came to the counter with a book, opened it, pointed at the £40 price label and said, 'What price is this? Surely not £40.' I explained that, yes, the book was £40. He dropped it on the counter, from where it bounced and landed on the floor, damaging one of the corners. He looked at it for a couple of seconds, then left without another word.

Most of the books sold today were from the collection of railway books I bought in Glasgow a few weeks ago. I wonder if word has got round the railway community that the collection ended up here. The same thing happened with an ornithology collection that I bought from a collector in Stranraer last year. For weeks there were twitchers in the shop, and it only took a few days for me to recoup my investment.

Till total £281.99
18 customers

SATURDAY, 24 MAY

Online orders: 4
Books found: 4

Sunny and warm all day. Nicky was in. She has bought a job lot of 1,000 pens on eBay. They are horrible little red things, and she insists on bringing them into the shop, despite the fact that I have a box of far better pens. At the moment there are about a dozen of them in various locations about the place. I keep putting them in the bin, but she retrieves them and redistributes them throughout the shop again.

When I took the mail sacks over to Wilma, I said good morning to William and commented on the warm, sunny weather. He replied, 'Aye, the rain won't be far behind it.'

At 11 a.m. there was a talk about Robert Service, the Canadian poet, by Professor Ted Cowan upstairs in the drawing room. As with most of Ted's talks, it was very well attended. Shortly after it had begun, two very smartly dressed young men in suits, with American accents, came into the shop and asked if we had a copy of *The Book of Mormon*. On closer inspection I spotted that they had black name badges with 'Church of Jesus Christ of Latter-Day Saints' printed on them. Nicky was visibly suspicious of them, just as the cat is when a dog enters the shop. When they were just out of earshot, she said, 'I dinnae like they people. They've got some very strange ideas.'

Till total £420.20
34 customers

MONDAY, 26 MAY

Online orders: 6
Books found: 5

At 9.05 a.m. a customer came in trying to sell a box of books on Christian Science. He told me that a load of Christian Scientists had already picked over the collection and taken some of them for free. He was telling me this as he was trying to sell it to me. If a bunch of Christian Scientists didn't want books on Christian Science for free, then I certainly was not going to pay for them, particularly when they were covered in cat hair.

Late in the day a customer, when asked if he'd like a bag, replied, 'Desperately.'

Over the past few days about £400 worth of books from the railway book deal in Glasgow have sold. They probably account for half of all the books I have sold in the last week.

Till total £408.88
46 customers

TUESDAY, 27 MAY

Online orders: 3
Books found: 3

As a customer was looking at the Birlinn reprint of Barnard's *The Whisky Distilleries of the United Kingdom* in our new books section, I happened to be passing to put new stock out and I heard the words 'cheaper on Amazon' whispered to his companion. He didn't even have the courtesy to wait until I was out of earshot.

Till total £426.50
21 customers

WEDNESDAY, 28 MAY

Online orders: 7
Books found: 3

After lunch Alastair and Leslie Reid called in to say hello. They live in New York and come over every year to enjoy the Galloway spring months. Alastair was born in nearby Whithorn, the son of the Church of Scotland minister. He is a writer of extraordinary talent, now in his eighties. He is a poet, and also writes for *The New Yorker*. In recent years he has come to appreciate what he describes as his 'flinty beginnings' in Galloway, and every spring he and Leslie return to the place where the warm embrace of childhood friends and the memories of that season, with its familiar smells and sounds, transport him to the time before his wanderlust took him around the world. He introduced the poetry of Neruda and Borges to Europe. Despite (or possibly because of) his roots he has made no secret of his dislike for some elements of Scottish life. In the introduction to his book *Whereabouts* he writes: 'The two pieces "Digging up Scotland" and "Hauntings" represent my coming to terms with my flinty beginnings, but while I am still haunted by some Scottish landscapes and weathers, I never feel at home in the wariness of its human climate.'

Those words were written in 1987, and I suspect that his annual visit is an indication that perhaps he now does feel more at home in Scotland's human climate. It is always the most enjoyable rite of spring to see them both, to have them over for supper, to drink whisky together and for that favour to be returned at least once every visit. It has been an enormous privilege to have come to know both Leslie and Alastair. His has been the most extraordinary peripatetic life, which, he is fond of saying, stems from the first time he saw Irish travellers passing the manse in Whithorn. He asked his father where they were going, to which his father replied, 'They don't know.' This fired Alastair's imagination, and I suspect that at any time in his life if he was asked where he was going, his response would have been 'I don't know.'

Till total £192
19 customers

THURSDAY, 29 MAY

Online orders: 5
Books found: 5

A customer appeared at 9.15 a.m. with a fishing waistcoat and an over-groomed moustache, leaned over the counter and pompously asked if we have a section on 'The Great Game', as though he was Clive of India.

An elderly couple bought a book on the music of Scotland and commented as they were paying that they had found a hardback book of poetry by Stevie Smith that was £1 when it was published in 1970. They were surprised by 'how much' I was selling it for, which, it turns out, was £6. Often when this happens I attempt to explain that not everything goes down in value as it gets older, and in any case it is all relative. If that book were to come out in print today, it would probably be selling for at least £12. John Carter (from whom I bought the shop in 2001) used to reply to customers who accused him of naked profiteering by selling a book that was two and sixpence for £1 that, 'If you've got two and sixpence, you can have it for two and sixpence.' John was very good to me when I took over the business, and accompanied me on my first few book-buying deals, as well as showing me the ropes for a month before the shop became mine. One of his many pieces of invaluable advice was 'My motto is the same as the Roman army: SPQR – small profit, quick return.'

At 3.15 p.m. four heavily built American men came in looking for 'old Bibles', so I showed them several from various periods going back as far as 1644. They didn't buy any of them, and all insisted on calling me 'Sir'.

Till total £271.49
13 customers

FRIDAY, 30 MAY

Online orders: 3
Books found: 3

Uneventful day. Spent most of it reading.

Till total £114.98
12 customers

SATURDAY, 31 MAY

Online orders: 3
Books found: 3

Another quiet day in the shop. Re-priced some of the stock in the antiquarian section, including a third edition (1774) of Thomas Pennant's *A Tour in Scotland 1769*. The mid-eighteenth century appears to have been a popular time for books about tours of Scotland, normally illustrated.

Probably the most well-known tour – largely because of the already established fame of its author and his companion – is that of James Boswell and Samuel Johnson in 1785, when they toured the Hebrides. On their travels, they took with them a copy of Martin Martin's *A Description of the Western Islands of Scotland* (1703), of which Johnson was (typically) critical. This copy of Pennant came from a large house in Ayrshire which contained a wonderful library of such things. Daniel Defoe got in before Pennant and Boswell, writing *A Tour Through the Whole Island of Great Britain* (1724–6), and among the other Scottish tours currently in the antiquarian section are Garnett's *Observations on a Tour Through the Highlands and Western Islands of Scotland* (1811), with maps and beautiful oval copperplate illustrations, and Campbell's *A Journey from Edinburgh to Parts of North Britain* (1802), again with fine copperplate illustrations. The descriptions of the landscapes, the people and their lifestyles, along with the contemporary illustrations, provide the most accurate impression of what life in that period must have been like, making them not only beautiful books but invaluable social historical documents. Finding such items in a collection is always a joy.

Callum and I had arranged to go for a bike ride after work, leaving here sharp at 5 p.m. so I was prompt with closing and started locking up at 4.55 p.m. I told the only customer in the shop – a woman who was in the Scottish room – that I had to close for an important meeting. She shuffled reluctantly into the front room and started looking at the cookery books. Just as I was explaining (again) about my important meeting and trying to manoeuvre her towards the door, Callum strolled in wearing what were clearly cycling clothes and holding a bike pump, shouting, 'Right, are you ready to go on this bike ride then?' The woman left amid a barrage of tutting.

Till total £179.48
24 customers

JUNE

There are always plenty of not quite certifiable lunatics walking
the streets, and they tend to gravitate towards bookshops, because
a bookshop is one of the few places where you can hang about for
a long time without spending any money. In the end one gets to
know these people almost at a glance. For all their big talk there is
something moth-eaten and aimless about them.

George Orwell, 'Bookshop Memories'

Things have changed a little since Orwell's day. Perhaps the
National Health Service has accommodated the 'not quite certifiable lunatics' who dogged his daily life in the bookshop back
then or perhaps they've found some other equally frugal means of
distracting themselves. We have one or two regular customers to
whom this description might apply, but far more common today
is the customer who will spend a few short minutes in the shop
before leaving empty-handed, saying, 'You could spend all day in
this shop', or the young couple who will find the most inconve-
nient place in which to park their vast, screaming Panzer of a pram
while they sit exhausted in the armchairs by the wood-burning
stove. Nowadays, when customers have that 'aimless' look about
them, it is almost a certainty that it is because they are waiting for
the pharmacist (three doors up) to fulfil their prescription or for the
garage in Wigtown to call and tell them that their car has passed its
MOT test and they can collect it.

SUNDAY, 1 JUNE

While Amazon appears to benefit consumers, there is an unseen
mass of people who suffer thanks to the punitive conditions which
it imposes on sellers – authors have seen their incomes plummet
over the past ten years, publishers too, which means that they
can no longer take risks with unknown authors, and now there
is no middleman. Amazon seems to be focused on matching if
not undercutting competitors' prices to the extent that it seems to

be impossible to see how it can make money on some sales. This puts the squeeze not only on independent bookshops but also on publishers, authors and, ultimately, creativity. The sad truth is that, unless authors and publishers unite and stand firm against Amazon, the industry will face devastation. Amanda Foreman wrote an excellent piece about this in today's *Sunday Times*.

MONDAY, 2 JUNE

Online orders: 3
Books found: 3

Laurie's first day back at work in the shop. Predictably, there were massive problems with Monsoon. Laurie is a student at Napier University in Edinburgh, a place that she loathes with undisguised contempt. She has worked in the shop for the past couple of summers. I have taken her on for this summer, which will probably be her last before she enters the hideous world of attempting to find a real job.

For the first time in the thirteen years since I bought the shop, I have been left with no choice but to turn the radio off. Terry Waite is guest of the week in Rob Cowan's *Essential Classics* on Radio 3.

Tracy, with whom I often compare notes about the general public, dropped in during her lunch break at the exact moment when a customer came to the counter. The customer put a book on the counter. When I picked it up to check the price, I noticed that there was an ancient '59p' written in pencil on the first page next to our price sticker of £2.50. During the ensuing argument over which was the correct price, I could see Tracy attempting to stop herself from giggling. When the customer reluctantly accepted the price and said 'I will just get rid of some change', she lost all control and began laughing hysterically. The customer took five minutes to work out the correct change, which consisted entirely of 2p pieces and pennies.

Till total £330.49
16 customers

TUESDAY, 3 JUNE

Online orders: 2
Books found: 2

Opened the shop five minutes late because the key jammed. The first customer of the day brought two Rider Haggard first editions to the counter, £8.50 each. At the same moment the thought 'Those are seriously underpriced' entered my head, he asked, 'Will you do them for £13?' When I refused to knock anything off them, he replied, 'Well, you've got to ask, haven't you?' so I told him that, no, you do not have to ask.

After work I went for supper with Alastair and Leslie Reid in the cottage they rent from Finn and Ella in Garlieston. Alastair spoke of his first trip to America, which he took via London. A lecturer at the University of St Andrews, from which he had recently graduated, had given him the telephone number of a friend of his in London called Tom. Alastair duly arrived in London and telephoned 'Tom' to see if he could put him up for the night. 'Tom' turned out to be T. S. Eliot. Stewart Henderson, another friend who was there for supper, asked him 'What did he smell like?' to which Alastair – with no pause for thought – replied, 'A musty pulpit, which is exactly what he would have wanted to smell like.'

Afterwards I asked Stewart – a poet who presents programmes on Radio 4, including *Pick of the Week* – what had possessed him to ask that question. He replied that he had once been interviewing the last survivor of a British brass band which Hitler had requested to perform a private concert for him before the Second World War. The interviewee was an elderly woman who evidently did not understand that Stewart was trying to extract more than 'yes/no' answers from her. Eventually, in despair, he decided that he would ask her 'What did Hitler smell like?', at which point she opened up completely and gave him all the material he could have hoped for.

Till total £125.38
19 customers

WEDNESDAY, 4 JUNE

Online orders: 3
Books found: 3

Today was surprisingly quiet in the shop, which afforded me the opportunity to sort through some of the piles of boxes of fresh stock that perpetually clutter the shop and price up some of it and put it on the shelves. With the constant stream of fresh stock coming into the shop it is a battle to keep the place tidy and organised, particularly now that we have to check prices online to see whether a book is worth listing. This has slowed the whole process down considerably.

The undoubted highlight of the day was when my mother appeared, excitedly clutching a book that I must have bought at least six years ago, back in the days when I used to store freshly bought stock in the shed at my parents' house. I thought I'd cleared it all away, but she'd found a box and started rummaging through it and discovered a signed, numbered limited edition of W. B. Yeats's *The Winding Stair*. The edition was limited to 642 copies, 600 of which had been signed by Yeats. It was unusual to see my mother, who is not a bookish person, so animated, but it was not about the value of the book – more because she had in her hands a book that the most famous poet of his generation from the land of her birth had once also held. I spent the rest of the day wondering how on earth I could have missed it when I bought it, and trying to remember where it had come from in the first place. No idea.

Till total £157.48
20 customers

THURSDAY, 5 JUNE

Online orders: 2
Books found: 2

At about 10 a.m. Nicky and I were gossiping about the perils of lending things to people when we were interrupted by a customer who asked if we had a 'rest room'. Blank looks were exchanged for some time before Nicky broke the silence, saying, 'There's a comfy seat by the fire if you need a rest.' For moments like this, Nicky's value is beyond measure.

Smelly Kelly appeared, doused, as always, in Brut 33. He now has a walking stick but assured me that he will be fighting fit in no time. His relentless pursuit of Nicky is most inspiring, particularly considering that not only has she failed to give him any positive signals, but on several occasions she has also told him quite bluntly that she is not interested.

Drove to Glasgow and bought fifteen boxes of books from a retired couple in Bearsden.

Till total £115.50
10 customers

FRIDAY, 6 JUNE

Online orders: 2
Books found: 2

Laurie was in, covering for Nicky, who put in an extra day yesterday, so I went fishing on the Luce. Didn't catch anything, but a worthwhile break from the shop. Eliot emailed to say that The Bookshop Band are going to be in the area this weekend and are looking for a venue for a gig, and could he come and stay for a few days. I replied that I would be happy to open on Sunday for them, and yes, of course he was welcome to stay too.

Till total £109.49
7 customers

SATURDAY, 7 JUNE

Online orders: 2
Books found: 2

Laurie fronted the shop today, which turned into a beautiful sunny day.

Her first customer was a Welsh woman who had brought ten boxes of Scottish books with her while she's here on holiday, with a view to selling them. Her husband brought them in from the car. Some were interesting – perhaps 20 per cent of the total – but they were all in terrible condition. As I was going through the first three boxes, the woman made a note on her list of the books that I had removed. This is always, without exception, an indication that someone has overvalued their books. Occasionally she would pick one up and mutter, 'Oh yes, that's very rare', or 'valuable' or 'first edition', as if this would somehow influence what I would offer her for the collection. When she eventually stopped talking, I offered her £60 for about twenty books. Immediately she replied, 'Oh no. Oh no no no no no', so I left the room at this point and went to make a cup of tea. When I returned five minutes later, both she and her beleaguered husband, and the books, were gone.

Eliot arrived at 4 p.m. and made himself at home, which, as always, meant dispersing the contents of his overnight case as widely as possible throughout the house.

Till total £128
20 customers

SUNDAY, 8 JUNE

I opened the shop at 2 p.m., just as The Bookshop Band arrived. They set up and started the gig at 3.30 p.m. They were wonderful. The Bookshop Band are Ben, Beth and Poppy. They were doing a tour of Scotland and the north of England, and Eliot persuaded them to come to Wigtown and perform in the shop. They brought their friend John along to give them a hand with setting up. Their USP is that they mainly play in bookshops, and all of their songs are based on books they've read. The shop was full for their gig: Callum brought his children along too. In the evening, once we'd eaten, the instruments came out again as the wine and beer began to flow and they sang folk songs (John's speciality). We drank and sang until 3 a.m.

MONDAY, 9 JUNE

Online orders: 3
Books found: 2

Awoke and opened the shop with the hangover from hell.

On Facebook today was a message from hater Paul: 'We've crossed swords before and before you patronise me with your explanation of exactly what your site is meant to be portraying, remember that due to the wide coverage of the internet, you are possibly doing your business more damage than good. I, for one, stopped visiting your shop a few years ago, due to your pathetic postings on Facebook and over-inflated self-belief and attitude. I really think you should stop doing this, as it is quite patently a childishly backhanded way of being rude behind your customers' backs. Grow up and find a more beneficial hobby for crying out loud.'

In the evening I went for a pint with Eliot and Natalie McIlroy, who is one of this year's festival artists in residence. Natalie's project is to find thirty-one Galloway pippins – apple trees native to this area – and create an indoor orchard in an empty building on the square. She is going to raffle them off at the end of the festival. I already have one in my garden. The fruit it produces is huge. This year there are three artists in residence – Natalie, a woman called Anupa Gardner, who paints on textiles, and Astrid Jaekel, who did an extraordinary silhouette installation in the windows of the County Buildings last year. This year Astrid is making plywood cut-outs of figures to go in front of each shop. Astrid is German but grew up in rural Ireland before moving back to Germany. She has a very unusual blend of accents.

Among the books from the Glasgow deal last week was a set of Scottish Mountaineering Club journals, which, with hindsight, I wish I had left behind. They are nearly impossible to sell, and the shelves in the Scottish climbing section are already bulging with them.

Till total £294
17 customers

TUESDAY, 10 JUNE

Online orders: 3
Books found: 2

Today Laurie was in, and I spent most of the day in the garden, so my only interaction with a customer was during her lunch break at 12.30 p.m. The customer asked, 'Do you have any pamphlets about the history of the area?', to which I replied, 'No, but we've got plenty of books about local history in the Scottish room. You're welcome to have a look there.' The customer parted – on the way out of the door – with 'Oh no, we don't want books. We're only interested in free pamphlets.'

The garden behind the shop is long and narrow (50m by 7m) and would have been a vegetable garden for the house during its heyday in the late Georgian period. Consequently it has been fertilised with lime, and as such is not conducive to the growth of rhododendrons, magnolias, azaleas and other ericaceous plants, which I like to grow. There is a healthy looking camellia, which flowers in April, but the flowers turn brown within days and fall off shortly afterwards.

When I bought the place, the garden was mainly rock gardens and dwarf conifers, but over the years I have replanted all of it, and now in spring it is an explosion of colour and scent, with gardenia, scented clematis, wisteria, viburnum, laurel, all manner of ground cover, native trees and shrubs. With the help of pots and ericaceous compost there are even azaleas and rhododendrons. It is my favourite place, and at this time of year, when the days are long and warm, sitting out there alone at night is a singular pleasure. At dusk the bats appear, and it is a joy to sit on the bench with a glass of whisky watching them flitting, silhouetted against the fading light. Once, one came so close to me in pursuit of its prey that I could feel the breath of its wings against my face as it wheeled away. Older Gallovidians refer to them as 'flittermice', probably something that fans of operetta would recognise.

Till total £184.89
19 customers

WEDNESDAY, 11 JUNE

Online orders: 2
Books found: 2

Laurie was in to cover the shop today.

While she was having her lunch break, a customer started rummaging through a box of unpriced books and found a Penguin edition of *The Day of the Triffids*, priced in pencil at 12p (presumably from a charity shop in the 1970s). When I told her that our price would be £1.50, she decided that was 'outrageous' and that if that was the case she'd 'just get it from the library'. I have a feeling that 'outraged' may well be her factory setting.

After lunch I drove to Dumfries and picked up Anna from the railway station at 4.30 p.m. Home by 5.45 p.m.

The swallows' eggs have all hatched: three in one nest, and four in the other. Hopefully Captain will not annihilate them.

Till total £127.50
15 customers

THURSDAY, 12 JUNE

Online orders: 6
Books found: 5

Laurie was in the shop again. Today was a beautiful sunny day, and Anna was clearly delighted to be back in Galloway and away from London.

My father telephoned shortly after the shop opened to see if I wanted to go fishing, so much of the morning was spent with him in a boat, trout-fishing on Elrig Loch. We caught six or seven wild brown trout. Elrig is a loch about six miles from Wigtown. Gavin Maxwell spent his childhood nearby and wrote about it in *The House of Elrig*. The house is now owned by a family called Korner, who left Europe in the 1930s, when the Nazi menace was starting to loom large. They took in the Austrian 'degenerate' artist Oskar Kokoschka during the Second World War, after he fled Europe in 1938. Stories abound locally of Kokoschka giving framed sketches to local farmers and other people who had shown him kindness, and of the recipients – unable to comprehend the artist's modern genius – politely accepting them, then throwing the sketches in the waste-paper basket and putting photographs in the frames instead.

My father and I often fish together, and drifting down the banks of Elrig on a warm day, with a good ripple on the water, is nirvana. When there is enough water, we go salmon-fishing on the nearby River Luce, a river that I have fished since early childhood with him. During the season we both become acutely aware of the weather: if it is warm enough to go to Elrig and there is a bit of cloud cover (not too bright) and a good enough breeze, we will meet at the boathouse and fish for trout. If there has been enough rain to push the Luce up over a foot, we will meet on the banks of the river instead and fish for salmon. The river always takes precedence over the loch if conditions are right for both.

My father first took me fishing when I was two, and that is the age at which I caught my first trout. No doubt, with hindsight, it was my father who caught it, but I reeled it in, and in that moment, like the trout, I was hooked. When I was a small child – four or five years old – I would insist on going to the river with him. As a passionate salmon fisherman, he didn't want the distraction of a boy pestering him. So he gave me an old, broken trout rod which had belonged to his father, and tied a length of baler twine around a tree, then paced out a short distance from the water's edge and tied the other end around my belt. This allowed him to fish every pool down, close enough to know that I was safe, and for me to flail the rod around pointlessly – but utterly convinced I would catch something – without any chance of falling into the water.

Arrived back at the shop after lunch to find that the best sale of the day was the Georgian mahogany chest commode. I bought it about ten years ago for £80 at the auction in Dumfries, and used it as a glorified plant pot for a Boston fern that lived in the drawing room for most of that time. Eventually I decided to get rid of it. I can't remember why. Perhaps I bought something that looked less like a loo for my Boston fern. We sold it for £200 to a charming woman who was delighted with it. Nicky, who mocked me relentlessly about it and was convinced it would never sell, will be furious to be proved wrong.

Till total £342.49
15 customers

FRIDAY, 13 JUNE

Online orders: 2
Books found: 2

Nicky and Laurie were both in the shop today.

Nicky arrived and stared at the space where the commode had been: 'Where's that hideous thing gone? Dinnae tell me that some idiot's bought it. Oh no, surely naebody could be that daft.'

A ferrety man wearing a beret came to the counter and said, 'Just thought I'd tell you, you've got a book in the railway section called *The Railway Man*. It's not about railways, you need to move it to the right section.'

No. I need to bludgeon you with it. There is a certain kind of customer who delights in pointing out that a book is in the wrong section, as though they're showing you that they know more about books than you do. More often than not, when a book is in the wrong section, it is because a customer has put it there, not a member of staff.

Among the books from the Glasgow deal on Thursday was one called *The Intimate Thoughts of John Baxter, Bookseller*, published in 1942. As with many book deals, it is hard to resist dipping into some of the titles as you price them up, and this one seemed particularly relevant so I put it to one side and began to read it after I had closed the shop.

Till total £164.50
15 customers

SATURDAY, 14 JUNE

Online orders: 3
Books found: 3

Nicky in. Drove to Dunkeld for a friend's fiftieth.

Till total £188.28
26 customers

MONDAY, 16 JUNE

Online orders: 1
Books found: 1

Laurie covered the shop today.

Anna and I drove from Dunkeld to Stuart Kelly's house in the Borders to pick up books, then spent the afternoon in Summerhall in Edinburgh with him. Stuart is a writer, journalist, literary critic and former Booker Prize judge. Because of the latter, he receives dozens of books every day from publishers, desperate for him to review them. These he puts in piles until there are enough to justify me driving over to his house and picking them up. He is a festival regular, an extraordinary intellect and a good friend. Summerhall used to be part of the Royal Dick School of Veterinary Studies, informally known as the 'Dick Vet', the veterinary school of Edinburgh University. It has been bought by an Irish philanthropist friend of his and is now full of artists and creative types. Wandering around it, I thought of my grandfather, who completed his PhD in the 1930s in the same buildings.

While we were away, I asked Laurie to make a note of a few things customers asked her during the day. Her note reads:

'Why is Wigtown called Wigtown?'
'Why is Wigtown a book town?'
'How many bookshops are in Wigtown?'

The last two are asked on average twice daily all year round. After fifteen years, that means that I have been asked those same questions 9,360 times. It's hard to muster any enthusiasm when I reply now. Perhaps it's time to start inventing fresh answers that have absolutely no basis in fact.

We arrived back in Wigtown at 7 p.m.

Till total £114.50
12 customers

TUESDAY, 17 JUNE

Online orders: 2
Books found: 2

Laurie was in again today, which turned into a balmy, sunny day after an unpromising start. Both of the online book orders today were AbeBooks, no Amazon, which is extremely unusual. I set her to work packaging the books for the Random Book Club's June mail-out. We are back up to about 140 members. She stamped them and processed them through the Royal Mail web site. The cost of postage this month was £244.12. I have alerted Wilma, and she will send the postman around tomorrow to pick up the five sacks.

As it was a pleasant day, I spent much of it working in the garden. By mid-afternoon it was too hot, so Anna and I went to the beach at Garlieston and had a swim in the sea.

When I was locking up the shop, the telephone rang. It was a local woman who had books to sell, mostly Folio Society:

> 'You'll have to come to my house to view them, I am housebound.'
> 'How would next Tuesday suit?'
> 'As long as it's not in the morning, the nurse comes on Tuesday morning to dress a wound on my leg. It's terrible. Weeping sore, had it for years. Oozes the most disgusting pus.'

I have arranged to visit her on the afternoon of the 24th.

Till total £237.49
17 customers

WEDNESDAY, 18 JUNE

Online orders: 3
Books found: 3

Today both online orders were Amazon, no AbeBooks orders – the reverse of yesterday.

Another day of blazing sunshine, but I was stuck in the shop as Nicky and Laurie were both unavailable. Jim McMaster arrived at 9 a.m. for a poke around the shop. He went through the boxes from the Glasgow deal, only a few of which we had processed and shelved in the previous two weeks. Jim is a book dealer from Perth-shire. He started out in the book trade as a runner for Richard Booth in Hay-on-Wye. A runner buys books to sell to the trade, usually on request – so, for example, Booth might say to Jim, 'I need 500 books on African wildlife', and Jim would set off in a car or van and scour bookshops throughout the country for bargains until he had 500. Jim has an encyclopaedic knowledge of books. When I started out, in 2001, he could scarcely have been more helpful, giving me pointers here and there each time he came to the shop. He is one of the few dealers who will still visit other dealers' shops in search of fresh stock, and on the occasions when I have bought large quantities of books from people – in 2008 I cleared 12,000 books from a house in Gullane, near Edinburgh – Jim has come down and sorted through them, shifting bulk quantities to his contacts in the trade. He is a well-known, well-respected and well-liked figure in the second-hand book trade. Oddly enough, I was reading *The Intimate Thoughts of John Baxter, Bookseller* this morning and came across a passage that reminded me of David McNaughton, from whom I acquired the book signed by Florence Nightingale. Jim and David belong to the old school, and Baxter's words resonated when I read them:

> I say that these old fellows are the backbone of the book trade. As they drop off one by one, like leaves from a tree, there is a gap which no modern pushful young salesman can fill, and they leave a memory that is a good deal more fragrant than the smelly hair-oil of those Smart Alecs who come asking me for a job in the confident tones of one who is quite prepared to teach me my own business.

Not that Jim is particularly old, or in danger of dropping off.

At 11 a.m. the telephone rang – it was Mr Deacon: 'My apologies for the quality of the line. I am in Patagonia. Could you order me a copy of *In Patagonia* by Bruce Chatwin? I will be back next week.'

An American woman spent an hour taking books off the shelves in the children's section and checking prices on Amazon on her laptop. Right in front of me, completely shamelessly. Before I had the opportunity to rebuke her for this practice, the postman arrived to pick up the Random Book Club sacks, and by the time he and I had loaded them into his van, she had vanished.

The shop was quiet all afternoon until 4.59 p.m., when a middle-aged couple wandered in, the man humming irritatingly to himself. Both headed straight for the boxes of fresh unpriced stock from Stuart Kelly and began raking through them, taking things out and piling them up all over the floor. They left at 5.10 p.m. without putting any of them back or buying anything, complaining loudly that the shop should be open until 7 p.m. Boxes of fresh stock attract customers like moths to a flame.

Any bookseller will tell you that, even with 100,000 books neatly sorted and shelved in a well-lit, warm shop, if you put an unopened box of books in a dark, cold, dimly lit corner, customers will be rifling through it in a matter of moments. The appeal of a box of unsorted, unpriced stock is extraordinary. Obviously the idea of finding a bargain is part of it, but I suspect it goes well beyond that and has parallels with opening gifts. The excitement of the unknown is what it's all about, and it's something to which I can relate – buying books is exactly that. Driving towards any book deal, whether a private collection, an institution or a business, there's always the same slight quickening of the pulse which comes with the anticipation that there might be something really special in this lot; and there often is, whether it's an early Culpepper, incunabula, an early Ian Fleming first in a mint jacket, a fine calf craft-binding or just something that you've never come across before. I have yet to find a book bound in human skin, but a dealer I know once found one in a house in Castle Douglas.

Till total £163.99
17 customers

THURSDAY, 19 JUNE

Online orders: 6
Books found: 5

Nicky was in today. Her plan to turn her van into a mobile shop has been temporarily put on hold because the back door won't open. She has decided instead that she is going to buy an old mobile library from the council and convert that.

In the morning I started going through Hamish Grierson's books, which he had dropped off when I was in Dunkeld. Hamish is a retired antique dealer and a book collector, so a regular customer. The books were mainly about prehistory and in good condition. When I was checking the prices of some of the more interesting books from his collection on AbeBooks to see what other people are selling them for so that I could work out a fair price for him, I told Nicky that I was going to offer him £100 for them, to which she replied, as she always does, that I ought to halve the figure.

Anna insisted that, since it was a clear, sunny day, we climb Cairnsmore, the granite lump of a hill on the far side of Wigtown Bay. We left at 3 p.m. and reached the summit at 4.30 p.m. and were back home by 6.30 p.m. It is always entertaining doing this sort of thing with Anna: it is always she who suggests it, then very soon into the adventure she will start complaining bitterly about it, becoming increasingly vocal and miserable. Then, once it is done, she will announce, 'Wow, that was awesome.' On one occasion we decided to cycle forty miles around forestry tracks in the Galloway Hills. After about twenty miles of steadily escalating complaints, she dismounted, lay on a rock and said, 'Leave me here. Save yourself.'

Till total £155.44
23 customers

FRIDAY, 20 JUNE

Online orders: 5
Books found: 5

Laurie was in the shop today, so I drove Anna to Dumfries in the morning to catch the train to London. I am not sure when she will be back in Wigtown again. It depends, I suppose, on how she gets on with her various projects, which now include the *Rockets* script, as well as a NASA documentary, a young adult novel and a romantic comedy script on which she has been working with her friend Romiley.

After lunch I telephoned Hamish Grierson to offer him £100 for his books. He was not very happy about it at all and complained that there were some valuable books in there. This is bad news, as Nicky has already priced most of them up and put them out on the shelves. He told me he will call back on Monday with more information.

At closing time a man telephoned to ask if I could look at his book collection at the Schoolhouse in Port Logan, a pretty fishing village south of Stranraer. I have arranged to go there tomorrow afternoon.

Till total £164.50
15 customers

SATURDAY, 21 JUNE

Online orders: 3
Books found: 3

Nicky in.

Just before 1.30 p.m. I remembered that I had arranged to look at the books in Port Logan and headed over there. I overshot and ended up at the neighbouring, almost identically named, Old

Schoolhouse. I knocked on the door and was met by an elderly couple, who explained that I had driven past 'Bob and Barbara's house' and pointed me in the right direction. As I was leaving, the old man said, 'Give my regards to your parents. Your father and I used to do the commentary at the Lochinch Game Fair.' I have no idea who he was, but, following their instructions, I drove the short distance to the correct house and was greeted by Barbara and her two dogs.

The house was a beautifully converted Victorian school with stunning views across the Irish Sea. There was a ruined pier here in days gone by, but that was replaced by a quay and a bell tower designed by Thomas Telford in 1818. What is left is what Seamus Heaney might have described as 'the hammered shod of a bay'. Bob and Barbara – a retired couple – showed me through the house to their library. Both Bob and I had to drop our heads because of the low door into the room. They left me to go through the books, which were mostly paperbacks in near new condition.

We chatted about living in so far-flung a village for a while, and I was surprised how well we got on: most book deals involve the minimum of conversation. I picked out five boxes' worth, gave them £65 and drove back. The books included some excellent, very saleable material: sets of Hemingway, Steinbeck, Chandler, Buchan, all in uniform editions, and a good number of Penguin Modern Classics. Their taste in books was remarkably similar to mine, and I wonder not only whether that was why I found them so agreeable but also whether I would have enjoyed their company as much had I not been aware that our reading tastes were so compatible.

Alastair and Leslie Reid came over for supper. Alastair's response to the question of what he would like to drink is invariably 'Whisky'. This time I was prepared and had a bottle of Laphroaig handy. It is unfortunate that Anna has gone back to London, because it turns out that Alastair used to share a lift to Sarah Lawrence College with her hero, Joseph Campbell. She would have been ridiculously excited. Alastair has rubbed shoulders with many of the greatest minds of the twentieth century, once famously incurring the wrath of Robert Graves in Spain by eloping with his muse, Margot Callas.

Till total £196.90
25 customers

MONDAY, 23 JUNE

Online orders: 8
Books found: 5

Laurie was in today. Her cat had kittens last night and she was up for most of the night looking after them, so she was barely functional today.

Hamish Grierson called again about his books. He had a list of the more valuable titles that he was cross about. Laurie checked and found that they had already been listed online. She had mistaken them as coming from the Glasgow deal from the first week of the month, which she had been working on. So at least we've found them and I can work out a fair price for him.

Till total £385.98
26 customers

TUESDAY, 24 JUNE

Online orders: 5
Books found: 5

Laurie was in today, so I brought the June random books over from the store in the garden for her to pack up. The number of subscribers is about 150.

After lunch I went to look at the book collection of the woman who telephoned last week with the weeping sore on her leg. The house was in Creetown, about ten miles away, and I bought about twenty Folio Society titles, including some good John Buchans as well as a few others. She is a very elderly woman, and is housebound. In the driveway to her house – a modern bungalow with a sea view – there was a rusting old Ford Capri, up on blocks with the wheels removed. A middle-aged man, who seemed to know even less about car mechanics than I do, was tinkering nervously with bits of the engine. The transaction was straightforward, and we had a chat about the reason she is selling the books. She retired here from Yorkshire, and her granddaughter has just been offered a place at Oxford, so she's trying to help her out financially by selling the books to raise some cash. I gave her £70 for a box and a half of books.

The Intimate Thoughts of John Baxter, Bookseller is turning out to be almost as entertaining as William Y. Darling's *The Bankrupt Bookseller*. In the editorial notes Augustus Muir (with reference to Jimmie Scriving) describes him as 'a young ruffian, with no thoughts higher than his stomach'.

Hamish Grierson called and we agreed a price of £225 for his books.

Till total £123
14 customers

WEDNESDAY, 25 JUNE

Online orders: 3
Books found: 3

Laurie in. One of the orders was for a book called *A Guide to the Orthodox Jewish Way of Life for Healthcare Professionals.*

Kate, the postie, arrived in with the mail at exactly the same time as Mr Deacon appeared. Among the post was a parcel containing his copy of *In Patagonia*. He paid for it and left, offering not the slightest clue as to what he had been doing in Patagonia, and not affording me the opportunity to ask. Not that I would have asked. It is none of my business, although the fishing there is among the best in the world and I admit that I am curious that he may have been over there in pursuit of trout.

I spent much of the day filming at the Galloway Activity Centre on Loch Ken. They have built two eco bothies and need videos to promote them. Over the years all the money I have generated from making films for people in the area has been ploughed back into that side of the business in the form of equipment, and we now have what amounts to an impressive amount of kit, including a jib, several very good camcorders, microphones and even a drone. Anna went to film school in Prague, but – apart from an MA in Creative Sound Production – I am completely self-taught and consequently probably incompetent. Although the income generated by Picto (the film business) is relatively small in comparison to that of the shop, I am confident that, if the bookselling business was no longer viable and I had more time, we could build this up into a good business. At the moment, though, it is more of a hobby for which I am paid, and I never actively seek out work: enough comes our way to be manageable. Any more would not be.

In the evening there was a piece on *Front Row* on Radio 4 about the author James Patterson's crusade against Amazon. He is a staunch advocate of bookshops and a vocal critic of Amazon. In his interview he announced that he intends to give £250,000 to UK bookshops in the form of grants of up to £5,000 each for initiatives that encourage children to read. It seems like a perfect fit for expanding the Random Book Club to include a children's section and overhaul the web site, which is now causing me enormous headaches.

Till total £343.67
33 customers

THURSDAY, 26 JUNE

Online orders: 3
Books found: 2

Online order for a book called *Experiences of a Railway Guard: Thrilling Stories of the Rail.*

Sandy the tattooed pagan came to the shop just after lunch and dropped off a dozen sticks. We have sold quite a few since his last visit. They sell particularly well at this time of year. He spent £33 of his credit on books about Celtic mythology.

In the early afternoon a young woman brought in three boxes of books to sell. Most of them were antiquarian calf-bound sets of the usual suspects: Gibbon, Scott, Macaulay, that sort of thing. Not particularly valuable or sought after, but they look nice on a shelf, and occasionally someone will buy them for this reason. They make good wedding presents. She had inherited them from her grandparents and wasn't interested in keeping them, so I gave her £200 for them. As I was pricing them up, I noticed that volume I of the set of Scott's *Poetical Works* (from around 1830) had eight different names written (in different hands) on one of the publisher's blank pages, each one a life about which I know no more than the name. I wonder whose name will be added to the list next.

Till total £184
15 customers

FRIDAY, 27 JUNE

Online orders: 4
Books found: 4

Nicky was in today. She turned up and asked me to give her a hand taking something out of her van that she wanted to sell in the shop. It was a beautiful day, and as soon as she opened the side of her van I saw, to my horror, a mobility scooter. She had been in Castle Douglas yesterday with her friend Iris, who, for reasons unknown, is an expert on mobility scooters. They had spotted it in a charity shop window, and Iris had told Nicky it was under-priced, so Nicky raced in and bought it. I told her that there was no way I was going to start selling mobility scooters in the shop and eventually conceded that she could leave it outside the shop with a 'For Sale' sign on it. She tested it by riding it to the co-op and back. We made a bet in the morning that she would never sell it. By 5 p m. she had sold it for £150 to Andy, a Wigtown resident, originally from South Africa, who had recently been diagnosed with terminal cancer.

So I lost the bet and had to take Nicky to The Ploughman (the pub in Wigtown named after a book by John McNeillie, *The Wigtown Ploughman: Part of His Life*, first published by Putnam's in 1939 and still in print today) and buy her a pint. We sat out on the pavement in the sun with Callum and a few other friends for an hour or two.

Today was the last day of term for the Scottish schools, so hopefully trade should pick up now as people come to Galloway for their holidays. The peaks and troughs of the business follow the timing of school holidays.

Till total £261.99
20 customers

SATURDAY, 28 JUNE

Online orders: 3
Books found: 3

Nicky was in again today, and is more or less back to her usual Friday/Saturday routine. I left at 5.30 a.m. to catch the ferry to Belfast, then the train to Dublin to visit Cloda. She is a friend from my time in Bristol. She now runs the family business, a pharmacy in Dublin, and we often exchange customer stories. Hers tend to be more dramatic than mine, and regularly involve heroin addicts, attempted robberies etc. Her friendship is invaluable, as it makes me feel that I am not the only person among my group of friends who is being driven mad by the public. And although Amazon has yet to branch into prescription medicine in the way that it has done with almost everything else, Cloda's business faces similar problems as an independent competing against chains such as Lloyds and Boots.

I arrived in Dublin in the early afternoon and made my way to Cloda's house in Stoneybatter. We had lunch, and I met her six-month-old baby, Elsa, for the first time, before we drove to the docks to pick up Anna, who had made her way over from London via Holyhead. Cloda had invited us over for an open-air concert in a park in south Dublin, headlined by Pixies and Arcade Fire. It was the first time I'd been to anything like that for years. Her partner, Leo, and her friend Roisin were there too. It was a warm, summer evening and a thoroughly good night. A scouser offered me half an E, after I had bought him a pint, but I politely declined.

Till total £143
15 customers

MONDAY, 30 JUNE

Online orders: 5
Books found: 5

I must remember to apply for the James Patterson grant.

Till total £203.45
15 customers

JULY

There are two well-known types of pest by whom every second-hand bookshop is haunted. One is the decayed person smelling of old breadcrusts who comes every day, sometimes several times a day, and tries to sell you worthless books. The other is the person who orders large quantities of books for which he has not the smallest intention of paying.

George Orwell, 'Bookshop Memories'

There is certainly still no shortage of people who darken the shop's door with the intention of trying to sell worthless books. Most days, particularly during spring, will bring a fresh wave of them to the shop. On average, I would say a hundred books a day come through the door this way. Of these – again on average – I would offer money for fewer than 30 per cent. The remainder I would rather they took away, but often they are clearing out someone's house – a dead aunt, grandmother or parent – and have no desire to have anything more to do with the books, so would rather leave them in the shop. In these instances, when dealing with the recently bereaved, the entreaty is often impossible to refuse. We used to stockpile these on pallets and sell them on eBay, but even that market seems to have dried up. What to do with this dead stock is increasingly becoming a problem for us and many booksellers.

Of the other type of person to which Orwell refers – the person who orders books without intending to pay for them – there certainly used to be such people until just a few years ago. Now we are rarely asked to order books thanks to the ease with which people can do it themselves from home. Or anywhere. Ordering books for customers was never a particularly lucrative exercise, but it was a small supplement to the shop's income, and one that is now lost.

Online orders: 4
Books found: 2

Laurie couldn't make it in to work today because her cat was hit by a car and had to be taken to the vet. Unfortunately it died, leaving her with four very small kittens to look after.

Among the orders this morning was one for *The Colliery Fireman's Pocket Book*, 1935 edition. For some reason Nicky had listed this as being shelved in the chemistry section, but it was not there.

The lease on Anna's flat runs out at the end of this month, so she has asked me if I can drive to London with the van and bring all her possessions back to Wigtown.

Matthew, a book dealer who sells at fairs and specialises in high-end material, came in and fished out a few things from the Glasgow deal, much of which was still boxed. He is another of the handful of dealers who still regularly visits the shop to buy. Fifteen years ago dealers were regular customers, coming in and buying up stock on their particular specialism. Now they are so rare that it is unusual to see them at all. Matthew deals in rare books, and mainly sells at book fairs: not the provincial fairs, but the big antiquarian fairs – Olympia, York – and the others where the average price of a book is in the thousands of pounds, rather than the tens. He only buys books in fine condition, and usually it is modern first editions. He travels all over Europe looking for books to buy and sell on at fairs, and he is like a terrier when it comes to negotiating.

Till total £291.44
21 customers

WEDNESDAY, 2 JULY

Online orders: 6
Books found: 6

Laurie was absent again today due to kitten-minding duties. One of today's online sales was to someone called Keith Richards in London, and another to someone with the unlikely name of Jeremy Wildboar-Hands.

Email from a widow in Norwich wanting to sell me her late husband's book collection. Emailed her to ask what it was.

Till total £280
21 customers

THURSDAY, 3 JULY

Online orders: 3
Books found: 1

Today I was supposed to drive to London to clear Anna's flat, but I have postponed it because Laurie couldn't make it in as she is on kitten duty. She didn't seem to mind, and the flat is hers until the end of the month, so she is not about to be turfed out onto the street.

Today was a warm day, although several customers came in dressed as though it was January.

The swallow chicks have started to fly. Captain is keeping a close eye on them.

The widow from Norwich replied to my inquiry about her late husband's book collection. Apparently it is mainly erotica. She is going to organise a courier to ship it up to the shop.

Till total £247.88
17 customers

FRIDAY, 4 JULY

Online orders: 4
Books found: 3

Nicky was in to work in the shop today. She was unable to disguise her delight on hearing the news that I would be away for the next two days, first to clear Anna's flat, and then on to Somerset for my cousin Suzie's wedding.

I bade Nicky as fond a farewell as our relationship permits and left for London in the blazing sunshine at 11 a.m., arriving in Hampstead at 7 p.m., after I had dropped books off at the auction in Dumfries *en route*. Normally I send anything really rare to Lyon & Turnbull's Edinburgh saleroom, and the Dumfries auction has become more fussy, so I can't dump rubbish there any more, but occasionally I find myself buying something that I know will sell there but not in the shop: sets of reasonably good bindings, for example. They tend to be bought by antique furniture dealers at the saleroom because – when they're selling bookcases – they are far easier to sell if they have nice-looking books on them.

Till total £307.89
36 customers

SATURDAY, 5 JULY

Online orders: 3
Books found: 3

Nicky covered the shop again, and since I haven't heard from her, I am naively assuming that all is well.

Anna and I drove from London to Taunton on the hottest day of the year. The van has no air-conditioning, and we were stuck on the M25 for three hours.

Suzie's wedding was a splendid affair, and everyone turned up to cheer them on. There was dancing and drinking long into the night: my mother had booked a huge holiday house about a mile from the reception, and a dozen or so of us stayed there, including Irish cousins, and my sister Lulu and her husband, Scott. There is always much amusement when we all get together, and people outside the gene pool of the family with whom we are in relationships compare notes about how indecisive all the Bythells are. All of our partners/husbands/wives formed a group and started telling stories about our emotional incompetence; there were frequent hysterics, which were invariably followed by a chorus of 'mine does that too'.

Till total £351.46
35 customers

MONDAY, 7 JULY

Online orders: 5
Books found: 4

Laurie eventually managed to make it back to work following a week of Pet Rescue with the orphaned kittens.

Anna and I drove back from Taunton and arrived home to Wigtown before 7 p.m., just in time for a meeting in the County Buildings about a proposed wind farm that is to be built on land at Kirkdale. We went along and objected, on the grounds that it will be clearly visible from Wigtown (across the bay), and it is unclear whether we will be within the eligible zone for the community cash bribe that usually accompanies such enterprises. The predicted annual turnover of the wind farm is somewhere in the region of £30 million, and the amount to be given to the residents (to be decided by committee) is just £100,000, or 0.3 per cent of turnover. As most of the visual impact of the development will be from our side of the bay, we are unlikely to benefit much, if at all, because we are furthest away. Those to whom the wind farm is nearest stand to gain the most, and very few of them will even see it. It has angered a great many people in the Machars.

Till total £213.48
17 customers

TUESDAY, 8 JULY

Online orders: 3
Books found: 1

The first order for a book today was about the history of level crossings.

Laurie made it in on another beautiful sunny day.

Much of today was spent editing the video for the Galloway Activity Centre on Loch Ken. When I came downstairs to cover Laurie's lunch break, she told me that she had been 'shhh-ed' by a customer for eating an apple too loudly. Apparently this was shortly followed by some deliberately audible whispering along the lines of 'Kids today' and 'Doesn't she know that this is a bookshop?'

A customer brought in three books on music, for which I gave him £10.

I received an extremely ominous text message from Nicky about working this week. It ended with the words 'Wait till you see what I have got for you THIS week! You'll love it!'

The time has come to replace the van. It has done 172,000 miles, and I have reached the point where I am starting to wonder if it can cope with long journeys, so I went to Wigtown Motor Company and spoke to Vincent about looking for a replacement.

Till total £254.98
25 customers

WEDNESDAY, 9 JULY

Online orders: 3
Books found: 3

Laurie made it in again today, but she had to bring the kittens with her because there was nobody at home to feed them.

The time may have come for a dreaded visit to the Polish dentist in Stranraer; I awoke with diabolical toothache this morning. My reluctance to visit the dentist is in no way a reflection on his ability as a practitioner, and has more to do with the memory of my last visit, during which he extracted a wisdom tooth. That trauma, however, paled into insignificance when I bumped into an old friend and two of her young children in Morrisons supermarket shortly afterwards. They all looked terrified. When I got back home and checked in the mirror, I understood why. Most of my face was frozen in a stroke-like state from the anaesthetic, and my chin was covered in blood, much of which had dribbled onto my shirt.

The depressed Welsh woman phoned again, the usual disappointment in her voice before I had even replied that there is nothing in stock for her.

Till total £334.99
28 customers

THURSDAY, 10 JULY

Online orders: 3
Books found: 2

Laurie in again today, yet another beautiful day.

Among the emails this morning were two, both from angry customers, each of whom complained that they had received the wrong book in the post. The customer who had ordered a book on bullfighting had instead received a book on creative candle-making, and the creative candlemaker had received the book on bullfighting. Despite the fact that we have agreed to refund them and rectify the mistake, the bullfighter left negative feedback on Amazon with the following comment:

> The book listed above, which I ordered, was not sent. Instead a book called *Creative Candlemaking* was sent by mistake. The 2 books could not be more different in content. I have contacted the suppliers – Wigtown Book Shop – to inform them of this mistake. They have acknowledged and have agreed to send the correct book when I return the book I did not order.

Vincent called to say that he has found a van in Inverary that has 50,000 miles on the clock and is £10,000, so I will speak to the bank about setting up another loan.

Till total £89.29
14 customers

FRIDAY, 11 JULY

Online orders: 2
Books found: 2

Nicky was back on duty again today – another beautiful sunny day marred only by her presence. She announced this morning that she will no longer participate in the videos we've been making for Facebook, in which she expounds her wisdom on various subjects, to the enormous amusement of the people who follow the shop's page, because I changed one after we had agreed on a final cut. She has, however, agreed to do the filming and make me the victim.

I found a customer in the garden, gazing into the pond, despite the gate with a 'Private' sign that she would have had to open before she could get near to it.

A customer brought three books to the counter, pointed to two of them and said, 'I'll take those two; you'll have to put that one back on the shelf.' He subsequently asked if he could pay for the two books that he wanted with Tesco Clubcard points.

Till total £149.90
14 customers

SATURDAY, 12 JULY

Online orders: 2
Books found: 2

Nicky was in once again. The weather has turned and is now damp and dreich.

The online orders are becoming fewer and fewer: possibly another problem with Monsoon.

Today was the start of Wigtown Civic Week, and Tam Dingwall, the former landlord of The Galloway, the pub directly across the square from my shop, marked the occasion by singing 'Achy Breaky Heart' to a small group of drizzled youths in the town square. Civic Week is one of the highlights of Wigtown's calendar. It involves all manner of curious activities and is squarely aimed at the local population, rather than tourists. There are quizzes, activities for children (such as a muddy nature walk on the salt-marsh), a raft race and all sorts of small town festivities, including the slightly anachronistic crowning of the Wigtown Princess. There are prizes for all manner of wonderful things, such as Best Decorated Toilet Roll. It feels very much like travelling back to the 1950s.

A customer asked one of his companions where the philosophy section was. He replied, 'I don't know, you'll have to ask the chappie.' Chappie? I don't think so.

An elderly man brought in a box of books that contained a Victorian family Bible. There is little demand for these nowadays, if there ever was. This one contained a handwritten letter dated 22 February 1879 and addressed from Carnwath:

Dear Mother we write
with the greatest delight
our promise to you to fulfill
so we're here safe and sound
on the old honoured ground
and we cannot complain very ill.
I am happy to tell
that our friends are all well
and hope you are all still the same
When Marion's away
Now mind what I say
Take care of yourself we shall blame
Janet means to go down
To that great big town
with Aleck on Monday forenoon
She's all ready to go
so this lets you know
She'll be back to Carluke very soon.
Yours affectionately,
Maggie.

Old letters are not unusual things to find in books, but one written in rhyme is rare. I once bought a copy of *The Seven Pillars of Wisdom* that contained over a hundred letters of condolence to a widow, many of which were from people who had never met her, but whose lives had been touched by her late husband. My curiosity is always piqued by such things, and it is hard not to speculate about who these people were, both the senders and the recipients.

Till total £367.91
33 customers

Online orders: 6
Books found: 5

Laurie made it in today. Clearly a family member is on kitten duty. Shortly after she had arrived, a customer came to the counter and said, 'Good morrow to you, sir! Would you mind, perchance, directing me towards any of your shelves which might contain any books on the subject of military history?'

The shelves were particularly untidy by the end of the day, an inevitable consequence of a multitude of children being in the shop. Some parents think that it is acceptable to let their offspring run riot around the shop, disturbing other customers and leaving a trail of devastation. Most, though, are fine and the children well behaved. There is an instinct that appears common to all boys of four years old when presented with a shelf of books, the spines neatly lined up with the edge of the shelf. They seem incapable of resisting the urge to push them back as far as they can, against the back of the bookcase. The sight of a neatly lined row of books is irresistible to small boys, and they can no more control their desire to make a mess of them than they can suppress the urge to pull a cat's tail or jump in a puddle.

Nicky reminded me recently that she thinks that my insistence on keeping the place ordered and tidy is some form of OCD and genuinely believes that customers like piles of books all over the floor and don't really much care for them being organised by subject or category.

Till total £223.98
21 customers

TUESDAY, 15 JULY

Online orders: 2
Books found: 2

Laurie was in charge again today. She came up to the office, where I was working, to tell me that a customer had brought in a print of Wigtown. It was a handsome framed print from the mid-nineteenth century and showed architectural features of the town that are no longer there. He wanted £50, which I was more than happy to give to him.

Callum and I are planning to go sailing tomorrow if the weather is good. Last year he bought a Hurley 22, a small sailing boat that claims to be four-berth, but which in reality would be uncomfortable for four small children, let alone two men, each over six feet tall.

Till total £374.96
37 customers

WEDNESDAY, 16 JULY

Online orders: 3
Books found: 2

Laurie arrived on time, but the sailing trip that Callum had planned was dependent on fine weather, and this morning it was pouring with rain, so he telephoned to say that we should postpone until it improves, so I didn't bother to pack or get organised. The moment the sun came out, he appeared without warning, ready to go, so I asked Laurie to pack and process the random books, and tell Wilma that they're ready for collection when she drops off the mail sacks from today's orders.

There are gaps appearing on the shelves, now that customers have started to come out of hibernation and are spending money – the Folio section and the railway section are particularly lean.

I packed hastily and said goodbye to Laurie, and we drove to Stranraer. We set sail at 1 p.m. and headed for Ailsa Craig, an uninhabited island in the Irish Sea, where we arrived at 7 p.m. The afternoon was cloudless and sunny, with the golden-orange sun silhouetting the island as we arrived. We moored at the pier and went ashore to explore the ruined buildings and old railway. Ailsa Craig is all that remains of an ancient volcanic plug. It is a granite lump off the Ayrshire coast. In its long history it has been a refuge for Catholic recusants in the sixteenth century, and is known locally as 'Paddy's Milestone', partly because it is half-way between Glasgow and Belfast, and partly because of the folkloric tradition which pitched two fighting giants against one another: one Irish, one Scottish. According to the legend, they threw rocks at one another, and Ailsa Craig was the last rock thrown.

Callum and I sat in the cockpit of his boat drinking beer until about midnight, watching as thousands of small jellyfish drifted by, occasionally disturbing the surface and making rings as though someone had dropped a pebble in the otherwise flat calm sea. I slept in one of the tiny berths at the back of the boat, which felt uncomfortably like being in a coffin.

Till total £242.49
19 customers

THURSDAY, 17 JULY

Online orders: 3
Books found: 3

We awoke at about 9 a.m. and went to explore the island further. We walked first to the northern foghorn, then I climbed to the summit, stopping to have a look at the castle on the way up. Callum stayed with the boat and anti-fouled the hull. I returned to the boat at about 1 p.m. and went for a swim before setting off for Lamlash. While I was at the summit of Ailsa Craig, I saw a boat motoring slowly towards Callum's boat, as if it intended to pull up and say hello. As it drew closer, I noticed it abruptly changed course and headed towards Girvan. When I returned to the boat, Callum was inside making a cup of tea. I mentioned to him that the other boat appeared to have taken a strange turn and he explained, 'Oh, that. After you'd headed up to the summit, I decided that I'd anti-foul the hull in the nude, since there was nobody about. I didn't hear that boat approaching, and I was hauling myself on board to get a brush, inadvertently pointing my bare arse right at them. It was only when I got back in the water that I noticed the boat, but by that time they were gone.'

We set off for Arran at 2 p.m., in an intermittent wind, so we motored and sailed, depending on what was most favourable.

We arrived at Lamlash at about 7 p.m., accompanied by a pod of porpoises. Callum inflated the tender, and we rowed ashore to The Drift Inn for a meal and a few drinks before heading back to the boat for the night.

Till total £102
11 customers

FRIDAY, 18 JULY

Online orders: 0
Books found: 0

Explored Holy Island just off Lamlash.
3 p.m. message from Laurie to say that there is a power cut.

Till total £389.45
29 customers

SATURDAY, 19 JULY

Online orders: 0
Books found: 0

I got back to the shop from the sailing trip at 4 p.m. to a startled Nicky, who had no idea when we were due to return. She was visibly upset to see me home safely. After I had shut the shop, a man telephoned to say that he is moving into a care home from his house, and wants to sell his book collection. He lives just outside Kelso, in a small village. I have arranged to visit him towards the end of the month.

Till total £288.98
38 customers

MONDAY, 21 JULY

Online orders: 0
Books found: 0

Laurie was in today, a lovely sunny day.

Monsoon was still not working, probably a consequence of the power cut on Friday, so I emailed their tech support team.

The first customer of the day was an Irish woman, who turned up at the shop at 9.09 a.m. and asked, 'Tell me now, does everything in Scotland open at 10 a.m.?'

After work I went to a meeting organised by the council, chaired by someone called 'The Shop Doctor', whose job it is to help retailers improve their businesses. It turned out to be a complete waste of time, and I spent three pointless hours being tortured by his PowerPoint presentation, an abomination rich with revelatory insights like 'If you keep your door open, more customers will come in than if it is closed' and 'The name of your business should reflect what you sell'. Well, I think I managed to nail that one. There's not a lot of ambiguity about 'The Book Shop'. I reached my limit and left when he showed a series of photographs of seriously run-down shops and asked us – like a group of pre-school children – 'Can anybody see what's wrong with this one?' By this point everyone was seething, and for a brief moment I feared a lynching, a fear that rapidly became a hope the moment he addressed me. 'You. You've been very quiet. What do you think is wrong with this shop front?' he oozed, as his projector clicked to a photograph of a shop with no sign, a smashed window and a burned-out car in front of it.

Till total £187.60
30 customers

TUESDAY, 22 JULY

Online orders: 4
Books found: 0

Laurie in again and another sunny day. She spent the day listing books for sale on Fulfilled By Amazon. Once we're up to four boxes she will organise for them to be taken to the Amazon warehouse in Dunfermline.

A customer came to the counter when Laurie was having a break, and pointed at a sealed box with an address label on, which contained a set of *Statistical Accounts* that we are shipping out to a buyer in the USA.

Customer: 'I am a bit confused, that box over there …'
Me: 'Sorry, the books in that box aren't for sale. They've already been sold.'
Customer: 'I thought not.'

I still have no idea what that was about.

Nicky sent me an email in which she described a customer on Saturday who had come into the shop in full Highland fighting dress: 'Glorious green gilet and hand-knitted socks, capercaillie feathers dancing on his bonnie Glengarry.' Apparently he 'marched proudly into the shop accompanied by a whinging dog which didn't shut up until he marched back outside. Kind of ruined his image. And he didn't acknowledge me. Probably English.'

Booked in to have my hair cut tomorrow by Richard, the barber three doors down the street from my shop.

Monsoon's tech support finally contacted us and managed to take over the computer and fix the problems.

Till total £268
27 customers

WEDNESDAY, 23 JULY

Online orders: 13
Books found: 9

Laurie in. Yet another stunning, sunny day.

I wandered down for a haircut at 10.45 a.m. Richard was, as always, friendly and chatty. As I was leaving, I met Mr Deacon coming in for whatever treatment he has applied to his comb-over. He faintly acknowledged me in a slightly confused fashion. Perhaps out of the context of the shop he couldn't place me.

Laurie managed to locate and pack all but four of the books that have been ordered since Friday. We had several angry emails and telephone calls about books that were ordered at the start of the month and still have not arrived. There might be a shipping problem with Historic Newspapers, so I will look into it.

Historic Newspapers is a local business that ships old newspapers around the world, and consequently they have a very favourable contract with a courier, DHL, so we put all our overseas orders through them. They drop in twice a week and pick up any parcels we have for non-UK customers.

After lunch I drove to Carsluith again to look at more of the books belonging to the woman with a weeping leg sore. She is slowly clearing her stuff out, and there was a lot of good Folio

Society material – one box worth. Gave her £55 towards her grand-daughter's Oxford fund.

After work I went for a swim in the sea at Monreith with Maltese Tracy.

Till total £236.49
16 customers

THURSDAY, 24 JULY

Online orders: 5
Books found: 3

Laurie opened the shop on what was the hottest day of the year so far: the garden thermometer read 29 degrees.

As we were putting books on the shelves, a couple came into the shop. The wife mauled her way through the antiquarian shelves, coughing and moaning, while he looked at books in the Scottish room. The moment he joined her, she complained loudly about having a headache, catarrh and sore knees. When she finally stopped talking, he offered her some sort of homeopathic crystal to cure her headache. Despite being remarkably annoying, they spent £250 on an eighteenth-century Scottish botanical book.

Laurie organised the collection of four boxes for sale through FBA. They will be delivered to the Amazon warehouse in Dunfermline, and sold and shipped directly through Amazon.

Possibly triggered by our brief encounter in the doorway of the barber's yesterday, Mr Deacon dropped in and ordered a copy of Alison Weir's *Eleanor of Aquitaine*. He looked suspicious when Laurie took his order, slightly as I suspect the character of Mr Pumpherston did in *The Intimate Thoughts of John Baxter, Bookseller*, in which Alec, the young apprentice, serves him instead of Baxter himself: 'I think he would admit he has his doubts about that young shaver', although, unlike Alec, Laurie is perfectly competent to deal with any customer.

Laurie and I spent the rest of the day packing and labelling books for the Random Book Club. Two subscribers failed to renew for another year. After we had finished with the Random Book Club I asked Laurie to sweep up the shop window. It was like a furnace in the summer sun.

Till total £449.99
16 customers

FRIDAY, 25 JULY

Online orders: 5
Books found: 5

Nicky was in the shop today. She spent the day dealing with the postage for the random books, a job that she particularly dislikes, and which I endeavour to ensure falls to her every month.

Just before closing, a customer brought in two large framed maps of Ayrshire, hand-coloured and dating from 1828. I gave her £60 each for them.

Till total £369.50
17 customers

SATURDAY, 26 JULY

Online orders: 3
Books found: 3

Nicky was up early tidying the shop – a significant reversal of her usual work-time activities, which largely comprise making as much of a mess as she possibly can. She asked me to find her an excuse to escape if Smelly Kelly came in to continue his Brut 33-scented wooing. Unsurprisingly, on seeing her blue minibus parked opposite the shop, he pitched up at about 11 a.m. I pretended that I had a parcel to collect from the post office in Newton Stewart and asked Nicky if she would mind picking it up for me, to which she readily agreed. Smelly Kelly then asked if she could give him a lift there as he wanted to visit his brother, at which point there was no option but to fall on my sword and tell Nicky that I would go to Newton Stewart, taking Smelly Kelly with me, if she could cover the shop. The journey was horrendous; the air in the cab of the van was barely breathable so dense was the cloud of Brut 33, even with all the windows open.

At 3 p.m. Mr Deacon appeared to inquire about his order. I told him that it should be here next week. He was clutching a tin of cat food.

Nicky and I spent the afternoon clearing out the van and tidying it up for Vincent to drive it to Inverary tomorrow. I dropped it off at Vincent's at 4 p.m.

Nicky has decided that she and her friend Morag are going to the Edinburgh Book Festival and intend to promote the Random Book Club. She has instructed me to produce business cards and flyers by Thursday.

Till total £367.46
13 customers

MONDAY, 28 JULY

Online orders: 6
Books found: 3

Laurie was off today, so I was alone in the shop. Vincent telephoned to tell me that the new van is here whenever I want to pick it up.

When I took the mail sacks over to the post office, Wilma asked how things were going with Anna. William overheard and muttered something unpleasant.

On Nicky's instructions, I spent an hour or two designing Random Book Club promotional material for her to take to the

Edinburgh Book Festival. After lunch I emailed it to J&B Print in Newton Stewart with a note that it needs to be ready for Thursday.

After work I picked up the new van from Vincent. It is silver with built-in satnav, electric windows and a tow bar, and much fancier than the old red one. It has a saltire flag on the back door, which should infuriate my pro-union mother.

Till total £434.44
39 customers

TUESDAY, 29 JULY

Online orders: 4
Books found: 4

Laurie made it in today. Apparently her dog has a punctured eye. The drama of her domestic menagerie continues. The kittens are doing well, though, apparently.

Amazon order for a book called *The Reforming of Dangerous and Useless Horses*. I ought to have sent this to my cousin Aoife, all of whose horses appear to fall into both categories.

Mr Deacon's book arrived, so I left a message on his voicemail.

Till total £341.48
33 customers

WEDNESDAY, 30 JULY

Online orders: 3
Books found: 3

Laurie was in today, which was largely a cloudy day.

Drove to North Berwick to look at a collection of books on

Catholicism in a beautiful Georgian town house. Gave the man
– a tall man, so wordless that I began to suspect that he may have
belonged to a silent order – £200 for five boxes of them, then drove
to Eyemouth and found a hotel to stay in.

Till total £541.90
44 customers

THURSDAY, 31 JULY

Online orders: 3
Books found: 2

Laurie covered the shop. She couldn't find one of today's orders,
which was for a book whose title was *Sewage Disposal from Isolated
Buildings*.

After breakfast I left Eyemouth and drove to a house near
Kelso, where I had arranged to look at another collection for sale.
This time it was the library of an elderly man whose wife had died
recently and who was moving from his bungalow into sheltered
accommodation. He seemed happy to be moving, probably for the
last time in his life. The bungalow was on a steep slope, and there
were a dozen or so steps up to the front door. As his mobility is
quite limited, I imagine that comfort is now his top priority, rather
than independence. The books were both his and his late wife's.
They were a good mix of fiction and non-fiction, in fairly good
condition, probably about 600 in total, including boxed Folio sets of
Wodehouse, E. F. Benson and Orwell. I left with about 100 books,
gave him £190 and drove home, arriving back at the shop at about
3 p.m. to be met with a customer in cheap polyester suit who asked,
'Do you remember me? I bought a book about bowling from you
five years ago.'

Alison from J&B Print dropped off the new Random Book
Club flyers with an invoice for £313.94. Nicky had better get a lot
of new subscribers to cover the cost of that.

Email from Helen, secretary of the Wigtown Agricultural

Society, reminding me that I have agreed to film and make a DVD of the cattle show on Wednesday. The long-range weather forecast looks dire for that day.

Till total £277.73
31 customers

AUGUST

Like most second-hand bookshops we had various sidelines. We sold second-hand typewriters, for instance, and also stamps – used stamps, I mean. Stamp-collectors are a strange, silent, fish-like breed, of all ages, but only of the male sex; women, apparently, fail to see the peculiar charm of gumming bits of coloured paper into albums. We also sold sixpenny horoscopes compiled by somebody who claimed to have foretold the Japanese earthquake. They were in sealed envelopes and I never opened one of them myself, but the people who bought them often came back and told us how 'true' their horoscopes had been. (Doubtless any horoscope seems 'true' if it tells you that you are highly attractive to the opposite sex and your worst fault is generosity.)

George Orwell, 'Bookshop Memories'

Perhaps various sidelines are more important to second-hand bookshops now than they ever were. When I can afford to and I have the opportunity, I attend the auction in Dumfries and pick up bits and pieces to sell in the shop. At the moment there is an oak Georgian bureau (£70), two pairs of Victorian crown green bowling balls (£25 per pair), seventeen jardinières and plant pots (various prices), a sturdy Victorian fire screen (£300), several prints and paintings and a mahogany table (£75), as well as an assortment of trinkets and costume jewellery that Anna has arranged into a corner of the shop that she has called 'The Littlest Antique Store in the World'. Not my idea. These things, carefully chosen, can add atmosphere to the place by referencing the building's history as a home prior to its incarnation as a shop – first as a draper's in 1899, then later as a grocer's in the 1950s, and since 1992 a bookshop. Add to that mix Sandy the tattooed pagan's walking sticks and there is hopefully enough to keep the non-reading companions of biblio-philes occupied while their partners browse.

FRIDAY, I AUGUST

Online orders: 4
Books found: 4

Nicky in.

Tracy dropped in this morning to say hello. It is her birthday today.

> Me: 'Happy birthday, Tracy, hope you have a lovely day.'
> Nicky: 'Well, Tracy, you're one year closer to death.'

Norrie turned up with prototypes of the concrete books that he has made to replace the spirals we had at the front of the shop. I used to make them from real books coated in fibreglass resin, but they were a lot of work in the making and needed to be replaced every three years. The concrete spirals will be expensive but should last for ever.

Mr Deacon dropped in to collect his copy of *Eleanor of Aquitaine*: 'I'm in Wigtown seeing the doctor in any case, so I thought I'd collect the book while I am at it.'

My parents called in for a cup of tea at about 4.30 p.m. My father retired from farming about fifteen years ago, around the time I bought the shop (with their enthusiastic encouragement). They sold the farmhouse and steading – which they had converted into holiday cottages when I was a child – and moved to a modern house about five miles away in 2000, thirty years to the day after they had moved into the farm. They kept the land and now rent it to a tenant. My mother, ever the entrepreneur, keeps busy with various projects, while my father has occupied himself with restoring old cars since his retirement. The first was a Bentley, and he is currently working on an Alvis. As I was locking up the shop five minutes after they left, I caught my mother picking the saltire sticker off the back door of the new van.

After work I went to The Ploughman for a pint with Callum and Tracy to celebrate Tracy being another year closer to death.

Till total £263.98
31 customers

Online orders: 4
Books found: 4

Nicky was in today, and miraculously turned up bang on time. It was a dismally wet morning, but it brightened up in the afternoon, in the middle of which I received a text message from Katie. Apparently I had offered her work for the summer, and she is coming in tomorrow. Oh dear. I will have to cut Laurie's hours as I can't afford two sets of wages.

Nicky was all set to go to the Edinburgh Book Festival on Wednesday to distribute propaganda about the Random Book Club, so I checked online to see what events and authors she should target. It turns out that it doesn't start until next Saturday, and she had misread the dates.

Anna Dreda from Wenlock Books (in Much Wenlock, in Shropshire) and her partner, Hilary, arrived. I had invited them to stay *en route* back from their holiday on North Uist. We stayed up late talking shop. It is rare to have an opportunity to compare notes with another bookseller, and it is always reassuring to hear that other people are facing the same problems, largely caused by the relentless march of Amazon. Anna has adapted to the situation by cutting paid staff and relying on volunteers – something that I hadn't considered – as well as organising events in her shop. They are here for a couple of days.

At closing time a man from Ballater, in Aberdeenshire, telephoned. He has a collection of books on polar exploration that he is keen to sell, so we have arranged that I will see him on Wednesday. If it is a good collection, it is the sort of thing that might sell well during the upcoming book festival.

Till total £495.49
36 customers

MONDAY, 4 AUGUST

Online orders: 7
Books found: 7

Bank holiday. Katie and Laurie were both in today. Katie's further education as a doctor seems merely to have served to make her more acerbic – I was barefoot in the shop when she arrived, and she told me that I made the place look more like a homeless shelter than a bookshop.

A customer brought in four boxes of books on medieval literature. I picked out a few and gave him £60 for them. Katie spent the day alphabetically organising the crime section, finishing the job started by Andrew before it became too much for him.

As I was tidying the shelves in the psychology section, I came across a book called *Atomic Structure and Chemical Bonding*, which had clearly been put there by Nicky. I will speak to her about it on Friday. I also spotted that she has created a new section called 'Home Front Novels', which I removed immediately and put in the boxes for recycling.

Hilary is very keen on Gavin Maxwell, so I took her and Anna on a tour that included the House of Elrig, his childhood home, the Maxwell memorial at Monreith and a quick look at Monreith House. Afterwards I went down to the cattle show ground to film some aerial shots using the drone, on which is mounted a small GoPro video camera, as the setting sun was stunning.

Several years ago a friend gave me a copy of one of her favourite books: *A Confederacy of Dunces*, by John Kennedy Toole. It has been sitting on my pile of books to read, so I began reading it after I closed the shop.

Till total £346
26 customers

TUESDAY, 5 AUGUST

Online orders: 0
Books found: 0

Laurie and Katie were both in the shop again today. I really need to split them, as I can't afford to pay them both. Next week they will work three days each with no overlap.

No orders today, so I suspect that there is a problem with Monsoon. I have emailed them to let them know.

Anna and Hilary left for Much Wenlock, but before they did, they told me that they want to come back with a book group and run a creative writing course in the shop in February. I warned them about the temperature. They didn't seem to be put off. I'm not sure how it would work financially, so I suggested that they could use the house for free the first year – they seem to think that the drawing room would be an ideal venue – and if it works, we can find a way of repeating it but with a small fee for the use of the house.

Katie spent the day ordering the poetry section, which has become chaotically disorganised.

Internet stopped working at 3 p.m.

Till total £550.34
52 customers

WEDNESDAY, 6 AUGUST

Online orders: 0
Books found: 0

When I came downstairs in the morning to open the shop there was still no internet connection, so I telephoned Titan Telecom, my new supplier, who told me that I would need a new username and password. When I explained that this was a matter of urgency, as we had no orders coming through, they said that a technician would call back soon, so I left Laurie and Katie with instructions to sort it out.

It rained heavily last night, and the morning was cloudy, but it turned into a glorious day in spite of the forecast. Just as well, as it was Wigtown Show day. I spent most of the day filming sheep, cows, horses and chickens and chatting to farmers. Wigtown Show is one of the oldest agricultural shows in Scotland. It has been held annually for 200 years, and it entails marquees filled with people selling country craft things and food. There's music and a bar and all manner of entertainment, as well as the pens full of livestock.

The Titan Telecom technician called at 3.45 p.m., and we were back online by 4 p.m., so the two sets of wages I paid the girls to list books online were, thanks to technical problems, wasted.

Laurie and Katie went to the post-cattle show party in the marquee and stayed overnight in the shop. I went to bed at about 1 a.m. and they still hadn't come home.

Till total £386.90
43 customers

THURSDAY, 7 AUGUST

Online orders: 6
Books found: 4

Laurie was up at about 8.50 a.m., Katie at about 9.15 a.m. Both looked pretty hungover and were relatively useless all day.

Till total £337.05
28 customers

Online orders: 3
Books found: 2

I left for Ballater at 7 a.m., so Laurie opened the shop today. Nicky was at home making things to take to Edinburgh next week to help promote the Random Book Club at their book festival. She is planning to go up on Wednesday and Thursday and hand out flyers and free books, most of which – she has now told me – she just removed from the shelves of the shop without asking me.

I arrived in Ballater just before noon and found the house, a small, unattractive bungalow in a scheme of identical small, unattractive bungalows, all with fussy rose gardens. The man who greeted me at the door was small and bearded, and wearing a dressing gown and slippers. His wife was identically attired. The house was small and cluttered, and a layer of dust and grime appeared to cover every surface. The books were in several rooms throughout the house, many of them upstairs in a converted attic with a very narrow staircase leading up to it. The wife made me a cup of tea, and I worked my way through the collection while they watched television. They were friendly enough but didn't appear to want to chat. The books were slightly disappointing – Nansen's *Farthest North* in a two-volume leather-bound edition in poor condition, the Penguin edition of Cherry-Garrard's *The Worst Journey in the World* and Admiral Evans's *South with Scott* – and most of the collection was in average to poor condition. There were none of the big hitters you always hope for in a polar collection – Shackleton's *South* in the first edition, or *The Heart of the Antarctic* in the de luxe edition, which is probably just as well as money is tight this year. After an hour or so I had amassed about six boxes of books, all about the Antarctic, and we agreed a price of £300. Both the man and his wife had been fairly uncommunicative but not unfriendly, and I had early on decided that he probably had little to say for himself, but as I was loading the boxes into the van I asked what had piqued his interest in Antarctica, at which point he became surprisingly animated. He had been part of the British Antarctic Survey in his thirties and had been there for several summers doing research. I really ought to be less dismissive of customers and people selling books.

Left Aberdeenshire at just after 1 p.m. and headed south. Home by 6 p.m.

Till total £196.98
19 customers

SATURDAY, 9 AUGUST

Online orders: 4
Books found: 4

Nicky was in the shop today, a glorious sunny day. I'm off for a few days' fishing next week, so we discussed the various jobs that need to be done in my absence. I have little or no confidence that she absorbed any of the information and expect that she will do exactly as she pleases while I am away.

As Nicky was leaving, someone on a mobility scooter almost ran her down on the pavement. Initially I thought it might have been Andy, who bought hers a few weeks ago. As I was musing at the irony of her being run over by her own mobility scooter, she came back into the shop to collect her hat, which she had left in a corner somewhere. I asked her if she had seen Andy lately, as I hadn't seen him for quite a while. She replied with the casual indifference that is the preserve of those who believe that death is the beginning rather than the end, 'He died last week.'

Till total £336.87
25 customers

SUNDAY, 10 AUGUST

Online orders: 3
Books found: 3

Drove up to Lairg for three days' fishing with friends Frederick and Fenella and the other guests they'd invited. The A9 is a tortuous road, particularly when you are on your own, as there is no radio signal for much of it. Normally, I can re-tune to long wave and listen to *Test Match Special*, but England beat India with a day to spare yesterday, so I was denied even that to keep me company. It rained heavily all the way, and the forecast is for more of the same all week. Ideally for salmon-fishing a falling river is best, but it looks very much like this is not going to be likely.

This trip is a highlight of my year, and I live in perpetual fear of not being invited again – probably for my inadequate fishing (and social) skills. Frederick's family shares the fishing rights for the River Shin and the Oykel with a number of other people, and they own a considerably extended cottage just outside Lairg. Every year for the past few years it has been my good fortune to have been invited to fish for a few days on some of the best salmon water in Scotland. By now I know most of the other people who are also invited – it changes every year – and this time, as well as Frederick's children from his first marriage, Wilf and Daisy, the guests include Biffy, with whom I was at school for a few years, and Will, a charming man whom I hadn't met before.

The Shin is a spectacular river; Mohamed Al-Fayed built a visitor centre near the Falls of Shin, where there is a platform from which anyone can stand and watch the salmon waiting in the falls pool burst out of the water and power up through the waterfall into the upper section of the river to spawn. The Shin is part of a hydro system, and cuts a deep and steep gorge through a beautiful broad-leafed landscape, dropping dramatically down into the Kyle of Sutherland. There is a sense of something truly ancient about the Shin – perhaps it's a connection to the Ice Age – huge boulders the size of houses are strewn along its path – or some form of geological transformation that you can't help but feel a part of, because the river is still carving and ploughing its way along the Silurian fault-line in the Moine Nappe to the sea. The upper waters of the Oykel have a similar appearance, but there the landscape is more open: the Shin is enclosed by high cliffs, trapped in the gorge and, as I discovered one year, at the mercy of the hydro scheme. I was kneeling on a rock in the middle of the river when a hydro technician must have decided to open the sluice. I was concentrating on trying to cover the water with my fly, so that I failed to notice that the rock on which I was kneeling had become submersed. By the time I was aware, the river between the rock and the bank had risen to such a level that the only way I could get back was to flood my waders and stagger, soaked, to the trees and the path home.

MONDAY, 11 AUGUST

Online orders: 4
Books found: 3

The sound of howling wind and driving rain woke me at 7 a.m. Frederick and I drove from the cottage down to the Shin to meet up with the ghillies. The Shin was unfishable at 5 feet, as was the Oykel at 11 feet. Far too much water to fish either, so we went to the falls of both rivers to see what they looked like with so vast a volume of water crashing through them.

Till total £467.46
45 customers

TUESDAY, 12 AUGUST

Online orders: 4
Books found: 2

Up at 7.30 a.m. with Will, one of the other guests – an old friend of Frederick. We drove to beat 3 on the Oykel, where the water was very high. I caught an 18lb. salmon at about 9 a.m., just as Peter, one of the ghillies, arrived. It turned out to be the only fish caught on the Oykel that day. In the afternoon I fished the Shin and lost a huge salmon above the falls, which took all of the line off my reel in a matter of seconds and kept going, leaving a 'V' in its wake. I am convinced that it must have been over 30lb. I doubt whether anyone believed me when I told them.

Till total £534.57
54 customers

WEDNESDAY, 13 AUGUST

Online orders: 5
Books found: 4

Spent the morning fishing. After lunch I said goodbye and left for Glasgow, where I spent the night in a hotel, and where I have a book deal nearby tomorrow morning.

Till total £297.70
25 customers

THURSDAY, 14 AUGUST

Online orders: 3
Books found: 3

Awoke at 8 a.m. and drove to a house in Glasgow to meet a young couple who are moving house and have decided to sell their book collection. It included an assortment of mountaineering books, and I picked out three boxes' worth and offered them £75. As I was writing the cheque on the desk in their office, I accidentally nudged the mouse next to the monitor, which activated the previously dormant screen. It brought up a swingers' web site on which there was a photograph of a very attractive young dark-haired woman. Thankfully, neither of them was in the room at the time, and when the wife reappeared to take the cheque, the screensaver had returned.

After I had loaded the boxes into the van, I drove home and arrived back at the shop by 12.30 p.m. to find both Laurie and Katie chatting and listening to music instead of working. The counter was a mess, the tables and workspace all littered with books and scraps of paper, so I attempted to give them a lecture about tidiness, to which they responded by calling me a fussy old woman and imitating me, so I checked the river levels online and decided to go to the nearby River Minnoch for the afternoon and try to catch another salmon, an enterprise that proved entirely unsuccessful.

At 4.30 p.m. I returned to the shop to discover my mother giving my cousin Giles a guided tour of the place. She is partial to giving people guided tours of my house. Once, a few years ago, during the book festival, I went to my bedroom to fetch a jumper and found her in there with a very uncomfortable-looking Joan Bakewell, whom she was lecturing on the subject of my tastes in interior design.

An elderly man came in just before 5 p.m. and asked if we could clear books from his late sister's house near Haugh of Urr (roughly 800 titles). He needs to clear them urgently as he is only here until Saturday, so I have agreed to go over and look at them tomorrow after lunch.

Till total £299.69
32 customers

Online orders: 3
Books found: 0

Katie was in today, covering for Nicky.

Monsoon was down again, so we couldn't access the locator codes to find the books that have been ordered, the title of one of which was *He Was Born Gay*, by Emlyn Williams.

After lunch I left for Haugh of Urr, a tiny village about thirty-five miles away, to look at a book collection. They were in a very pretty, small whitewashed cottage. The place was a mess, but full of beautiful antique furniture and paintings, and a mixed collection of books. There wasn't much exceptional material, and a lot of the better books were mouldy and water-damaged from a flood in March, but I found a copy of *Don Quixote* from 1755 in two volumes and some A. A. Milne firsts. The books, paintings and furniture had come from a stately home, and had been divided among the family when the bigger house was sold. They looked out of place in the tiny cottage and had clearly been bought with a far grander location in mind. The old man was there with his grandson, and said very little. I noticed that I had the same trainers as his grandson, and when I pointed this out to him, he looked horrified. Left with twelve boxes of books and wrote the old man a cheque for £525.

I returned to the shop to find a list of things to do left by Katie before she went home, including 'Fix Monsoon'. This is becoming far too frequent a problem, and it is probably time to look into an alternative system. It is now inoperable about 25 per cent of the time, and although the tech support is good, they are based in Oregon and so are eight hours behind us. Conveniently, they start work as I am closing up.

Till total £217.98
26 customers

SATURDAY, 16 AUGUST

Online orders: 5
Books found: 0

On my own in the shop all day, and Monsoon was still down this morning, which means that we can't even find locator codes for the books that have been ordered overnight. Nicky was at the Edinburgh Book Festival, dispensing Random Book Club flyers and wisdom in equal measure. I received a text message from her at 4 p.m. to say that she had given up and gone to the pub.

By lunchtime I had already had a disagreement with a customer about whether or not ghosts exist, and another who had brought in a carefully bubble-wrapped odd volume of Burns (one from a set of four – the other three were absent) from 1840, believing it to be worth a fortune. She looked quite insulted when I told her that I wouldn't even take it if she offered it to me for free. Odd volumes are difficult to sell – the chances of finding a buyer who is missing the volume you have, and in a matching binding, are extremely low, so unless it is something exceptional, or an illustrated book with fine woodcuts or copperplate engravings, we – and most book dealers – tend to avoid them.

Helen, the secretary of the Wigtown Agricultural Society, emailed me about the video, which I have yet to start editing.

There was a delivery of two boxes of books this morning. It turned out to be the erotica collection from the widow in Norwich. I had forgotten all about it. I checked their values online and decided to offer her £75 for the lot. It is difficult buying erotica, as very little of it can be sold on Amazon or eBay because they violate the puritanical sensibilities of the prudes in charge of both organisations.

Eliot arrived at 7 p.m. for a board meeting and seemed to be in pretty good form, although his shoes were on the floor in the kitchen within minutes of his arrival.

Till total £407.97
29 customers

MONDAY, 18 AUGUST

Online orders: 6
Books found: 5

Katie was working in the shop today. She complained about being ill, so I made her a Lemsip. By lunchtime I was starting to feel pretty unwell too.

Monsoon was down until 2 p.m., at which point one of their tech support team in Oregon woke up and finally took over the computer again and fixed it, so that we were able to process the orders and find the books.

In the afternoon a customer asked where we keep the 'illustrated poetry books'. I explained that we don't have a specific section and that he would have to trawl through the whole poetry section. He emerged two hours later, looking delighted with a pile of £200 worth of books, explaining that he had just taken up book-collecting and thought that illustrated poetry was an interesting subject on which to build up a collection. I genuinely thought that this type of person had ceased to exist. I could have hugged him.

By the time it came to close up I was feeling pretty rotten – sore throat, headache, runny nose. Callum called by, and we went for a pint.

I still haven't unloaded the van from the Haugh of Urr deal on Friday, so I really ought to prioritise this and start listing the more valuable books online to recover some cash.

Till total £469.33
36 customers

TUESDAY, 19 AUGUST

Online orders: 3
Books found: 3

Katie called in sick, so I was on my own in the shop. I suspect that I have the same malady she has; I felt awful all day, but the Random Book Club mail-out is due tomorrow so I packed all of the books up and processed them on the Royal Mail web site. We are back up to 153 members. The postage was £247.53. When I dropped off the orders this morning, I asked Wilma if she could send the postman over tomorrow to collect the six sacks. William greeted my 'Hello William, lovely day again' with his customary 'What's lovely about it?'

Till total £270.98
30 customers

WEDNESDAY, 20 AUGUST

Online orders: 2
Books found: 2

Both Katie and Laurie called in sick, Laurie at 11 p.m. yesterday, Katie at 8 a.m. today. Tremendously inconsiderate of them both to be ill at the same time.

As I was tidying the shelves in the garden room, I found a copy of *The Odyssey* in the fishing section. I have yet to question Nicky about this, but the answer will almost certainly be, 'Aye, but they were on a boat for some of it. What do you think they ate? Aye. Fish. See?'

The postman came and picked up the Random Book Club parcels just after I had locked up, but fortunately I was still in the shop and heard him knocking on the door.

After closing I texted Katie, who has promised that she will cover the shop despite being ill, so that I can drive to Grimsby and collect books from Ian, a bookseller with whom I have had a long working relationship.

Till total £276.70
30 customers

THURSDAY, 21 AUGUST

Online orders: 4
Books found: 4

Katie managed to struggle in today. I left at 5 a.m. for Grimsby and arrived at 10.45 a.m. Ian's place is an old church right in the middle of Grimsby. He took it on three years ago with the intention of listing ten thousand or so books online. He has now decided to pack it in because it is becoming impossible to compete with the mega-listers, who put through such volume that Amazon and Royal Mail give them massive concessions that smaller dealers do not get.

Ian and I went through the boxes of stock I had sent to him two years ago to list online for me. I took out about ten boxes of material that I thought I could sell in the shop and sold the remainder to him for £500. He then offered me £1,500 for the books that he had already listed but hadn't yet sold, which I accepted gladly.

My back is stiff after thirteen hours of driving and shifting boxes. Tonight I will sleep like Chichikov after his successful day of harvesting the names of the deceased in Plyushkin's estate in Gogol's *Dead Souls* – 'a deep and sound sleep, into that wonderful sleep which only those fortunate folk enjoy who are unacquainted either with haemorrhoids, or fleas, or overly powerful mental capacities'.

Picked up a copy of Faulkner's *As I Lay Dying* from the Penguin Modern Classics section of the shop and began reading it again before going to bed. It was on the curriculum when I sat my 'A' levels, and I remember enjoying it back then.

Till total £603.63
41 customers

FRIDAY, 22 AUGUST

Online orders: 3
Books found: 2

Laurie was in today.

A less than friendly email this morning among this morning's messages:

> It is now 22nd August and I HAVE STILL NOT RECEIVED POMFRET TOWERS.
>
> I LIVE IN CUMBRIA JUST ACROSS THE SOLWAY FIRTH FROM WIGTOWN.
>
> A BOOK ORDERED VIA ABEBOOKS FROM SOUTH AFRICA ARRIVED IN TWO DAYS AND ALL OTHER ORDERS HAVE BEEN DESPATCHED AND RECEIVED PROMPTLY.
>
> 12 DAYS TO RECEIVE A BOOK FROM WIGTOWNSHIRE TO CUMBRIA IS FRANKLY UNACCEPTABLE. PERHAPS YOU SHOULD CONSIDER AN ALTERNATIVE METHOD.

After lunch I went to my parents' house to get my shotgun and shoot a Kindle (broken screen, bought on eBay for £10), imagining it was the missing copy of *Pomfret Towers*. It was remarkably satisfying to blast it into a thousand pieces.

Before closing a man brought in three Ian Fleming first editions, including *Dr No* (lacking jacket), for which I gave him £150, then immediately regretted it. With hindsight, £100 would have been more than adequate.

Till total £296.47
20 customers

SATURDAY, 23 AUGUST

Online orders: 2
Books found: 2

All the girls were off today. My back is excruciating, and now my left leg is numb. I called Carol-Ann, who has recently done something to her back. She told me that these are the symptoms of sciatica.

Two emails from Amazon customers complaining that they had been obliged to collect their parcels from the post office and pay extra because we had not stamped them. They were sent out on 14 or 15 August, so I checked the diary. On the 14th both Katie and Laurie were working in the shop. On the 15th it was just Katie. Someone is going to get a roasting when they recover and return to work.

I was looking for this morning's orders when a customer asked, 'What's the oldest book you have in stock?', then demanded to see it. It is a book called *Martialis*, dated 1501, so it misses the holy grail of being incunabula (the grandiose name for any printed book published before 1501) by the slenderest of margins. She then told me that she had an older book. I had been unaware that it was a competition. Our copy of *Martialis* – although not an incunable – has the distinction of being published by the Aldine Press, one of the most prestigious early Venetian printers, and famous in the world of typography for introducing italics to printing and for being the first printer to publish smaller books in the – now standard – 'octavo' size. It is also iconic for its device: an anchor with a dolphin weaving around it.

Till total £270.85
28 customers

MONDAY, 25 AUGUST

Online orders: 2
Books found: 2

Katie managed to shuffle in to work today. I brought up the subject of the parcel with the missing postage stamp on it. She conceded that it had probably been her fault.

Sandy the tattooed pagan brought in five sticks to replenish the stock.

My back is still agony. I had planned to go to the doctor but forgot that it is a bank holiday, so I telephoned my pharmacist friend Cloda. She recommended co-codamol, after which I went to the chemist only to discover that it was shut too, so I ended up buying paracetamol and ibuprofen from the co-op.

Telephone call from Mr Deacon asking if he could order a copy of Alison Weir's *Eleanor of Aquitaine*. I asked him if he was quite sure, as we had recently ordered a copy for him. He paused, then replied, 'Oh yes, I can see it on my desk. Where's my list? Yes, I meant David Starkey's *Henry*. Could you order that?' I assured him that it would be here by the end of the week.

I left Katie in charge and drove to Glasgow to drop off forty boxes of reject stock at Cash for Clothes in Partick.

My memory is terrible, so I have made another note to apply for the James Patterson grant. It is now on my expanding list of things I will kick myself for not doing.

Till total £367.05
72 customers

TUESDAY, 26 AUGUST

Online orders: 2
Books found: 1

Laurie was in to work today. Moments after she arrived an enormous woman with a ginger Fu Manchu moustache bought a book about the making of the *Lord of the Rings* film.

A book dealer whom I hadn't previously met came to the counter and asked if we had any rare firsts, so I told him that he could have the three Flemings that I had just bought for £200. He declined, but bought our *War of the Worlds* first edition for £225 and paid by cheque. He is the first person who has used a cheque in the shop this year. We used to bank two or three cheques a week when I first bought the shop, but now it's mainly credit cards.

I had an appointment at the opticians in Newton Stewart after lunch. Following several tests Peter, the optician, told me that my eyesight was very similar to four years ago, when I was last there for a test. When I explained that I was having trouble reading in the bath, he asked, 'Can you read in there better during the day?' to which I replied that, yes – I could. He suggested changing the light bulb. We spent most of the appointment discussing mountain-biking and sailing, as usual. On the way out I ordered two new pairs of glasses.

Carol-Ann came round at 6.30 p.m. and asked if she could stay tonight. I called Callum and invited him for supper. Anna and Carol-Ann drove to the Chinese restaurant in Newton Stewart and picked up a take-away. This is what passes for 'cooking' in Anna's world.

Till total £287.96
56 customers

WEDNESDAY, 27 AUGUST

Online orders: 3
Books found: 2

Nicky in.

Foodie Friday has apparently moved to Wednesday this week, and this morning I was greeted by a grinning Nicky: 'Look, eh, I've brought you a packet of caramel digestives. They're all melted into one massive lump though.' She also brought in a bike to sell. I told her that there was no way anyone would be stupid enough to buy it. Shortly after she had put a 'For Sale' sign on it and leant it against the bench in front of the shop Smelly Kelly appeared and asked how much she wanted for it. She told him that he was a bit optimistic buying a bicycle, considering he is now walking on two crutches.

An older woman, probably in her late seventies, came in with a bag of books to sell. They were all erotica, and all photographic books from the 1960s. I checked one or two of them and they were reasonably valuable, so I gave her £50 for them. Just before she left she picked one of the books up and said, 'See if you can work out which of the models in this book is me.'

Carol-Ann stayed the night again.

Till total £461.39
34 customers

THURSDAY, 28 AUGUST

Online orders: 5
Books found: 5

Katie was in today.

To my enormous irritation, Nicky's bike sold. Her Facebook update read:

> Sorry people, the bike has sold!
> In its place though is a bespoke wooden table with a lift-up
> lid! How cool is that! Yours for £20.

An elderly woman came to the counter with a book: 'I'll take this book, thank you. It's for my son, you see. He's a primary school teacher and he's teaching the children about dinosaurs. I don't know anything about them, and neither does he, so I have bought him this book. I'm seeing him next week and I'll give it to him then. It's his auntie Florence's seventieth birthday. Do you know, she doesn't look a day over sixty ...' And so it continued for a further ten minutes.

AbeBooks emailed to tell me that our account has been suspended because we have dropped below their order fulfilment minimum of 85 per cent for a month. I replied and asked how we could be reinstated.

An old man with a walking stick accosted Nicky as she was rifling through a box of books that was destined for Cash for Clothes – 'I'm looking for a book, but I don't know what it's called. I know what it looks like, though. It's a very old book.'

Sandy the tattooed pagan turned up with some more sticks. Sold one straight away.

Till total £388.03
39 customers

FRIDAY, 29 AUGUST

Online orders: 1
Books found: 1

Nicky in again today. For Foodie Friday today she brought in bhajis and pickle – as always, pillaged from the Morrisons skip.

AbeBooks emailed me with a ridiculously complex explanation of how to reinstate our account, which involves me explaining why our fulfilment levels dropped, and what we are going to do to make sure that they improve. It felt very much like apologising for being caught smoking at school. I blamed Laurie and told the woman at AbeBooks (Emma) that I had sacked her for being lazy, and that this was my strategy for improving order fulfilment. She seemed quite satisfied with that.

In the afternoon I drove to Dumfries to look at the library of a retired Church of Scotland minister. He had recently lost his wife, but seemed surprisingly cheery in spite of this. Or perhaps because of it. I took one box of mixed material away and gave him £75. The only reasonable book was a copy of *Galloway Gossip*, which used to command a price of £40 but now makes less than £20.

Got back to the shop at 3.30 p.m., just in time to overhear a customer saying to her crumbling wreck of a husband, 'I have just had a wander through the garden. There's a gate with a sign which says "Private" but I went through anyway. It's lovely.'

Nicky found a book called *Working with Depressed Women*, which she has decided to keep for herself. We went to the pub after closing the shop, and she spent the night in the festival bed.

Till total £328.89
27 customers

SATURDAY, 30 AUGUST

Online orders: 3
Books found: 3

Today we had our first AbeBooks order since June. They have clearly, finally, let us back on as sellers.

While Nicky was taking the mail bags to the post office, a customer found an 1876 edition of *Daniel Deronda* priced at £6.50 and brought it to the counter asking 'How much could this be?' I was sorely tempted to tell her that it 'could be £7.50'. She didn't even bother waiting for a reply, and went completely off-piste, saying 'I found Venice terribly disappointing. It was full of tourists', the perpetual complaint of the pretentious tourist.

I left Nicky in charge and drove to Glasgow airport with Anna, who's going to visit her family in America.

Till total £211.86
29 customers

Amazon Kindle
Shot By Shaun Bytholl
22nd August 2014
Near Newton Stewart

Caroline McQuistin

SEPTEMBER

We did a good deal of business in children's books, chiefly
'remainders'. Modern books for children are rather horrible things,
especially when you see them in the mass. Personally I would sooner
give a child a copy of Petronius Arbiter than *Peter Pan*, but even
Barrie seems manly and wholesome compared with some of his later
imitators.

George Orwell, 'Bookshop Memories'

The children's section of the shop is always a mess. No amount of
tidying will keep it neat for more than a day or two, although we
maintain the Sisyphean effort of trying to keep it so. As much as
I'd like to blame the children who make it a mess, I suppose it's just
what children do. It gives me a glimmer of hope for the future of
bookselling, though, to see a child reading, their attention rapt in the
book to the total exclusion of everything else. In general, it appears
– in my shop at least – that girls are more committed readers than
boys. It was certainly something in which I had a limited interest as
a child. Neither boys nor girls ever pick up Barrie, though. Of the
Scottish writers of that period only Stevenson and Buchan seem to
have stood the test of time, still selling well in the shop.

Andrew Lang's Fairy Books are good sellers too, but to collectors rather than children. I once bought a set of them from another
dealer, and took them to a book fair (another part of the trade
that, with a few notable exceptions, appears to be exhaling the
last rattling gasp of its dying breath). The most lucrative trade at
book fairs takes place between dealers as they're setting up stall,
before the public comes in. This was no exception, and – less than
a week after I had bought them for £400 – I sold the set of Lang's
Fairy Books for £550 to another bookseller at the Lancaster Book
Fair. Since then I have not gone to another fair. The cost of travel,
accommodation and the stall and the pitiful prices that people are
prepared to pay for books these days have made all but the top-end
fairs almost entirely financially unviable.

MONDAY, I SEPTEMBER

Online orders: 3
Books found: 2

Laurie was in the shop today. After she arrived I drove to Newton Stewart to lodge last week's takings at the bank and pick up my new glasses from the optician's. Isabel turned up at 3.30 p.m., spotted my new specs and said, 'Oh, they make you look quite intelligent.' She could give lessons in damning with faint praise.

Till total £153.54
15 customers

TUESDAY, 2 SEPTEMBER

Online orders: 4
Books found: 2

Laurie in bright and early. At 2 p.m. a customer with a very neatly trimmed moustache came to the counter and said, 'I've been looking for a copy of Apsley Cherry-Garrard's *The Worst Journey in the World* for years after I lent mine to a friend who never gave it back to me. I see you have a copy, but it's £23. It seems a lot of money for an old book.' So, after years of looking for a copy of *The Worst Journey in the World*, he finally found one, and a scarce edition too, but £23 was too much.

As I was sorting through the boxes of books from Haugh of Urr, I came across a copy of Collins *French Phrasebook* in a box. You really would have to be on the most dismal holiday to find the following phrases useful:

'Someone has fallen in the water.'
'Can you make a splint?'
'She has been run over.'
'Help me carry him.'

'I wish to be X-rayed.'
'Leave me alone.'
'I do not like this.'
'The chambermaid never comes when I ring.'
'I was here in 1940.'
'Eleven hostages were shot here.'

Till total £218.93
20 customers

WEDNESDAY, 3 SEPTEMBER

Online orders: 3
Books found: 3

Laurie opened the shop at 9 a.m., but neglected to turn the sign from 'Closed' to 'Open'. By the time I noticed it, 10.30 a.m., not a single customer had entered the shop.

A Shearings coach stopped outside the shop at 3 p.m. This invariably results in a busload of Yorkshire pensioners invading the shop, complaining about absolutely everything, taking anything that's free, then leaving ten minutes later, urgently demanding to know where the nearest public toilet is. Today's onslaught was made slightly more bearable by the coach driver, who was the only one of them to buy anything. We shared a look of mutual pity. Shortly after they all left, a woman wandered through the shop shouting, 'Liz! Karen!' at the top of her voice. It turned out that the Shearings coach was waiting for them before it could leave. The post-invasion tranquillity of the shop was briefly shattered by her high-pitched bawling.

The proposed wind farm at Kirkdale has been rejected by the planners. Although this is good news, the company pushing for it is well known for its ability to have local planning decisions overturned by Holyrood.

Laurie left at 3 p.m. Today was her last day. She is being employed by the Festival Company, though, to work upstairs as a venue manager later in the month. During the festival my drawing room is converted into the 'Writers' Retreat', an area exclusive to visiting authors who are giving talks. We bring in a caterer, and writers are fed and plied with wine during their visit to Wigtown. Laurie will be given the job of making sure that everything runs smoothly, which it never does. One year one of our house guests had a bath on the morning of the first day of the festival, and, through no fault of his, the bath drain started leaking the moment he pulled the plug, and a torrent of water crashed through from the bathroom, soaking the electric cooker, which exploded with a bang. I had to telephone Carol-Ann and ask her to pick a new one up from Dumfries and bring it over with her. The surge in power when the cooker blew also destroyed the wireless router, so we had no internet, and later in the day the washing machine stopped working. Of all the essential facilities we need during the festival, these three are the most vital.

Till total £173.49
15 customers

THURSDAY, 4 SEPTEMBER

Online orders: 3
Books found: 2

Today was Katie's last day, so I gave her a hug as she was leaving. She hates physical contact, so it was particularly gratifying to see how uncomfortable it made her.

Till total £304.38
25 customers

Online orders: 5
Books found: 4

Nicky in. Within minutes of arriving she had thrown her bag on the floor in the middle of the front room of the shop, her coat had been tossed in a corner, and she'd opened several boxes and covered almost every available surface in the shop in unpriced, unsorted books. She found the missing order from yesterday, though, which I had failed to find, and admitted that she had put it on the wrong shelf.

While I was repairing a broken shelf in the crime section, I overheard an elderly customer confusing E. L. James and M. R. James while discussing horror fiction with her friend. She is either going to be pleasantly surprised or deeply shocked when she gets home with the copy of *Fifty Shades of Grey* she bought.

A short, chubby customer in tartan polyester trousers blocked the doorway to the Scottish room as I was attempting to put new stock out. She stared at me for a while before saying, 'You don't recognise me, do you?' After an awkward silence, to which I admitted that, no, I had no idea who she was, it eventually transpired that she was author of many very perplexing posts on the shop's Facebook page and clearly a woman with an impressive, if entirely unjustified, belief in her own genius. She told me that we had spoken once on the telephone; she is the author of *No, I Am Not Going on the Seesaw*, her unsurprisingly as yet unpublished autobiography. To my horror, she spotted one of the signs that Nicky had put up inviting customers to read extracts from their favourite book for us to video and post on Facebook. She disappeared to her car and returned with a book that she insisted I record her reading from. It was an autobiography of one of her ancestors, written just before the First World War. The dreary monotone of her reading of it was punctuated occasionally by fits of wailing and wildly gesticulating enthusiasm at inappropriate points in the text.

Before she left, she told me that she plans to come to the festival to 'get an idea of the atmosphere' so that she can know what to expect when she comes to visit as an invited speaker following the impending success of her book. She asked me if she could book the festival bed in the shop. I should really have seen that coming but stupidly was caught completely by surprise. I blurted out a feeble excuse that absolved me of responsibility and blamed Eliot, saying that he had decided that we would not be doing it again this year. This, despite the fact that I have taken two bookings for it already.

After work Tracy called round for a cup of tea and began describing the most obnoxious person that she has ever had in the RSPB visitor centre. It was the same woman.

Nicky stayed the night in the festival bed.

Till total £246.60
14 customers

SATURDAY, 6 SEPTEMBER

Online orders: 3
Books found: 3

Nicky was up early and had tidied the kitchen by the time I came down. We had an order for a book called *Incontinence*.

Posted a photo on Facebook of the Scotland's War of Independence mug, which sparked a few orders. Bev produced the mugs, based on a pamphlet from the 1920s that I scanned and emailed to her. I am sorely tempted to give one to my mother as a Christmas present.

A customer brought in eleven boxes of books at 10.30 a.m. – a mix of Italian art, physics and statistics. As I was going through them, an Australian woman stood uncomfortably close by and watched, grinning. After a while, she asked me if the books were being donated. I explained that nobody donates books, and I pay for everything. She then watched as I wrote a cheque for £120 for the books I wanted from the collection and gave it to the man who had brought them in. As she was leaving, the Australian woman told her husband, 'All his books are donated, you know.' By the end of the day I had sold six of the art books to a delighted customer who had been looking for two of them for several years.

Sandy the tattooed pagan dropped in with a friend and browsed for a while. He and Nicky had a ferocious argument about metal-detecting, of which they are both enthusiasts. There is something about the appeal of metal-detecting to which book collectors could probably relate. Both are scouring their fields for buried treasure, and I can see a keenness in Sandy's eye when he is in the shop that is, I imagine, the same look he has when he is out searching for Viking hoards.

After lunch I had a meeting with Anne Barclay from the Wigtown Book Festival Company, who has asked me to produce a video for a funding application for Wigtown, The Festival (WTF) – the young adult strand of the book festival. I have arranged to video three of the organisers next Saturday. Anne is the Operational Director of the festival (Eliot is the Artistic Director), and she takes care of all the logistics, bookings etc. She is an exceptionally hard worker. The light in her office is often still on when I go to bed (I can see it from my bedroom window as I draw the curtains), and in the run-up to the festival it is invariably still bright at 1 a.m.

Till total £496.96
36 customers

MONDAY, 8 SEPTEMBER

Online orders: 6
Books found: 5

Nicky was in today. The first business of the morning was an argument about her refusal to co-operate with my request for her to sort through boxes one at a time, and to not leave piles of books randomly distributed around the shop. By the close of the shop there were nine open boxes, and piles of books left in seven locations around the shop. When I pointed this out to her, she blamed customers.

At 11 a.m. I drove to Murray's Monument with the drone to

film a trailer for Stuart McLean for The Dark Outside, an event he set up last year, and for which he invited people to submit previously unheard pieces of music that they had written and recorded. Using an FM transmitter based at Murray's Monument (a few miles away), he broadcast twenty-four hours of new music to anyone within a four-mile radius. He then destroyed the hard drive on which they were stored, meaning that – essentially – each piece only really existed for that one broadcast.

Anne Brown, former chair of Wigtown Festival Company, has requested some audio pieces for Wigtown Radio, a station that will be broadcasting during the book festival, so this afternoon I went round the square and recorded short interviews with people who work in shops and businesses. Wigtown Radio started last year and runs throughout the festival. It is based in the Martyrs' Cell in the County Buildings, a tiny vaulted room, and is nearly all live, with a presenter, a producer and a seat-of-the-pants line-up of guests whom the producer has to run out and find during broadcasts while the presenter holds the show together.

Finished *As I Lay Dying* this evening. A customer saw me reading it this afternoon and suggested that, if I liked it, I might also like Nick Cave's book *And the Ass Saw the Angel*. I found a copy in the paperback fiction section and have started on it.

Till total £242.30
18 customers

TUESDAY, 9 SEPTEMBER

Online orders: 3
Books found: 1

No Nicky today, so I was on my own in the shop on a warm, sunny day. Failed to locate two of the three orders. Nicky's locator codes have been extremely inconsistent lately

In this morning's emails:

Subject: I have no money, I love books, please give me a job
Message Body:
To the Book Shop,
I am writing to inquire into job vacancies as I am a writer and like most writers, I am out of pocket. Normally I would resort to waitress work but I am crossing my fingers for a job that involves being in close proximity to a lot of books.

I live in a campervan and am parked up in the area as my husband is currently working with local potter Andy P (he told me to mention him, so I cannot be judged for name-dropping ...). I have plenty of experience working with other people and good customer service skills but what I believe qualifies me for a job at your book shop is a deep love and reverence of books in all shapes and sizes. I have always loved books and I always will. If it was legal then I probably would have married one.

I have a hard-working and friendly nature and I can provide references if needed.

I know this is a hopelessly unprofessional plea for a job in the Book Shop but I assure you that I can be professional when needed/forced.

Kindest Regards,
Bethan

I replied telling her that her timing was perfect as the run-up to the festival is frantic, and we need as many pairs of hands as we can muster, but that there will only be work until a few days after the festival finishes.

Carol Crawford, the Booksource rep, called in at around 12.30 p.m. She always times a visit before the festival to ensure that I am well stocked up from her iPad full of new books. I ordered about fifty titles, including three copies of *Scotland's Lost Gardens*, one copy of which I intend to keep for myself. Again I feel consumed with the questionable rationale of buying from a distributor when Amazon is supplying the same titles cheaper than I can buy them from the publisher. I suspect that things can't continue like this for much longer. Increasingly customers are using the shop merely as a browsing facility, then buying online. This is particularly the case with new books, which will almost certainly be for sale for less than their cover price on Amazon, but not so much so with second-hand books, where there is a good chance that they will be more expensive online.

In the early afternoon a customer entered the shop and asked if we have a copy of 'the book called *Kidnapped*'. I told him that, yes, we have several copies in the Scottish room. Without even bothering to reply, let alone check, he left the shop.

I made a wooden shield mount from an old tray, mounted the shot Kindle and hung it in the shop.

There has been no sign of Captain, the shop's cat, since Sunday. When I spoke to Anna on Skype and mentioned it, she seemed very worried and depressed about it, imagining all sorts of unlikely fates that may have befallen the unfortunate creature.

Till total £235.47
27 customers

WEDNESDAY, 10 SEPTEMBER

Online orders: 3
Books found: 3

Nicky came in to work today. She managed to find the two books that I couldn't find yesterday. She had listed them, then put them on completely different shelves from the locator codes on the database.

The depressed Welsh woman telephoned again, with the usual consequences. I wonder whether she might have a vast list of bookshops and spend all day every day telephoning them and asking the same question. By my reckoning such a list must be long enough to occupy her for two months before she has to start at the top again, which coincides more or less with the frequency of her calls.

At 11 a.m. Norrie and Muir turned up with the concrete books and the steel rod to make the new spirals, amid much excitement and consternation from passers-by.

I offered Nicky a cup of tea at about 3.30 p.m. She replied, 'Aye, but only if it's in a bone-china cup and saucer. I do not want one of your rubbish mugs.'

After work I filled in the application for the James Patterson bookshop grant. I will check it later and send it in.

Still no sign of the cat.

Till total £273.94
24 customers

THURSDAY, 11 SEPTEMBER

Online orders: 4
Books found: 3

Nicky was in again today. She brought me a present of four bashed-in tins of tomatoes that were heavily discounted in the co-op.

At 10 a.m. I drove to Newton Stewart to pick up building supplies. I have to create a performance space in the back of the shop for the festival. While I was at the builders' merchants, I bumped into Ronnie, the electrician, and reminded him that he has not yet sent me an invoice for some work he did for me three years ago.

Wigtown's co-op closed at 4 p.m. for a refit. We now have to go to Newton Stewart for food shopping. It opens again on the 18th. This news is being greeted with at least as much excitement by some people of the town as the Scottish independence referendum on the same date.

Till total £411.44
19 customers

FRIDAY, 12 SEPTEMBER

Online orders: 4
Books found: 4

Nicky back in again. The first thing she said was, 'Do you want some bramble jam? Well, it's not really jam. And it's pretty disgusting, it's far too sweet and I put chilli powder in it too. It might be quite nice with some meat.'

We found all of the orders, and I asked Nicky to deal with Royal Mail and drop the parcels off with Wilma at the post office. At 5 p.m. I noticed that they were still sitting in the shop, so I confronted her about it. She replied that they could wait until tomorrow. When I pointed out that this means that customers who ordered books on Thursday will not receive them now until Monday or Tuesday, and that we promise delivery within forty-eight hours, she replied, 'They wilnae mind.'

After lunch I drove to Glasgow airport to pick up Anna, who spent most of the journey home articulating her various implausible theories about what might have happened to Captain, the errant cat.

As I was closing the shop, I spotted – on the shelf where Nicky had previously housed her 'Home Front Novels' (which I had removed) – a new shelf label called 'Real-life trauma/abuse'. I removed it immediately. She clearly put it there to annoy me.

Nicky told me, on leaving, that she might come in on Monday, but only if she feels like it.

Till total £141.22
17 customers

SATURDAY, 13 SEPTEMBER

Online orders: 6
Books found: 4

At 10 a.m. a very pretty blonde woman appeared and introduced herself as Bethan, who had emailed me on the 9th. She seemed charming and bright, so I have offered her a few odd days between now and the end of the festival, depending on when Nicky can or cannot work.

A customer picked up a copy of a Lyn Andrews book and announced to her friend, 'I am reading that on me Kindle at the moment.' I sincerely hope she stumbled across my mutilated trophy Kindle and considered the potential implications that the e-readers might have on bookshops, but I genuinely doubt that her mind is particularly troubled by thoughts of any nature.

At lunchtime a customer with his left trouser leg rolled up to his knee and his right one at his ankle, and a flat cap, bought a book about tantric sex.

At Anna's insistence I printed off 'Missing Cat' posters and distributed them about the town.

Supper with friends in the Isle of Whithorn, which largely consisted of loud arguments about the independence referendum. Anna, who initially had been against independence because of her understandable dislike of nationalism (her maternal grandparents were both Holocaust survivors; her grandfather was a prisoner in Auschwitz when it was liberated), seems to be coming around to the idea that nationalism and independence are not necessarily the same thing. Half of us at supper were pro-independence, the other half against it. If the result on the day is as evenly split as we were, then it should make for an interesting night as the votes are counted on the 18th.

One of the unlikely outcomes of the evening was a discussion about poetry. Christopher, our host, is a farmer who read pure mathematics at university, and the last person I would have suspected to have a passion for poetry. I have known him all my life, but until tonight I had no idea that he had even the slightest interest in anything other than rainfall statistics and crop yields.

Tonight he recited Yeats's 'The Song of Wandering Aengus' by heart. It was extraordinary and surprisingly moving.

Till total £239
17 customers

MONDAY, 15 SEPTEMBER

Online orders: 5
Books found: 5

Nicky couldn't come in today, so I emailed Bethan and told her that she was welcome to work if she was free.

Our Amazon rating has dropped from Good to Fair, probably due to unfulfilled orders. Of today's orders, one was sent to Belgium and another to Germany. This usually happens when sterling is weak, which it is at the moment, in part – so the anti-independence campaigners say – due to uncertainty caused by the referendum on Thursday.

Bethan turned up at about 1 p.m. I showed her around the shop and started her on tidying shelves, which has the twin benefits of making the shop look smarter and teaching her where the various sections are in the shop.

Shortly after Bethan arrived, Anupa, one of the festival artists in residence, dropped in for a cup of tea. I was desperately trying to catch up with a backlog of jobs, but we chatted for an hour or so anyway. We discussed Thursday's vote, and the possibility that when we next meet, in a week or so, it might be in an independent Scotland. If nothing else, at least the co-op will be open again.

A shuffling old man with a beard asked for books on 'Cumbriana and Northumbriana', further fuelling my dislike of people who try to make themselves sound more intelligent by using unnecessary words. Philately will get you nowhere in The Book Shop. A few minutes later he returned, unable to find the topography section, and asked 'Where's Northumbria?' Resisted the urge to tell him that it is just south of Scotland. His wife came to the counter with seven books on Northumbria, including a mint first edition *Highways and Byways*. The total was £27. He looked at the floor and mumbled, 'What's your best price?'

Till total £211.17
28 customers

TUESDAY, 16 SEPTEMBER

Online orders: 1
Books found: 1

Bethan was in again this morning, so I spent most of the day building the 'creative space' in the old warehouse for Allison's puppet show during the festival. Last year I converted part of the warehouse into a sort of clubby drawing room, and we advertised it as The Festival Club. Maria, who catered for the whisky supper back in the Spring Festival, supplied food, tea, wine, beer and soft drinks, and it was an enormous success. But this year Maria is catering for the Writers' Retreat during the festival, and we haven't been able to find a replacement caterer, so it is being used as an events venue, mainly for Allison.

A woman arrived in the shop at 4 p.m., wiping blood from her arm. She was convinced that she had found Captain near the tennis court and had tried to bring him back to the shop, but when she got to the co-op the cat started scratching her and hissing, then ran away.

In the afternoon I did a short interview with Border TV about the impending book festival. Life in Galloway, with its thinly spread population, often involves being badly served by things that other people take for granted, such as public transport, but nothing quite encapsulates this epic failure in the way that our local television station does. They do their best, but Galloway is not part of the Borders, and our 'local' television station is broadcast from the far coast of another country. Gateshead, the headquarters of ITV Border, is in England and nearly 200 miles from the west of

Galloway. This would be analogous to London's local news being broadcast from Swansea and attempting to cover everything in between the two places.

Till total £152.49
13 customers

WEDNESDAY, 17 SEPTEMBER

Online orders: 0
Books found: 0

Bethan was in again today.

As we were going through the last of the boxes from the Haugh of Urr deal, Bethan came across a copy of *The Collected Poems of Kathleen Raine*. Ordinarily I would expect to know little or nothing about most of the authors whose works are on our shelves, but Kathleen Raine is someone whom I learned a little about when I was buying books from an elderly man who lived near Penpont, about forty miles from Wigtown. Six years ago he had telephoned me to tell me that he was selling his books, so I drove to his house – an attractive laird's house with an Andy Goldsworthy sculpture in the garden. Before I started to work my way through his substantial library, we sat down to a pot of soup which he had made, and over which he explained that he had recently been diagnosed with terminal leukaemia. He was clearly struggling to accept the diagnosis, repeatedly telling me that two years previously, on his seventy-fifth birthday, he had climbed Kilimanjaro. His wife had died some years ago, and he had obviously expected to live considerably longer than the medical experts had now told him he could reasonably expect. There was a clear and understandable sense of injustice and anger in his language. Of his library of about six thousand books I bought about 800, and paid him £1,200. The most interesting thing among it was a letter to him from Kathleen Raine, which he had used as a bookmark in Gavin Maxwell's *Ring of Bright Water*. When he produced this and showed it to me, I had to confess that I had never heard of Kathleen Raine, so he explained that she and Maxwell had been good friends until, during a visit to Camusfearna (his home at Sandaig on the west coast of Scotland), he banished her from the house during a storm in 1956. Raine cursed Maxwell under a rowan tree in the garden. She blamed all his subsequent misfortunes – which were swift and many – on this curse and believed that Maxwell's friends also blamed her for the series of disasters that befell him. The letter in the copy of *Ring of Bright Water* was a reply to an invitation to the opening of the Gavin Maxwell memorial at Monreith, near where Maxwell grew up. Raine turned down the invitation because she believed that Maxwell's friends would be hostile towards her. The elderly man died within a few months of selling me his books.

There was a reported sighting of Captain at the Martyrs' Stake car park, at the bottom of Wigtown hill. Anna set off straight away and returned with him. Clearly the cat found at the tennis court yesterday was not Captain, which would explain why he started scratching the well-meaning woman who attempted to relocate him.

No sign of the swallows on the wires any more.

Till total £158.50
16 customers

THURSDAY, 18 SEPTEMBER

Online orders: 2
Books found: 1

Bethan and Nicky were both in today, so I set them to work picking and packing the Random Book Club mail-out. I don't think I trust either of them enough to pick the sort of books that I imagine the subscribers would enjoy, but with the festival looming I am stretched to capacity, so I have no choice but to delegate. Nicky asked Wilma if she would mind sending the postman to collect the sacks tomorrow.

One of the books from today's orders that we couldn't find was one that I had sent to Ian in Grimsby when he had taken our online stock, but which I had failed to remove from Monsoon back then, so it was still listed as available from us. This normally results in negative feedback, as we are obliged to cancel the order.

I spent some of the afternoon interviewing more local business people for the radio station that will be broadcasting from the Martyrs' Cell in the County Buildings during the festival. One of the interviewees was Nicky, who described me as 'a big ginger conundrum'.

The co-op re-opened today, to much excitement, but by the end of the day everyone was complaining that they couldn't find anything any more.

Referendum day: I had my own vote, and Callum gave me his proxy vote. He has gone off on the *Camino* – the pilgrim route to Santiago de Compostela. After the shop closed, Eliot and the festival interns, Beth and Cheyney (they get the glamorous jobs, such as stacking chairs and answering the office telephone), came round and we watched the results coming in. Eventually went to bed at 2 a.m., depressed at what was obviously going to be a 'no' vote to Scottish independence.

Till total £237.96
20 customers

FRIDAY, 19 SEPTEMBER

Online orders: 3
Books found: 3

Bethan and Nicky both in the shop again today.

Spent the day recording more interviews for the festival radio station, leaving Nicky in charge. She arranged for the postman to pick up the six sacks of random books at 3 p.m. This time next week the festival will be starting.

Till total £157
10 customers

SATURDAY, 20 SEPTEMBER

Online orders: 2
Books found: 2

Nicky arrived ten minutes late, gloating over the referendum result.

Twigger emailed: 'Hey Shaun you colossal ginger bastard – insult a few writers for me will you!

Love to all my friends in WIGTOWN, Rob.'

This year is the first year in a long time that Twigger won't be at the festival – he is off exploring somewhere in the Himalayas for his next book, which is, I think, going to be a sort of topographical biography, similar to his last book, *Red Nile*.

As I was unloading some boxes from the van, Carol Carr, a local sheep farmer, was passing. We exchanged pleasantries and she asked how I was, so I told her that I was fine, apart from my back. She looked surprised and told me that Rob, her husband, has a bad back, as do most farmers. It had not occurred to her that book dealers spend a good deal of time lifting boxes of books in and out of vehicles and off the floor in uncomfortable, awkward spaces. I calculated that I lift about fifteen tons of books every year, and those fifteen tons will be moved a minimum of three times.

Six days until the festival begins.

Till total £193.50
17 customers

MONDAY, 22 SEPTEMBER

Online orders: 5
Books found: 5

Nicky and Bethan in. Nicky brought in a cake that was made to look like a giant caterpillar. It had been reduced to 49p in Morrisons and she picked it up at the weekend. It looks absolutely revolting, covered in the most hideous icing.

The festival begins on Friday, just four days away, so most of this week will be spent in frantic last-minute preparation.

Bethan spent the day pricing up and shelving the Penguins that Bev brought in earlier today.

Zoe and Darren arrived. They are actors with whom Anna is going to be doing some performance art during the festival. Rehearsals start tomorrow. They are going to be re-enacting scenes that are set in bookshops from famous films – *The Big Sleep*, *Notting Hill*, *The NeverEnding Story*.

Checked the status of the delivery of FBA boxes to Amazon in Dunfermline – the boxes that UPS picked up have not arrived there yet.

Today brought some very sad news. Alastair Reid died yesterday. I will write to Leslie, his widow, tomorrow. Finn telephoned to let me know at lunchtime.

Till total £145
22 customers

TUESDAY, 23 SEPTEMBER

Online orders: 4
Books found: 4

Nicky and Bethan in. As the festival is looming, they spent the day making sure the shelves are full and tidy. Three days until it begins.

After several whiskies I wrote to Leslie, Alastair Reid's widow. Springtime will lose some of its lustre now that I know that it will no longer be marked – along with the bluebells and the swallows – by his arrival.

Till total £372.96
21 customers

WEDNESDAY, 24 SEPTEMBER

Online orders: 2
Books found: 1

Bethan in today, but no Nicky.

I moved the furniture from the big room and set it up for the Writers' Retreat. Davy Brown, the friend and artist who holds art classes upstairs, arrived and hung his paintings there. They will be there for the duration of the festival. The Writers' Retreat began in the relative infancy of the festival's history, when Finn was director of the Festival Company. He had invited – among others – Magnus Magnusson to speak one year. His talk was at 8 p.m. At 6 p.m. he decided to find something to eat. In those early years, when the audiences were relatively small, most of the cafés, pubs and restaurants stopped serving food at 6 p.m. and, unable to find a meal anywhere, Finn called me in desperation and asked if they could come here for something to eat, so I quickly made some soup and a plate of leftovers, and the three of us sat down and had a meal in the house. Afterwards, Finn asked if I would consider keeping a supply of cheese, oatcakes and soup at the ready for the rest of the festival in case such an emergency reoccurred. It did. Several times. After a few years this had grown to the point at which we required a caterer to come in and manage it, and we had official opening hours. Nowadays, we feed up to seventy people on busy days, and at the weekends we treat them to fresh local lobster.

The marquee went up in the town's central gardens today. More lorries arrived with chairs, flooring, heating and sound equipment, and another marquee. Just two days until the festival starts.

I spent an hour on the phone to UPS and Amazon in an effort to track down the missing six boxes of books we sent up to Amazon's Dunfermline warehouse as part of our FBA shipment, but without any success. I appear to have entered a hellish world of corporate three letter acronyms.

One of the festival volunteers borrowed the van to pick up Astrid's plywood cut-outs for the festival from her studio in Edinburgh and bring them down here. (Astrid is one of the artists in residence this year.)

This afternoon I made a stage from plywood and timber for Allison's play. She wanted parquet flooring, so I've found some stick-on vinyl and ordered it.

Made a determined effort to plough through *And the Ass Saw the Angel* and finish it before the festival begins. Just thirty pages to go.

Till total £146.49
9 customers

THURSDAY, 25 SEPTEMBER

Online orders: 3
Books found: 3

Nicky and Bethan were both in today.

The actors (Zoe and Darren) rehearsing in the shop caused even more consternation among the customers, particularly now that they have found props and costumes.

Amazon telephoned to say that they have tracked down the missing shipment, and it is now listed and available online.

The actors, Anna and I went round to the house that Eliot has rented for the festival, and he cooked supper for us and the interns, Cheyney and Beth. When we got home, Nicky offered me the last bit of the chocolate caterpillar cake that she had bought for 49p. All that was left was its face; she had eaten the rest of it.

Carol-Ann arrived. Stuart Kelly arrived too, so the house is fairly full. The two Italians who are staying in the festival bed should arrive some time tomorrow, so I went into Newton Stewart to have spare keys cut so that guests can come and go as they please.

After work I spent a frantic hour or two putting an audio piece together for Stuart McLean for 'The Dark Outside' event, which starts at noon on Saturday.

The festival begins tomorrow.

Till total £227.49
15 customers

Online orders: 4
Books found: 3

I finished *And the Ass Saw the Angel* before the shop opened. Nicky and Bethan were both in again today.

Maria, who is catering for the Writers' Retreat this year, came to set up the kitchen. This seemed mainly to involve the pair of us moving fridges around.

Nicky and I spent the morning organising things for the festival, such as making sure we have enough loo roll and washing-up liquid and that sort of thing, as well as putting up signs directing people to venues and finding seating for events. The parquet tiles arrived for Allison's stage. Laurie, Nicky and I had our annual argument about where the apostrophe belongs on the sign for the Writers' Retreat.

Anna was uptight today, as the performances she has been rehearsing with the actors begin tomorrow. Apparently this is 'immersive theatre'.

Received an email from the Italians who were supposed to be in the festival bed to say that they can't make it. I suppose the silver lining is that it is now available for any friends who need a bed for the night.

The festival was launched (as always) with fireworks at 8 p.m. Nicky brought some home brew in with her and had a couple of pints of it before we headed down. Nobody else dared to touch the stuff. She was dancing away to the Creetown pipe band as though it was hardcore 1980s acid house.

After the fireworks we dutifully trooped to the festival opening night party in the marquee. Zoe read one of Alastair Reid's poems after Eliot had welcomed everyone, then Lauren McQuistin performed a setting of 'Ye Banks and Braes'.

Till total £346.75
30 customers

SATURDAY, 27 SEPTEMBER

Online orders: 3
Books found: 2

Nicky was in, but Bethan took the weekend off to chop logs for the winter.

I opened the shop at 9 a.m. to find an author waiting outside. Before I had even put the lights on, he was in the door and demanding food, so Nicky told him that the Writers' Retreat isn't open until 10 a.m. Maria hadn't even arrived with the food.

I found two of today's orders and took the mail bags to the post office. William's choler rises to an extraordinary level during the festival, and he complains bitterly that – despite the thousands of people who come to the town because of it – his newspaper sales drop. This he attributes to the fact that it is difficult to find somewhere to park, so that locals go elsewhere to buy their newspapers.

Nicky decided that today – traditionally the busiest day of the festival – would be a good day to paint the shop windows and spent most of the morning doing that while I dealt with customers and the chaos of the first day of the Writers' Retreat. This normally involves me searching for extension cables for the soup kettle, fuses to repair it when it has blown immediately after it has been plugged in, unblocking the sink, filling log baskets and lighting fires.

As well as all of that, Anna asked me if I could film her theatre performances in various bookshops throughout the town. They appeared to meet with an equal measure of confusion and excitement from customers wherever they were performed. One bookseller found the whole thing so perplexing that he telephoned me and said that that they were not welcome back in his shop.

Lou and Scott, my sister and brother-in-law, and their children arrived in the morning. They are loyal supporters of the book festival and always come down for Wigtown's Got Talent, an event that happens on the first Saturday night of the festival. I fed them in the Writers' Retreat at lunchtime, during which we heard a fairly harrowing story about necrophilia from a visiting writer. Thankfully, the children were playing with Captain in the snug at the time.

In the afternoon I produced Wigtown Radio for an hour between 3 and 4 p.m.

After the shop closed I went with Anna, Carol-Ann, Astrid and Stuart to Anupa's opening night. Nicky, Stuart and I then went on to Lauren McQuistin's Art Song event, then finally to Wigtown's Got Talent. Stuart seemed particularly impressed by Lauren's event. Drinks back here afterwards, Astrid slept in the festival bed, which the Italians had conveniently left free.

Till total £989.30
95 customers

SUNDAY 28 SEPTEMBER

Online orders: 4
Books found: 3

Nicky in at 9 a.m. Maria arrived hot on her heels, and told me that the fridge wasn't working, so I stripped the plug and replaced the fuse, then drove to the dump in Newton Stewart with all the empty bottles and bin bags of paper plates from yesterday.

Lee Randall, a journalist who chairs events during the festival, asked me if I could find some books in the shop with unusual titles for an event she is chairing – Robin Ince's Bad Book Club. I managed to find her a few, including a huge medical book called *The Rectum*. She looked through it briefly before putting it on the counter and announcing, 'Very interesting. I have got almost every condition in that book.'

Anna and the actors performed scenes from *The Big Sleep* and *Notting Hill* in the shop, once more to the confusion and joy of all who witnessed it. I overheard a young woman whispering, 'It's immersive theatre' to her bewildered mother.

I spotted Mr Deacon chatting to Menzies Campbell outside an event as I was walking from the shop to the festival office to see Eliot about an author who needed a projector for his talk. I have been to a few talks that Mr Deacon has also attended. If he ever asks a question – and he usually does – it is always met by the speaker to whom it is directed with the response 'That is a very interesting question.'

Nicky found a book by Ian Hay in which the main character is called Nicky. Rather than work, she spent most of the day reading it and chuckling. Apparently there is another character in it called Stiffy, who she has decided is me, and she is editing it to suit her own narrative.

The Writers' Retreat was busy all day: Kate Adie, Menzies Campbell, Clare Short, Kirsty Wark and Jonathan Miller, among others. For a brief moment they were all chatting in the shop. It was like a literary salon.

It was, unsurprisingly, a late night here, with Eliot bringing a crowd of writers back. At one point Stuart Kelly had poured himself a glass of wine which Eliot snatched from his hand and began to drink, leaving Stuart looking perplexed. Later, to compound the offence, Stuart was tidying up the Retreat (at about 2 a.m.) when he discovered a pair of shoes under a table, so he moved them and put them in the hall. When Eliot discovered that they were his, he asked Stuart to go and get them for him. At this point Stuart was carrying a large pile of newspapers, which he dropped on Eliot's feet, saying, 'Extra, extra, read all about it. Festival director unable to fetch his own shoes.'

Till total £447.98
44 customers

MONDAY, 29 SEPTEMBER

Online orders: 3
Books found: 3

Nicky, Bethan and Flo were all in today. Flo is a student who worked in the shop last summer, and is admirably disrespectful to customers, but considerably more so to me. It would have been handier to have them all in over the weekend, and I struggled to find things for them all to do.

The Writers' Retreat was fairly quiet, except when Clare Balding was in. I spent most of the day filling the log basket and taking bin bags full of lobster carcasses and paper plates and bottles out of the kitchen and down to the bins.

Nicky brought me in some homeopathic stress relief pills and made me take two, washed down with a pint of her vile home brew.

Till total £467.12
51 customers

TUESDAY, 30 SEPTEMBER

Online orders: 2
Books found: 2

Bethan and Flo in, though Bethan missed the bus and didn't appear until 10 a.m. Flo failed to find one of the orders this morning, *Tokyo Lucky Hole*, in the erotica section, and another in the poetry section. I found both in about a minute and asked her to package them. When I returned about ten minutes later, she was engrossed in the fairly graphically erotic *Tokyo Lucky Hole*.

In the evening Allison, Anna, Lee Randall and I formed a team for Stuart Kelly's Literary Pub Quiz. We came third, with 25 out of 35. Anupa came back to the house afterwards for a few drinks.

Till total £291.49
27 customers

OCTOBER

First edition snobs were much commoner than lovers of literature, but oriental students haggling over cheap textbooks were commoner still, and vague-minded women looking for birthday presents for their nephews were commonest of all.

George Orwell, 'Bookshop Memories'

First edition snobs are, sadly, a dying breed, although many people who bring books into the shop in the hope of selling them will point to the verso of the title page, where the edition is displayed, and expectantly await an offer of untold wealth. Now, I rarely check the edition unless it is a pre-1960 Ian Fleming, or a well-known author's first title or something similar. In non-fiction – with a few exceptions – it barely makes any difference what edition a book is, yet people still cling to the notion that first editions are somehow imbued with a magical and financial value. Textbooks are something we don't even bother with in the shop these days. Every year they appear to be very slightly revised and republished. Students (oriental in Orwell's case, of every kind in mine) are expected to be armed with the latest edition, rendering all previous editions essentially worthless. Commonest of all these days are not 'vague-minded women' but men trying to track down a particular title. Their disappointment at being told that we don't happen to have a copy in stock is matched only by their sense of smug satisfaction on hearing that information. Should the quest for their holy grail ever be completed, many of them would have no further purpose in life. By far the favourite is the search for an odd volume to make up a complete set of something. It has to be the same edition, same binding, same colour. Most booksellers don't stock odd volumes unless it is a particularly interesting title, or a volume with fine illustrations, so the benighted crusader searching for his missing third volume of Gordon's *The Works of Tacitus* (fourth edition, Rivington, London, 1770, tree-calf, five raised bands, purple title panel) can be confident that his quest will continue until he can no longer remember what he was looking for.

WEDNESDAY, 1 OCTOBER

Online orders: 4
Books found: 4

Nicky and Flo both in today.

Today was my forty-fourth birthday, so at lunchtime I went to Rigg Bay for a swim in the sea with Anna to mark the occasion in the same way that I have done for the past thirteen years.

The Writers' Retreat was unusually busy by lunchtime for a weekday. Among the retreating writers were the journalist Allan Little and Richard Demarco, who must be in his eighties now. Richard was instrumental in setting up the Edinburgh Festival, and Allan, who grew up in the west of Galloway, was one of the BBC's finest journalists. At its busiest time there must have been thirty people in the room, at which point Maria, who was bringing in a tray of food, spotted something on the floor that looked suspiciously faecal. She quietly gestured to Laurie, who came over, and they hatched a plan for her to find a cloth and remove it before anyone else saw it. Maria discreetly stood over it to ensure that nobody trod in it. As she was guarding it, Allison marched into the room, saw it, pointed at it and said, 'Oh look, a shit!' before Laurie had the chance to remove it.

The source of the shit became the subject of discussion for the rest of the day, Nicky leading the investigation with forensic scrutiny, which included rifling through the bin to retrieve it so that she could measure it. She became increasingly convinced that an elderly visitor had done it without noticing, and that it had slipped down their trouser leg. Other theories included the suggestion that it was actually icing from my birthday cake, which Anna had made. When Stuart suggested that the turd may have been Captain's, Nicky's instant and vituperative response was, 'Nae chance, the bore's wrong'.

The interview recorded earlier in the month with Border TV was broadcast on their magazine programme *Border Life*. Mercifully, I missed it.

Till total £395.93
45 customers

THURSDAY, 2 OCTOBER

Online orders: 2
Books found: 2

Flo and Nicky in.

I spent most of the day editing a promotional video about Wigtown that I've been putting together purely because of the diabolical lack of attention that Visit Scotland pays to this corner of the country. For decades it has been referred to as 'Scotland's Forgotten Corner', and many visitors appreciate that element of it, but it ill-becomes our publicly funded tourist agency to forget it. On the Visit Scotland web site, under the blurb about Wigtown, there is a photograph of the golf course at Glenluce, twelve miles away. It really can't be that difficult to find a picture of Wigtown. I have even emailed them one of my own, but they have yet to substitute it and probably never will.

Lunched with two Italian women – journalists who were over because they had read Anna's book and wanted to visit Wigtown. I am quite convinced that *Rockets* has done far more for tourism in Wigtown than Visit Scotland ever will.

Nicky and I did a slot on Wigtown Radio between 3 and 4 p.m. Unfortunately someone had muted the music on the computer, so Nicky had to keep talking until I worked out how to fix it, which took about half an hour. She dried up a few times and was clearly not enjoying it, but she did a decent job of presenting. As soon as her shift was over, she left the cell and demanded whisky.

The comedian Robin Ince arrived at about 6 p.m. He wanted to browse in the shop, so I put all the lights back on and left him to it. He bought a pile of books. Nicky and I went to his event in the County Buildings at 7.30 p.m.

I posted the video of Wigtown that I had been editing on Facebook.

Till total £319.05
40 customers

FRIDAY, 3 OCTOBER

Online orders: 3
Books found: 3

Flo and Nicky in.

A customer asked Nicky if we had any rare John Buchan titles in stock. She found a copy of *The Scholar Gypsies*, which was £100, and told her that she could have it for £80 since she was doing an event. She turned out to be his granddaughter, Ursula Buchan.

In the afternoon I picked up the Italian journalists and we drove to Cruggleton church, a Norman church in the middle of a field, with no glass in the windows or electricity.

The event in Cruggleton consisted of Tom Pow reading poetry, accompanied by Wendy Stewart on harp and Alex McQuiston on cello. Entirely candlelit, it was an extraordinarily beautiful event. On the journey home in the van I was emptying my pocket to show one of the journalists the programme (she wanted the performers' names for her blog) and produced from it a teabag in a pouch that I had taken from the Writers' Retreat. Unfortunately it looked exactly like a condom. Both of the Italians saw it and there was an awkward silence while I pathetically attempted to demonstrate that it was actually just a teabag as they edged slowly away.

Allison's event – a play about Borges – was on at 6 p.m. in the old warehouse at the back of the shop. Anna had been directing her rehearsals here all week. We had to change the access from the garden to via the road because the lighting on the path in the garden had fused, so I led people there in small groups in the driving rain. In no time I was completely soaked. The event went well, although Anna did not look particularly pleased.

Heavy rain continued into the night. Before long the gutter was blocked and water was pouring into the Writers' Retreat, so Laurie, Nicky, Anna, Stuart and I spent some time frantically racing about with buckets and saucepans. Despite our efforts to limit the damage, the water came down through the floor of the Retreat and into the shop.

Till total £239.05
38 customers

Online orders: 4
Books found: 2

Flo, Bethan and Nicky in.

Nicky opened the shop to find water still flooding into the building from the blocked gutter. We tried to clear the blockage with a broom handle from the bedroom window, but it wasn't long enough, so I went down to the cellar and found a drain rod. Half hanging out of the third-floor window in the torrential rain, with Laurie holding my ankles, I eventually managed to clear it. It stopped dripping into the Retreat at 10 a.m., just as we opened.

Sally Magnusson and Margaret Drabble were in the Writers' Retreat when I appeared, soaked, to check that everything was ready. Lucy (Maria's helper) cornered Sally to ask her about journalism, which she very obligingly and enthusiastically discussed for a few minutes. Damian Barr bought some books from me. I had no idea who he was at the time.

At the start of the day I set up the GoPro camera behind the counter to make speeded-up video of life in the shop, just as Dylan Moran came in. I now have video of him buying a book from the shop. Flo served him. She was annoyingly unflapped about it.

Flo overheard a woman ask a man, as they walked through the shop, 'So they didn't have the book you're looking for?' To which he replied, shaking his head, 'Aye, they did, but just the one copy.'

Ceilidh in the big marquee in the square in the evening. It was packed. Lots of girls dancing with girls and boys with boys, as well as the more traditional arrangements. In the early days of the festival nothing was particularly well attended, but the ceilidh was undoubtedly among the worst. For the first few years there were just a handful of us, and to avoid embarrassment we would all end up joining in every single dance. Now it is different. The event has to be ticketed and always sells out. It has become enormously popular. At one point I was standing next to Damian Barr, who was dancing with another man. I drunkenly asked him which of them was being the woman, then later discovered that he is gay. If he was offended, he hid it extremely well. *Faux pas* of the festival so far. Went to the house to try to convince Nicky (who had decided not to attend) to change her mind and come along. Bumped into Jen Campbell and her parents outside the shop, so they came in for a drink and a chat.

We all stayed up late: Colin, Peggy, Stuart, Nicky and Natalie Haynes, who was on the Booker panel of judges with Stuart. Peggy runs the Dundee Literary Festival and could easily have emerged from the same clutch of eggs as Stuart Kelly. Colin, her partner – who generally answers to the name of 'Beard' – is running the social media side of the festival. They are both Wigtown Festival institutions, and have helped carve the identity of the event as much as Eliot, Stuart, Twigger and Finn.

The shop was heaving all day: the last gasp before the long winter of penury.

Till total £1,274.03
87 customers

SUNDAY, 5 OCTOBER

Online orders: 6
Books found: 4

Nicky and Flo in. I bumped into Nicky in the kitchen at about 8.30 a.m. She told me, 'You smell as good as a bacon roll.'

As always on the final day of the festival, there's a sense of end-of-holiday blues, as the party begins to wind down. Despite it being the last day, there was the usual chaos going on in the Writers' Retreat, with the staff and Maria being magnificently serene.

Eliot roped Anna into chairing Jen Campbell's event, a talk about her new book, *The Bookshop Book*. It went extremely well, apart from me asking a particularly stupid question. Both Anna and Jen were erudite and entertaining.

As with every year, on the last day of the festival, we turned the

Writers' Retreat into a cinema. This year we set up the projector and watched *Dr Who* with Stuart, Beth and Cheyney.

Till total £568.75
32 customers

MONDAY, 6 OCTOBER

Online orders: 5
Books found: 4

Nicky and Flo in. We spent the day shifting furniture and trying to get the place back to normal. Maria came in at lunchtime to sort out her stuff in the kitchen. Anna and I drove to the dump to get rid of cardboard boxes and empty wine bottles.

Nicky made herself cheese on toast for lunch and ate it in the middle of the shop, surrounded by customers.

This morning a busybody of an old man for whom I have always had an intense dislike came into the shop to try to persuade me to stock the self-published novel he has written. I am frequently presented with this sort of thing, and I take it on sale or return for purely diplomatic reasons. Without exception, one year later, I end up returning every single copy.

The big marquee came down today, leaving a pale yellow patch of grass beneath where it had stood, a reminder throughout the long winter of what had been here until it starts to green up again as the soil temperature warms up in March.

Anna and I went for supper at The Ploughman with the volunteers.

Till total £123.97
14 customers

TUESDAY, 7 OCTOBER

Online orders: 5
Books found: 3

Nicky was in today.

The shop received an anonymous postcard this morning, so I posted it on Facebook. Hopefully it will trigger more. It was a picture of a bronze lion, and on the back it just read: 'a large portion of the *Oxford English Dictionary* was written by a murderer from a mental institution'.

After lunch I dismantled the framework I had put up for Allison's event in the old warehouse. Everyone had a slight case of post-festival come-down today.

We spent most of the day continuing the clear-up operation. After the shop was shut I cooked for the interns and we watched *Wings of Desire* on the projector in the Writers' Retreat.

The timing of the festival was originally intended to prolong the tourist season for shops in the town and it has succeeded to such an extent that the infrastructure is starting to creak with Hotels and B&Bs nearing the capacity they experience at the summer peak. The extent to which it brings people and money to the town more than justifies the costs of putting it on.

I rarely have the luxury of attending any events, and spend my time driving to the dump and the recycling skips with bin bags and bottles from the Writers' Retreat; but when I am in the shop, I have the opportunity to meet writers and other famous (or not) visitors in the Retreat, where they tend to be far more relaxed than at their events, so it is an extraordinary privilege to have the chance to talk to them in a more natural environment.

Eliot is excellent at making a point of introducing me to people although if he's not around, occasionally – seeing me help clearing up plates, or filling up the log basket – they will assume that I am hired help, and a few behave disparagingly.

One year, as I was putting logs on the fire, a well-known newspaper columnist who was sitting at the table in the Retreat drinking free wine and eating free lobster, clicked his fingers and shouted 'sugar' at me, while pointing at an empty sugar bowl on the table.

Those are the visitors whom I dislike second-most. Worse than them, though, are those who – once they find out that it is my house – suddenly start to treat me differently from the girls helping Maria in the kitchen or the Retreat, or Nicky and Flo, or Bethan in the shop. I suppose the charge could be fairly levelled at me that I don't make a great deal of effort to find out about my customers, but I am never rude to waiters, waitresses, cleaners or shop staff and hope that I have never treated anyone as a second-class citizen, and instead merely reflect rudeness back at people who are rude to me. I can afford to be rude back to customers – it's my shop, nobody is going to fire me – but most people who work in shops are not in this position, and to exploit that by not showing them the slightest courtesy is something that offends me greatly. And while I do make observations about the appearance of some of my customers, they are just observations – not judgements. In most cases.

Till total £143.90
14 customers

WEDNESDAY, 8 OCTOBER

Online orders: 6
Books found: 4

Just before lunch a customer offered £10 for a book that we have priced at £80. I told him that if he asked politely he could have £10 off. He slammed the book down on the counter and walked out in 'disgust', at which point I decided that escapism from customers was the order of the day, and found a new book to read and hid in the office with *Kidnapped* – a fate I would quite happily have seen befall that last customer.

Till total £264.49
19 customers

THURSDAY, 9 OCTOBER

Online orders: 3
Books found: 3

All of today's orders were from Amazon.

The shop was quiet today. The contrast with last week is extraordinary.

One of the few customers was a woman who spent ten minutes wandering around the shop before coming to the counter and asking, 'So what is The Book Shop? Do you sell the books or what? Do people just come in and take them?' Temporarily stupefied, I was unable to answer. Thankfully, she broke the silence and ploughed on, 'I am not from here, I am a tourist. Do people just hand you the books in? What happens in here? Is that what happens in here?' I began what with hindsight was a pointless attempt to explain the basic principles of retail, which frankly, she ought to have grasped by the age of roughly fifty, but she meandered out of the shop while I was explaining it to her.

Sandy the tattooed pagan appeared at about 3 p.m. and found two books. Have deducted them from his credit.

Till total £222.45
19 customers

FRIDAY, 10 OCTOBER

Online orders: 3
Books found: 2

The missing book from today's orders was yet another one that we had failed to delist before sending our old warehouse stock to Ian.

At 11 a.m. a customer came to the counter with some maps of Ireland, demanding to know the year in which each was published. He then started the dreaded 'Let me tell you why I am looking for old maps and books about this area, it's because I am doing family history research and my great-grandfather …' for about five minutes before I could explain that the maps were undated, but probably from around 1910.

I am going to get a mask and paint 'I DON'T CARE' on the forehead and put it on when such occasions arise in the future.

Someone in the planning department came to inspect the book spirals. It appears that a complaint has been made about them, so now I have to get planning permission. She was remarkably decent about it all and said that if it were up to her she would just ignore the fact that I hadn't applied for permission for them, but because there has been a formal complaint and the shop is a listed building, they have no choice but to go through the process.

The *Guardian* published 'Weird and wonderful bookshops worldwide'; we are number 3 again. I'm not sure if these things go in cycles, or whether bookshops are suddenly becoming fashionable places. Perhaps it is the hipster movement driving the trend to be seen with vinyl and real books instead of iPods and Kindles.

Till total £133
15 customers

SATURDAY, 11 OCTOBER

Online orders: 2
Books found: 2

Nicky was in today, so I went to the river with my father in the morning. He caught a 12lb salmon; I blanked. We were fishing a pool called Wilson's, on the top beat of the river – the pool in which I caught my first salmon (under my father's watchful eye). It was 9lb, caught on 9 September, and I was nine years old. If I believed in luck, I suppose that nine ought to be my lucky number.

I returned to the shop at lunchtime and gave Nicky a break, during which a customer came to the counter and announced, 'I don't want to appear rude, but your railway section is mainly pot-boiler coffee-table-type books, and I am looking for something very specific blah blah blah …' He continued in this vein for a couple of minutes before getting to the point and telling me the title of the book he was looking for, by which time I was incandescent and his wife was cringing and mouthing 'sorry' at me from behind him.

Within a minute of being told the title I had located a copy of the book, at which point he decided that he didn't actually want it after all.

Prefacing a sentence with 'I don't want to appear rude, but …' flags up the same alarm bells as 'I am not racist, but …' It's quite simple: if you don't want to appear rude, don't be rude. If you're not a racist, don't behave like a racist.

Till total £312.30
22 customers

MONDAY, 13 OCTOBER

Online orders: 4
Books found: 2

Flo in.

As I came down the stairs with two cups of tea at 11 a.m. I literally bumped into Mr Deacon, covering his shirt with hot tea. He didn't seem to mind in the slightest and pointed out several other stains he had inflicted on the shirt while he was having his breakfast that morning. He asked if we could order him a copy of Kate Whitaker's *A Royal Passion*.

Went to the river after lunch and caught a 7lb salmon.

Till total £352.99
27 customers

TUESDAY, 14 OCTOBER

Online orders: 2
Books found: 2

Two complete strangers came into the shop at the same time and in an extraordinary coincidence both asked at the same time for a copy of Gavin Maxwell's *House of Elrig*. Sadly we don't have a copy or I could have orchestrated a bidding war.

Ronnie the electrician turned up when the shop was full of customers and started loudly describing the various ways in which we could blow up Kindles. He has a disconcertingly comprehensive knowledge of bomb-making. I will probably go for a sugar/sodium chlorate mix, although he seems quite keen to try an oxyacetylene bomb. Customers who arrived half-way through the conversation gave him a wide berth.

Quiet day compared with yesterday.

Till total £72.30
11 customers

WEDNESDAY, 15 OCTOBER

Online orders: 2
Books found: 2

Flo was in today. She seems to have mastered her pout, and spent most of the day demonstrating it.

When I was at the counter, an old traveller man who had not been in the shop for years arrived with a coffee table that had been made to look like two giant books. He wanted £60 for it. We settled on £35. The last time I saw him (about ten years ago) he came in and asked for a copy of *The Tinkler-Gypsies*. My father was in the shop at the time and instantly recognised him. Apparently he'd 'bought' scrap machinery from Dad about thirty years ago, when he was farming, but had never returned to pay him. He asked me if I had a copy of a book he was looking for, and when I replied, 'Yes, *The Tinkler-Gypsies*', he looked quite taken aback. *The Tinkler-Gypsies* is a book written by a lawyer from Newton Stewart called Andrew McCormick in 1906. It is a detailed account of the Galloway traveller community at the time and a valuable historical and social record. For a while copies would quickly sell for over £100 and were snapped up, but I see that it is now available as an e-book, which means that values have probably crashed.

Ecotricity, the company behind the proposed wind farm, have appealed to the Scottish government to have the council's decision to reject it overturned.

Till total £382.32
30 customers

THURSDAY, 16 OCTOBER

Online orders: 2
Books found: 1

In the inbox today was an email from Stuart Kelly, to which he attached the following rejection letter from a friend of his who had applied for a job in a bookshop:

> Dear XXX,
> We have too many people here. That they are all idiots is neither here nor there. I like them. They are firm, and peachy bottomed. I pay them £3 an hour. As a man with ambitions to enter the world of publishing, where artistic talent is sucked dry for profit, I imagine this sort of wage won't appeal.
> One of them now is prattling about Bonnie Prince Charlie. Do I care? No, I do not. But I am fond of her. She pulls her weight. She 'mucks in', so to speak. Would you

muck in? I doubt it. I think you'd run away to Italy and live out your life in indolence and drunkenness.

PROVE ME WRONG. COME IN AND WORK FOR FREE FOR MONTHS ON END WHILST RECEIVING ABUSE, SOME OF IT SEXUAL. YOU WILL WEAR A DUNCE'S CAP, AND A LOINCLOTH, AND BE FORCED TO EAT RAW SHRIMP, DAY IN, DAY OUT. DO YOU _LOVE_ THE SECOND HAND BOOK INDUSTRY ENOUGH TO HACK IT? WELL DO YOU? This is what we call an 'internship'. It looks good on CVs.

I suppose we'll see.

Yours,
XXX

Another anonymous postcard arrived in the post this morning. This one reads: 'The Bookshop has a thousand books, all colours, hues and tinges, and every cover is a door that turns on magic hinges.' I suspect that posting the first one on the shop's Facebook page last week may well trigger even more of them.

Mr Deacon's book arrived, so I called to let him know.

Till total £309.49
26 customers

FRIDAY, 17 OCTOBER

Online orders: 3
Books found: 1

Nicky appeared just a moment after I had opened the shop and thrust what at first glance looked like something from a hospital clinical waste bin under my nose. It was fleshy and covered in what appeared to be blood. 'It's a jam doughnut from the Morrison's skip. It got a bit squashed in the back of the van. Try it, they're delicious.' It was even more revolting than it looked. 'It's Foodie Friday,' she reminded me.

As we were chatting about what to do for the day, it occurred to me that I hadn't seen Smelly Kelly, her irrepressible suitor, or had my nostrils assaulted by the lingering stench of Brut 33 for a while. I asked Nicky if she had seen him recently, to which she nonchalantly replied, 'Did you not hear? He died three weeks ago.'

Three people turned up with boxes of books to sell today, including a very tall, well-spoken man in his seventies who arrived with seventeen large plastic crates full of all sorts of books, including one illustrated and signed by Aubrey Beardsley. I gave him £800 for them.

We were chatting about families, and he told me that his had been extremely wealthy until his great-grandfather lost everything on 'drink, gambling and women'. His grandfather became the first male heir in generations to be forced to secure a proper job, so he went to Cambridge and became a gynaecologist. Because the family was well connected, he ended up becoming gynaecologist to the royal family: 'He was Queen Mary's cunt mechanic.'

Two more anonymous postcards. One read: 'Friends may come and go, but enemies accumulate', while the other read: 'Be advised, my passport's green. No glass of ours was ever raised to toast the Queen.' The second seemed vaguely familiar, so I googled it. It is by Seamus Heaney in 'An Open Letter', and is his brilliantly petulant response to his inclusion in *The Penguin Book of Contemporary British Poetry*.

After the festival every year Anna and I have a night away in a hotel of a better standard than we would normally enjoy. This year Anna chose Glenapp Castle, near Ballantrae, so we left the shop at lunchtime and headed over there. I spent much of the afternoon lying on an enormous bed reading *Kidnapped*.

Nicky will open the shop tomorrow.

Till total £228.44
21 customers

SATURDAY, 18 OCTOBER

Online orders: 3
Books found: 3

Nicky stayed last night and opened the shop this morning. Anna and I returned from Glenapp at about lunchtime.

A customer came in with four bags of books, mainly rubbish, but they included a book called *Once a Customer, Always a Customer*, which I suspect he put in there deliberately to annoy me.

At 4 p.m. an unusually smart-looking Mr Deacon appeared to pick up his book. I commented that he was looking quite sharp, to which he simply replied 'Funeral' on his way out of the shop.

A couple with a young boy came in and bought books. The boy spotted Nicky's notice inviting customers to be filmed reading from their favourite book and asked if he could read from his. He was seven and called Oscar. He read very clearly from a Harry Potter book, and afterwards Nicky asked him if he was reading anything now, to which he replied '*To Kill a Mockingbird*'. Nicky was visibly impressed, and his parents looked justifiably proud. They explained that, although there are elements of it that are not particularly suitable for child to be reading, they didn't think that he was old enough to understand the full implications of the 'crime' for which Tom Robinson was being tried. Apparently Oscar had asked if he could read it.

Till total £245.49
19 customers

MONDAY, 20 OCTOBER

Online orders: 2
Books found: 1

Nicky came in today so that I could drive Anna to Dumfries to catch the train to London for meetings. After that, she will fly to America to work on a film for which one of her friends has raised the funding. On returning to the shop I discovered that the traveller who had sold me the giant book-shaped coffee table had been back in for our copy of *The Tinkler-Gypsies*. He had asked for a discount, but Nicky refused to budge on the price.

Three more anonymous postcards today, all with book-related facts.

Today in Scotland legislation came in to force that makes it compulsory to charge 5p to customers who wish to have a bag. The penalty for failing to charge for a bag is a £10,000 maximum fine. It might explain why I haven't seen the rep from Marshall Wilson for quite a while. Marshall Wilson is a Glasgow-based company from whom we used to buy carrier bags. The rep would appear every quarter, although even before this legislation was first discussed I had noticed a steady decline in the number of customers asking for a bag and in the frequency of his visits. In 2001, when I bought the business, I didn't even ask people if they wanted one – customers expected their books to be put in a carrier bag. Over the years, though, that has changed, and now when I ask customers if they would like a bag there is a more or less even split between those who do and those who do not. It will be interesting to see how this affects the demand for plastic bags. I feel a considerable degree of sympathy for the staff at Marshall Wilson, whose jobs are probably now on the line. I suppose a well-intentioned piece of legislation can have an unintended consequence on a small business whose trade is in such things. If the VAT rate on books rose from zero to 20 per cent, it would probably have a seriously detrimental effect on the trade in the same way that the 5p tax has impacted on the plastic bag industry.

Till total £250
23 customers

TUESDAY, 21 OCTOBER

Online orders: 3
Books found: 3

The first customer of the day came in with a box of books to sell that included a copy of *Biggles Takes it Rough*.

Kate, the postie, brought today's post at 11 a.m. It included two more anonymous postcards. I asked her if she could tell Wilma that the six sacks of random books are ready to pick up, and if she would mind asking the postman who collects the mail at the end of the day to drop in and collect them.

A woman spent about ten minutes looking around the shop, then told me that she was a retired librarian. I suspect she thought that this was some sort of a bond between us. Not so. On the whole, booksellers dislike librarians. To realise a good price for a book, it has to be in decent condition, and there is nothing librarians like more than taking a perfectly good book and covering it with stamps and stickers before – and with no sense of irony – putting a plastic sleeve over the dust jacket to protect it from the public. The final ignominy for a book that has been in the dubious care of a public library is for the front free endpaper to be ripped out and a 'DISCARD' stamp whacked firmly onto the title page, before it is finally made available for members of the public to buy in a sale. The value of a book that has been through the library system is usually less than a quarter of one that has not.

The postman appeared at 4.30 p.m. and collected the sacks for the Random Book Cub.

Just before I closed up there were two telephone calls, the first of them from a retired vicar in Durham with approximately a thousand books on theology. I have arranged to view them on Friday. The second call was from a woman whose parents lived in Newton Stewart. Her mother, a widow, died during the summer and the house is going on the market next week. She is up from London and has to have the books removed from the house by tomorrow evening.

Till total £166.99
17 customers

WEDNESDAY, 22 OCTOBER

Online orders: 2
Books found: 2

Nicky was in, so I drove to the book deal in the house in Newton Stewart shortly after she arrived. There was some good local history material. Clearing the house was obviously going to be a fairly onerous task; it was full of cheap furniture and had not seen a hoover for a year or two. Normally Nicky works Friday and Saturday, and once the summer students go back to university it is just me in the shop for the rest of the week, but she is very obliging and flexible, and will come in on other days too if I can't schedule a book deal for Friday or Saturday.

Both Nicky and I keep forgetting to charge customers for carrier bags. We have resolved to rectify this by not even offering them a bag and leaving it up to them to ask.

Nicky took a telephone call from a man in Lochmaben with books to sell. I have scheduled him for Monday evening.

Till total £203.55
14 customers

THURSDAY, 23 OCTOBER

Online orders: 6
Books found: 4

One of the missing orders this morning is called *Alien Sex: The Body and Desire in Cinema*. Bethan had listed it in the theology section.

I spent much of the day checking the prices of our antiquarian stock to make sure we were the cheapest online. In most cases, when we originally listed the books on Monsoon, we made sure that we undercut the competition, unless the only other copies were ex-library or in poor condition. If we sell our stock online at a fixed price, we make sure that we are the cheapest available. Only the cheapest copy will sell. Often we are undercut shortly afterwards, but unless we go back into the system and check, we have no way of knowing this, and if our copy is not the cheapest it will never sell. Most of our antiquarian stock has now been undercut, not just by other antiquarian copies but by Print on Demand copies. When a book is out of copyright, anyone is permitted to reprint it.

Until relatively recently this involved scanning or retyping the book and having a few hundred (or a few thousand) copies run off. This involved a cost, and also a financial risk, so most antiquarian books that were reprinted were local history books which the reprinters knew they could sell in their locale. In the first few years of this century, though, technology emerged by which anyone with a POD printer could print off single copies of out-of-print books at a relatively low cost. The consequence of this is that a search for a rare book on AbeBooks and many other web sites will throw up numerous cheap copies of books that do not exist until a customer orders them. It has driven the values of what were once rare books right down, as the seller is now competing in a market-place that is flooded with reprints, and we now rely on customers who want the original book for its own sake, rather than just for the information it contains. Couple this with the Google Books project, which plans to digitise and make free copies available of the 130 million or so unique titles that it has estimated exist in the history of publishing, and you have a lethal cocktail for those few of us left in the second-hand book trade.

Till total £852.50
9 customers

FRIDAY, 24 OCTOBER

Online orders: 2
Books found: 1

Nicky arrived with a substance that bore no resemblance to food. 'Chocolate éclairs. Delicious.' And so began another Foodie Friday.

At 9.15 a.m. I was about to head off to County Durham to look at the theology library when she remembered to tell me that the minister had telephoned on Wednesday to say that he had already sold them to another dealer.

Diana, Anna's friend, emailed to say that Eva, her fourteen-year-old daughter, will be arriving in Dumfries on Monday afternoon for a week's work experience. I had completely forgotten that I had agreed to take her on for the week, but I remember her being a very charming girl, so hopefully it will work out well.

A customer asked me if I could help her find Christmas presents for her four daughters, but she couldn't tell me what they were interested in or what her budget was, and since I have never met her children I had no idea what to suggest, although I was extremely grateful that she had decided to buy their Christmas presents in a second-hand bookshop. I recommended Philip Pullman and C. S. Lewis, both of whose works seem to have a broad appeal.

There has been a noticeable decrease in the numbers of people asking for bags, although English customers often look quite affronted when asked for 5p. I suspect that they are unaware that it is now a legal requirement and think they are being fleeced by greedy Scots.

A retired teacher from the nearby seaside village of Garlieston dropped in a few boxes of books, mainly book club fiction in poor condition, but I found a handful of interesting equestrian books on trap racing and gave him £20 for them.

Finished *Kidnapped*. It was a relatively early edition in a pictorial binding, so I put it back on the shelf. It is a title that always sells quickly.

Till total £149.39
16 customers

SATURDAY, 25 OCTOBER

Online orders: 2
Books found: 1

Nicky stayed last night and opened the shop.

Captain spent the afternoon sleeping in an empty cardboard box in the Scottish room, to the delight of the customers.

Till total £170.99
12 customers

MONDAY, 27 OCTOBER

Online orders: 6
Books found: 5

Nicky in again, and Kate the postie delivered three more anonymous postcards.

The telephone rang at 9.05 a.m.

Me: 'Good morning, The Book Shop.'

Caller: 'Oh, hello. Are you open today?'

The first customer of the day was a man with an extremely ill-advised Rolf Harris beard and high-handed tone: 'Do you have any Folio Society books? You have heard of the Folio Society, haven't you?' This is tantamount to asking a farmer if he knows what a tractor is, so I told him that, yes, I have heard of the Folio Society, and have a stock of about 300 books published by them. He bought two of the most beautifully illustrated of the Folio titles, *Heart of Darkness* and *Lord of the Flies*. As he left, he apologised for his earlier tone, explaining that the last three bookshops he had been in had no idea what the Folio Society was.

After lunch I drove to Dumfries for an appointment with the back specialist at 3.15 p.m., then picked up Eva from the railway station. She is here until Friday. Once I had picked her up we drove to Lochmaben to look at books in a bungalow. The books were mainly slasher crime fiction paperbacks. The man was selling the books as his wife had advanced cancer, and he was moving her into a care home. He had bought a small flat so that he could be close to her, but there wasn't enough space for the books. I gave him £40 for about sixty books.

In the van on the way home Eva was curious to find out about acquiring stock, and what factors determine which books I buy and how much I offer for them. I did my best to explain, but it caused me to reflect on quite how complex the process is. There are no rules, other than those you make for yourself.

I emailed Flo this morning to see if she can come in tomorrow for a few hours, just so that Eva has some company nearer her own age. I have arranged for her to work in the festival office on Wednesday (Anna's suggestion) by way of a change of scene.

Till total £205.90
27 customers

TUESDAY, 28 OCTOBER

Online orders: 2
Books found: 1

Eva eventually appeared at about 11 a.m. As with all new members of staff, I asked her to go around the shop and tidy the shelves to familiarise herself with the layout of the shop.

Kate the postie delivered a postcard this morning with this on the back: 'Do not go gently into that good night, another double Scotch should see you right.' The anonymous postcard trend seems to be gathering momentum. The postmark was Edinburgh.

Flo turned up at about 3 p.m. and taught Eva a few bad habits, including the importance of being rude to me and ignoring all of my instructions. Fortunately, Eva seems to be far too polite and well brought up to follow Flo's feral example.

Till total £314.46
30 customers

WEDNESDAY, 29 OCTOBER

Online orders: 1
Books found: 1

Eva spent the day in the festival office. She came back at lunchtime exhausted from a morning of data entry, then headed back to an afternoon of more of the same. When she came back to the shop at 5 p.m., she told me that she had 'nearly slipped into a boredom coma'.

Kate the postie delivered four more anonymous postcards.

A customer looking for books on dogs kept talking over me as I attempted to direct her to the right section. I finally gave up and timed how long it took for her to stop talking. Two minutes and forty-three seconds.

After I closed the shop, I went for a walk with Eva to show her some of the more interesting parts of the town, including the martyrs' graves, the medieval well and the monument on Windy Hill.

Till total £106
26 customers

THURSDAY, 30 OCTOBER

Online orders: 6
Books found: 4

Today's post brought four more anonymous postcards, including one quoting from *The Meaning of Liff*, a book in which Douglas Adams and John Lloyd took an assortment of British place-names and ascribed them meanings, as though in a dictionary. One of the postcards today read: 'Moranjie (adj.) Faintly nervous that a particular post box "won't work" when posting an important letter.' But I think my favourite definition in *The Meaning of Liff* is 'Mavis

Enderby (n.) The almost-completely-forgotten girlfriend from your distant past for whom your wife has a completely irrational jealousy and hatred.'

Shortly after I had opened the shop, a family of five came in. The father – wearing a baseball cap and drinking a can of Tizer – wandered about muttering 'ferret books' repeatedly to himself. I had no idea it was still possible to buy Tizer.

At about 1 p.m., as I was sitting at the counter chatting to Eva, a large man came into the room from the back of the shop with his wife and headed towards the front door. As they were leaving, the wife asked him, 'Are you going to buy anything?', to which he replied, 'No, I haven't seen anything I like.' Eva stared at me in open-mouthed disbelief, then told me that he had been sitting in the armchair by the fire since 10 a.m. working his way through a large pile of books that he had accumulated. Needless to say, he hadn't bothered putting any of them back on the shelves, a task that Eva and I split evenly once he had left.

Eva's mother emailed this morning asking if she could come home tonight because they are unexpectedly going away for a few days, so I telephoned Flo and asked if she could cover the shop for the afternoon – her first time locking up. Amazingly, she didn't make a mess of it. I drove Eva to Dumfries in time to catch the 5.58 p.m. train. Sad to see her leave; she was splendid company to have in the house as the winter draws in and I am left alone with the cat.

Till total £292.99
32 customers

FRIDAY, 31 OCTOBER

Online orders: 2
Books found: 1

Nicky in.

This morning Kate the postie delivered a Halloween anonymous postcard bearing the message that 'Ray Bradbury was a descendant of one of the Salem witches.' I asked Nicky to judge the postcards that had come in this week and pick a winner. She took it much more seriously than I had anticipated, going so far as to devise a system based on five criteria:

1. She had to understand the quotation on the back.
2. The picture on the card had to relate to the quotation on the back.
3. The card had to be recycled.
4. It had to make her laugh.
5. The quotation had to have some sort of reference to literature.

Just before closing, Mr Deacon appeared with two women who I would guess were about half his age. This time he was not looking quite so smartly dressed, and his shirt appeared to have acquired an impressive new tapestry of stains. I assume he wears the same shirt for funerals as he does for gardening. He bought a copy of Antonia Fraser's *King Charles II*, then introduced his companions, who, it transpired, were his daughters. They had both seen the video of the shooting of the Kindle, as had Mr Deacon, much to my surprise. I didn't imagine that he owned a single piece of technology, and that was why he bought books through me rather than Amazon or AbeBooks, but it appears that he is pretty *au fait* with computers – he just prefers to support local shops. Prior to meeting his daughters, I had assumed that Mr Deacon was a bachelor, and this tiny insight into his life somehow seemed like a sweeping canvas of information, compared with what little I knew about him before.

After work Tracy and I went for a drink to mark the end of her contract with the RSPB. Her summer of sitting in the Osprey Room of the County Buildings telling people that there are no ospreys in the nest has finally drawn to an end.

Till total £245.99
8 customers

your second-hand
bookseller is
second to none
in the worth
of the treasures
he dispenses.

the bookshop
17 NORTH MAIN STREET
WIGTOWN
DUMFRIES + GALLOWAY
DG8 9HL

"The Bookshop has
a thousand books
All colours, hues and
tinges
And every cover is
a door
That turns on magic
hinges"

CHRYSANTHEMUM

The Bookshop
17 North Main Street
Wigtown
Dumfries/Galloway
Scotland
DG8 9HL

The Bookshop
XVII North Main Street
Wigtown
DG8 9HL

NOVEMBER

Given a good pitch and the right amount of capital, any educated person ought to be able to make a small secure living out of a bookshop. Unless one goes in for 'rare' books it is not a difficult trade to learn, and you start at a great advantage if you know anything about the insides of books. (Most booksellers do not. You can get their measure by having a look at the trade papers where they advertise their wants. If you do not see an ad for Boswell's *Decline and Fall* you are pretty sure to see one for *The Mill on the Floss* by T. S. Eliot.) Also it is a humane trade which is not capable of being vulgarised beyond a certain point.

George Orwell, 'Bookshop Memories'

If it was dealers confusing authors and titles in Orwell's day, it is customers who are guilty of it today. I have been asked if we have a copy of *Nineteen Eighty-Four* by Aldous Huxley on a number of occasions, and it's not unheard of to be asked for a copy of *Tom Jones* by Helen Fielding. Nicky reminded me recently that *Homage to Catalonia* has been attributed to both Ernest Hemingway and Graham Greene in the past month by customers. And the 'trade papers' to which Orwell refers have all but disappeared in the age of the internet. Even when I took over the shop, there was a good deal of trade within the industry, and networks whereby dealers contacted others to try to track down a book for a customer were still reasonably healthy. Now, of course, customers do not need us to track down titles. Two minutes online and they have a copy on the way to them. Occasionally now I still have a visit from a dealer looking for the odd bargain or – if they are a specialist – combing through a particular section to find titles they need to maintain a credible stock, but this is a rarity. Back in the early years it was common; one or two a week would make their presence known and eventually turn up at the counter with piles of books, present their business card and receive the standard 10 per cent trade discount. These days even customers demand a discount, and it is usually a lot more than 10 per cent. The demise of inter-trade business has also put an end to the career of the 'runner' – someone who would know the trade and a number of dealers and trawl the country's bookshops, loading a van with stock bought from shops, which they knew they could sell at a small profit to other dealers. Much of the runner's stock-in-trade would be topography – prior to the internet, a book about Galloway would be of little value to a bookshop in Dorset, and vice versa, so the runner would clean up by redistributing these things to a more appropriate geographical location. It makes no difference on Amazon now, though, where on the planet that book is. As for the 'humane trade' – it certainly was, but Amazon has rendered it cut-throat and barbaric.

SATURDAY, I NOVEMBER

Online orders: 6
Books found: 6

Nicky stayed overnight and opened the shop this morning. When I asked her which was the winning postcard from the competition, she pointed to one that she had obviously written herself. It even had our Royal Mail stamp on it:

> *'Cinderella!' roared the wicked step-mother, splattering the customers in saliva and red hairs, 'WHY is the stove lit and WHY are those 40 boxes of mouldy books neatly stacked and WHY have you dealt with all the orders efficiently?' 'You drive me INSANE! Go and water down the soup and spoon feed cream to the cat.' 'AND WHY is all this money in the till?' 'No more mouldy trifle for you, wretch.'*

I've decided to read Andrew McNeillie's biography of his father, John McNeillie, who wrote *The Wigtown Ploughman*, a novel published in 1939 whose depiction of the crude standards of sanitation and hygiene in rural Scotland revolutionised social welfare in the country. Andrew and I have been friends since I bought the shop, and I'm curious to see how he writes, and to see what use he made of a letter that his father wrote to one of his readers that I found in a book and gave to him as part of his research material.

Till total £233
15 customers

MONDAY, 3 NOVEMBER

Online orders: 7
Books found: 7

Five orders from AbeBooks, two from Amazon.

One postcard in the mail today: 'The walls of books around him, dense with the past, formed a kind of insulation against the present world and its disasters.' It had a local postmark. Kate the postie dropped off a ticket from Royal Mail telling me that there is an item for which no postage had been paid. It is in the sorting office in Newton Stewart. I will collect it tomorrow.

Callum came in to rebuild the counter area. We are going to incorporate an oak gantry that I bought at a farm sale on the Buccleuch estate about ten years ago. It is intended to form a more substantial barrier to protect me from customers.

A man in his thirties with a luxuriant beard came in and asked if we would be interested in 2,000 books he has in a farmhouse outside Newton Stewart. I said that we would; he will be in touch soon. Just as he left, another customer asked, 'Do you have a toilet in here?' I told him that we don't, but that there's one in the town hall, just at the end of the square. Customer: 'Oh, that's very disappointing. And it's raining outside.'

Till total £238
15 customers

TUESDAY, 4 NOVEMBER

Online orders: 6
Books found: 5

Callum came in again at 9 a.m. to continue with fitting the gantry.
He had to dismantle some of yesterday's work to get the plaster-
board in.

Eliot arrived at 9 p.m. for a board meeting later this week. I
lit the fire, which he sat in front of, complaining about how cold it
was. Presumably that's the reason he didn't kick his shoes off the
moment he arrived in the kitchen, as he normally does.

Till total £82.50
8 customers

WEDNESDAY, 5 NOVEMBER

Online orders: 2
Books found: 1

Awoke at 6.30 a.m. to the sound of doors slamming and stomping
feet, then I remembered that Eliot is staying, so went back to sleep.
Finally got up at 8.30 a.m. to brush my teeth, to find that Eliot was
having a bath, so I went downstairs to make some breakfast. His
clothes were all over the kitchen floor. I made a cup of tea and went
into the big room to find the evidence of his breakfast all over the
table – plates, mugs, cutlery, crumbs. He had also managed to shut
the cat in there. He doesn't consciously do these things, and I am
quite sure it is because his mind is awash with the information that
he will have to present to the board at the meeting.

This afternoon Mrs Phillips telephoned ('I am ninety-three and
blind'), looking for a copy of Helen Macdonald's *H is for Hawk*. We
had a copy in stock. Helen Macdonald was one of the speakers at
this year's festival, and hers was one of the most popular events.

Callum was in after lunch to continue work on the counter. As he was underneath it, he was startled by a voice saying 'Hello' and – temporarily distracted – let go of the hammer at a vital moment, sending it crashing through a pane of glass. The guilty party was Mr Deacon, who was in to order a copy of Nancy Mitford's *Love in a Cold Climate* – 'Not for me, that sort of thing. Present for my daughter. Don't read fiction. It's largely written for women.' We had a copy on the shelf, so I didn't have to order it for him.

Very quiet in the shop. Not a single customer after 11.45 a.m., apart from Mr Deacon. The day was saved by an online order for the two-volume set of *Don Quixote* I bought on 15 August from the cottage in Haugh of Urr. It made £400 and sold to a customer in Japan.

Till total £152.50
5 customers

THURSDAY, 6 NOVEMBER

Online orders: 3
Books found: 2

No postcards today.

Nicky has asked if she can have my Facebook password so that she can update the thousand or so people who follow the status updates from her perspective. She has also told me that there is a bit of the new counter area that Callum has built that she doesn't like and she's going to remove it the next time I'm away. As always, there was a complete absence of any rational explanation as to why she has taken exception to that particular bit of the counter: 'I just dinnae like it.'

The winner of last week's anonymous postcard competition (the prize is a book of their choice, value up to £20) was from London, and the card read: '"Do you know Yeats? The wine lodge? No, W. B. Yeats, the poet…" and so to assonance, getting the rhyme wrong.' Apparently it is a quotation from Willy Russell, who came to the book festival a few years ago.

Isabel came in to do the accounts. She was very taken with the new book spirals.

I reached the point in Andrew McNeillie's biography of his father in which he quotes from the letter I gave him. My surname is often spelled incorrectly, but Andrew's interpretation of it is very unusual: 'Bithyll'.

Till total £88
5 customers

FRIDAY, 7 NOVEMBER

Online orders: 3
Books found: 2

A significant number of customers recently have been asking for Terry Pratchett novels. His sad decline with Alzheimer's may well have something to do with it. Pratchett, like John Buchan, P. G. Wodehouse, E. F. Benson and many others, is an author whose books I can never find enough of. They sell quickly and usually in large numbers. In one day last year we sold our entire Penguin Wodehouse section of over twenty books, all bought by three customers.

Till total £198.77
15 customers

SATURDAY, 8 NOVEMBER

Online orders: 2
Books found: 1

Reasonably busy day – spent much of it reading Andrew McNeillie's biography of his father, *Ian Niall: Part of His Life*. Ian Niall was John McNeillie's *nom de plume*, and the title is a reference to his father's most famous work, *The Wigtown Ploughman: Part of His Life*.

Till total £132.83
17 customers

MONDAY, 10 NOVEMBER

Online orders: 2
Books found: 1

A customer at 11.15 a.m. asked for a copy of *Far from the Maddening Crowd*. In spite of several attempts to explain that the book's title is actually *Far from the Madding Crowd*, he resolutely refused to accept that this was the case, even when the overwhelming evidence of a copy of it was placed on the counter under his nose: 'Well, the printers have got that wrong.'

Despite the infuriating nature of this exchange, I ought to be grateful: he has given me an idea for the title of my autobiography should I ever be fortunate enough to retire.

I have stapled the anonymous postcards along one of the shelves in the gallery, the room in the middle of the shop that used to be used for hanging paintings in the time when John Carter owned the place. We still call it the gallery, despite the fact that there isn't a single painting there. Similarly, there is a pub in Wigtown which for a hundred years at least was known as The County Hotel. When it was taken over about six years ago, the new owners changed the name to The Wigtown Ploughman. Locals still refer to it as The County, and I suspect they always will.

Till total £57.99
6 customers

TUESDAY, 11 NOVEMBER

Online orders: 3
Books found: 3

I am rapidly running out of space for the anonymous postcards and may have to start stapling them to Nicky.

A customer came to the counter with *Highways and Byways in Galloway and Carrick*, by C. H. Dick, published in 1916 and bound in blue buckram with gilt titles. This copy was in fine condition and priced at £16.50. When I asked her for the money, the customer – an elderly, well-spoken woman – spat '£16.50? That's daylight robbery, I am not paying that for an old book.' I followed her to the door and watched as she got into her brand-new Range Rover and drove off.

Highways and Byways is a truly wonderful glimpse of the area a hundred years ago. Surprisingly little has changed around here since then. Particularly the fact that – as Dick observed – the 'district has remained unknown to the world longer than any other part of Scotland, with the possible exception of the island of Rockall'.

Till total £125.03
7 customers

WEDNESDAY, 12 NOVEMBER

Online orders: 2
Books found: 2

One of the online orders was for the Penguin edition of Huxley's *Eyeless in Gaza*, a book I hadn't even realised we had in stock.

Just before lunch a customer brought in four boxes of grubby trashy fiction. I fished out a few and offered him £15 for them. He proceeded to complain that £15 wouldn't even cover the cost of the petrol he used to drive here with them. When I pointed out that I neither asked him to bring them here nor even knew that he was going to, he continued to complain until he finally left, muttering that he had a large library of rare antiquarian books that he 'most certainly won't be bringing to this establishment to sell'.

Winter is really setting in, and the shop is noticeably colder than it was a few weeks ago, despite the heating being on and the stove in the shop having been lit every day since the start of October.

Till total £67.95
7 customers

THURSDAY, 13 NOVEMBER

Online orders: 4
Books found: 2

Ran down the stairs at 8.55 a.m. to answer the telephone, which had been ringing for a while. *En route* I managed to spill tea all over my crotch. I reached the telephone to be asked, 'Do you know what time the next bus for Wigtown leaves Newton Stewart?'

Wrote grovelling apologies to the two Amazon customers whose orders I couldn't find, in the hope of avoiding negative feedback.

As I was attempting to put up a poster up in the shop for the Random Book Club, I noticed that the staple gun didn't appear to be working, so I tested it on my hand, at which point it decided to work.

Till total £34.50
3 customers

Online orders: 4
Books found: 3

Nicky arrived, bright and early with some hideous flapjacks from the Morrisons skip. She hijacked Facebook and posted the following:

> Todays Offers!
> Always wanted that copy of 'The Fly-Fisher's Entomology' with it's hand coloured Marlow Buzz, Little Yellow May Dun etc but you just did not have £70 to spare – well this weekend it could be yours! Let's BARTER!
> Firewood, whisky, hens, piebald cobs all taken in part exchange! Bring 'em in!

A small boy, probably five years old, came in on his own and asked if we could help him find a birthday present for his mother. He had £4. On inquiring, we discovered that she likes gardening, so we found him a book on container gardening priced at £6. Nicky let him have it for £4.

After lunch I drove to Rhonehouse, near Castle Douglas, to look at a book collection that a retired Church of Scotland minister's widow was selling. I arrived at 2 p.m. and met her and her son, a man a few years younger than I am who had moved back from Edinburgh to help look after her in old age. She made us all a cup of tea, then showed me to the dining room, in which she had laid out all the books – spine up – on the dining table. As she was discussing them she produced an extremely loud whistling fart, which she sustained over a period of several seconds. Shortly afterwards she left and wandered off into the garden, at which point her son entered the room, clearly detected the fart and shot me the filthiest of looks.

I left with four boxes of crusty theology and a reputation for flatulence.

Till total £105.90
11 customers

SATURDAY, 15 NOVEMBER

Online orders: 2
Books found: 2

Nicky stayed overnight and opened the shop this morning.
First telephone call of the day:

> Caller: 'I am just calling to confirm your advertisement
> in *Crime Prevention Publication*. We've got you down
> for a quarter-page advert. You agreed to it when you
> signed up back in August', followed by some uncon-
> vincing flannel about circulation and readership etc.
>
> Me: 'I don't remember any such conversation, and I would
> never advertise in anything called *Crime Prevention
> Publication*. It sounds like you've just made it up.'
>
> Caller: 'But you agreed, back in August; it's all written
> down here.'
>
> Me: 'I don't think so. What's your number and I'll check
> and call you back?'

They hung up.

Oh, the irony. *Crime Prevention Publication* scam. This sort of call happens about twice a year. Quite often the publication I have supposedly agreed to sponsor will be called something like *Be Nice to Sick Children*.

Till total £145.98
20 customers

MONDAY, 17 NOVEMBER

Online orders: 3
Books found: 2

Nicky came in today. I drove to Lockerbie and took the train to

Edinburgh for a meeting at the National Library of Scotland to discuss the possibility of using their out-of-copyright classical recordings to set up a radio station to which businesses could pay a small subscription and avoid the punitive fees imposed by PPL (Phonographic Performance Limited) and the PRS (Performing Right Society), two organisations whose *raison d'être* appears to be to extract money from anyone who plays recorded music in the workplace. On the train I was sitting next to a group of people, one of whom had a Kindle. He spent an hour lecturing his slack-jawed companions about the wonder of the bloody thing at considerable volume while the rest of us attempted in vain to read books, magazines and newspapers. Eventually – and with no sense of irony – he barked. 'Of course, I can't possibly read if someone in the room is talking.' Every head in the carriage simultaneously snapped towards him in a collective scowl.

Today's Facebook post from Nicky:

> Very harassed yesterday – sent lots of our best stock off to a new customer in Germany, shelves are looking empty!
>
> Customer of the day had to be the woman, along with her adult daughter, who handled most of our lovely antiquarian stock & dropped one on the floor, snapping off the leather boards. Then when she asked did we have any Steinbeck books ('yes, we do', big smile, customer is always right) sneezed ALL OVER ME.
>
> No, she did not buy anything.

I spent the night in Edinburgh with my sister Lulu and her family.

Till total £170.99
14 customers

TUESDAY, 18 NOVEMBER

Online orders: 3
Books found: 3

Left Edinburgh at 10 a.m. Nicky was in the shop, and I'd asked her if she would mind packing the books for the Random Book Club. Arrived home just after lunchtime, and to my surprise she had done it and had organised the postman to collect the seven sacks.

As I was sorting through boxes, I found an old guide to Wigtownshire which contained an advert for the shop when it was a grocer's in the 1950s. Occasionally a visitor to the shop will drop in to tell me that the shop was Pauling's, the grocer, when they lived in Wigtown, or that they were related to the people who ran it when it was a grocer's shop.

Till total £90.50
5 customers

WEDNESDAY, 19 NOVEMBER

Online orders: 5
Books found: 3

At 11 a.m. a teenage boy shuffled awkwardly to the counter and placed a paperback copy of *The Catcher in the Rye* in front of me, with the £2.50 change required to pay for it. Few books have affected me the way that book did when I was around the same age as that boy, and going through the tortuous transition into adulthood. Salinger's portrayal of Holden Caulfield's disengagement with the world in which he is forced to live must have resonated with millions of teenage readers over the decades since its first publication in 1951.

Till total £48
9 customers

THURSDAY, 20 NOVEMBER

Online orders: 3
Books found: 3

Nicky came in and carried on listing the books from the Rhone-house deal. It is now one month since the 5p bag tax was introduced, and Nicky has calculated that the number of people asking for one has gone from about 50 per cent to under 10 per cent.

Till total £149
10 customers

FRIDAY, 21 NOVEMBER

Online orders: 2
Books found: 2

Nicky has taken to hijacking Facebook regularly now. Here is her post for today:

> The customers were complaining of the HEAT yesterday when we lit the stove & burned the books we did not like, I mean, did not want, i.e. those without proper 'speechmarks' so – no more Roddy Doyle or Irvine Welsh – what a shame!
> Would you like to nominate any books for burning today?

Today's Foodie Friday treat was a packet of out-of-date oatcakes.

Mr Deacon came in to order a book but couldn't find the scrap of paper he had written it down on.

In a moment of boredom I worked out that we have posted out over a ton of books this year. No wonder I have to sit down before opening the Royal Mail invoice.

Till total £57.30
5 customers

SATURDAY, 22 NOVEMBER

Online orders: 3
Books found: 1

Nicky was in, so I went for lunch in the Steam Packet in the Isle of Whithorn with some friends. I returned in the middle of the afternoon to discover that she had taken it upon herself to wallpaper the section of wall near the children's section with illustrations of wild animals she had cut out from an encyclopaedia.

I despair. She is a law unto herself.

Mr Deacon telephoned. He wants a copy of Evelyn Waugh's *Decline and Fall*. When I reminded him that he had told me that fiction was for women, he replied, 'Most of it, but not all of it.'

A customer who had driven down from Ayr brought in two boxes of books to sell. Mostly Victorian guidebooks to Europe, but not in very good condition. She had bought them at an auction by accident, thinking she was bidding on a samovar. I gave her £200, which she assured me gave her enough profit to have made the journey worthwhile.

Nicky, on leaving at the end of the working day: 'I've got a great idea, why don't we turn the shop into a disco?'

Till total £345.99
19 customers

MONDAY, 24 NOVEMBER

Online orders: 5
Books found: 4

Yesterday I had the slightly unsettling experience of waking up after a lie-in, going downstairs to the kitchen, making myself a cup of tea and wandering into the sitting room with my dressing gown a-flap to encounter the window cleaner staring into the room from his ladder. I beat a hasty retreat. Neither of us spoke of it this morning when he dropped in to collect his £5.

A customer came to the counter with a book on Scottish history, leather-bound, dated 1817. He pointed at a price marked in pencil on the endpaper of £1.50, which was clearly not our price. I checked on our database and we had it priced at £75, and our copy was the cheapest online. I told him that there was no way he could have it for £1.50, and he stormed out. Nicky later told me that she had seen him writing something in a book in the shop and suspected that he had removed our sticker and written the price in himself. Years ago there was a notorious book dealer who would regularly trawl the bookshops of Wigtown, waiting until he saw a fresh face at the counter – someone who he suspected knew less than he did – and erase pencil prices in rare books and reduce them to steal himself a bargain. As far as I know, he is now dead.

The last customers of the day – a young couple who bought a few sci-fi titles – told me that they spend their holidays visiting second-hand bookshops all over the UK. A glimmer of hope still flickers for us.

Till total £78
7 customers

TUESDAY, 25 NOVEMBER

Online orders: 7
Books found: 4

Forgot to set the alarm and slept in. Opened the shop at 10 a.m. to discover that the ladies' art class was supposed to have started at 9.30 a.m. and they were waiting, shivering, outside.

Till total £64
3 customers

Online orders: 2
Books found: 1

Decline and Fall arrived in this morning's post, so I telephoned Mr Deacon to let him know.

Sandy the tattooed pagan came in with his friend. He dropped off six sticks and found a book on Celtic mythology.

Customer came in at 4 p.m. with a box of modern paperback fiction which included a copy of José Saramago's brilliant book *Blindness* and a copy of *Pereira Maintains*, by Antonio Tabucchi, both of which had been given to me by an Italian friend who was horrified by my ignorance of contemporary European fiction. *Pereira Maintains* was a book I greatly enjoyed, but *Blindness* was astonishing. There are few other books in which I have felt so completely immersed and – ironically – visualised so clearly. The filth and pathetic chaos of a world in which everyone has gone blind, the fragility of the social contract and the rapid disintegration of society following the loss of a single sense are so vividly painted by Saramago that it draws the reader in almost as a participant in the story rather than an observer and – like Hogg's *Justified Sinner* – spits you out at the end asking more questions of the world around you.

Till total £90.55
9 customers

THURSDAY, 27 NOVEMBER

Online orders: 8
Books found: 6

The Christmas tree went up in the square today.

A group of three Russian women came into the shop, and one

of them (clearly the only English-speaker) asked if we had any books in the Russian language. She seemed genuinely surprised that we had quite a few, but they didn't buy any.

We received an AbeBooks order this afternoon from a customer in Ireland. It was for an eight-volume set of books which had clearly been incorrectly priced on Monsoon:

Title:	*European History: Great Leaders & Landmarks*
Author:	Rev. H. J. Chaytor, William Collinge, Walter Murray
Price:	£3.48
Shipping:	£8.85
Total:	£12.33

The total weight of the set is 8.2 kg, which would put the postage to Ireland at £88. I emailed the customer and explained the situation.

Three people independently asked 'Do you buy books?' one of whom brought in three Harry Potter books and very ponderously showed them to me, pointing out the fact that one of them was a first edition. When I told him that the later Harry Potter books had such huge first-edition runs that they're practically worthless, he hastily put it back in the bag he had brought it in and left. I don't think he believed me.

While locking up, I was treated to the extraordinary sight of Mr Deacon sprinting towards the shop as only an overweight man in late middle age can. The tails of his ill-fitting jacket (slightly too small) flapping about and his comb-over (which had flipped up vertically) appeared together like a pair of vestigial wings and the dorsal fin of a sailfish: the former struggling to push him along, the latter to steer him. He was clearly trying to get to the shop before it closed. I held the door open for him, and he paid for his book, then shuffled off, panting, into the half-light.

Till total £88.99
6 customers

FRIDAY, 28 NOVEMBER

Online orders: 1
Books found: 1

Nicky arrived at 9.15 a.m., as usual. Straight away she offered me a plastic tray of what might have passed for food were it a few days fresher, asking, 'Would you like a cinnamon roll?' (Tesco 'Reduced to 27p' sticker clearly visible). I replied, 'I'd love one, thanks, Nicky.' And as I reached for one, she swatted my hand aside and said, 'I wouldn't go for that one. I licked the icing off it on the way into work this morning.'

The only order this morning was for a book called *A Toast-Fag*.

While I was pricing up books from the many boxes from various book deals piled up in the shop, I found a copy of a book called *The Restraint of Beasts*, by Magnus Mills. Finn had recommended this to me, so I put it aside and will start on it when I have time.

Nicky decided to stay the night so that we could drink beer and gossip. Predictably we both drank too much. I offered her a bottle of Corncrake Ale and she told me that she doesn't like any beer that has a bird's name in it. This is the kind of logic that she applies to all of her decision-making.

Till total £62.50
5 customers

SATURDAY, 29 NOVEMBER

Online orders: 1
Books found: 1

Nicky opened up, so I had a lie-in.

Today's order was for a book called *A Young Man's Passage*, by Mark Teller. Julian Clary used the same title for his autobiography, but I can't imagine he chose it for the same reasons.

As Nicky and I were putting fresh stock out, we both

commented at the same time (as we went into the gallery) that it was extremely cold in there. And the fire was lit too. Since we put in the air source heater at the bottom of the stairs last year, the gallery has gone from being the warmest room in the shop to one of the coldest, probably because it has a stone wall with no lining or insulation, so I telephoned Callum to see what he thinks about it. He is going to come over and have a look at it.

Till total £100
10 customers

DECEMBER

At Christmas time we spent a feverish ten days struggling with Christmas cards and calendars, which are tiresome things to sell but good business while the season lasts. It used to interest me to see the brutal cynicism with which Christian sentiment is exploited. The touts from the Christmas card firms used to come round with their catalogues as early as June. A phrase from one of their invoices sticks in my memory. It was: '2 doz. Infant Jesus with rabbits'.

George Orwell, 'Bookshop Memories'

Christmas and the run-up to it is possibly the quietest time of the year in the shop. The business is so dependent on footfall from tourists – of whom there are barely any in December – that we would almost be better-off closing the shop between November and March. The few people who give second-hand books as gifts for Christmas are usually eccentric, though, so it is worth opening purely for the entertainment these characters afford. They are the most interesting customers. And it wouldn't do to close; if the shop wasn't open, it would disappoint those few souls who do venture into rural Galloway in the winter months, and they would be unlikely to return another time. Occasionally they spend some money, and the short, cold winter days permit little by way of alternative occupation if I was to close the shop, so it is better to be open on my own and take what slim pickings there are than to be closed and take nothing. The one week for which it is certainly worth opening is that between Christmas and Hogmanay – that's the week when people return to the area to spend the festive period with their loved ones, whom they quickly discover that they love considerably more from a distance of several hundred miles than they do when confined to the same house as them. During that week the shop is busy, bustling with people who have spent far too much time in close confinement with their kin during the year's darkest month; desperate for any means of escape, they flock to the shop and while away the hours browsing, and – usually – buying books.

MONDAY, 1 DECEMBER

Online orders: 1
Books found: 1

Saint Andrew's day, a bank holiday in Scotland.
    A customer telephoned looking for a book:

> Woman: 'I was in your shop during the book festival and found a book about old ruined gardens of Scotland in your new books section. Could you tell me what the title is?'
>
> Me: 'No, I am afraid not. I know the book you're after and would be happy to sell you a copy, though.'
>
> Woman: 'Why won't you tell me the title?'
>
> Me: 'Because as soon as I do you'll just go and buy it on Amazon.'
>
> Woman: 'No, I'll send my mother round to pick it up from you.'
>
> Me: 'Oh good, in that case can I take your credit card details and your mother's name? I'll put it to one side once you've paid for it.'

At this point she hung up.
    Tracy and I went for a pint in the pub after work today. A local farmer dropped in and asked, 'Does anyone want a turnip? I've got some in the pick-up.' Laura, working behind the bar, told him that she would like one. He appeared with the most enormous turnip I have ever seen. Apparently he had a bumper crop this year.
    Started reading *The Restraint of Beasts*.

Till total £28
4 customers

TUESDAY, 2 DECEMBER

Online orders: 3
Books found: 2

Callum dropped in, and we discussed the possibility of insulating the stone wall in the gallery. It should make a significant difference to the temperature. He has agreed to do the work, starting some time this week.

Today was a golden, sunny day; the low light of December and January illuminates the Penguin section in a way that never happens at other times of the year. The undoubted highlight of the day was selling a book called *Donald McLeod's Gloomy Memories*, published in 1892, to a customer who had been looking for it for six years.

Till total £33
2 customers

WEDNESDAY, 3 DECEMBER

Online orders: 4
Books found: 2

Cold morning, so I lit the fire and processed the online orders. As I was walking to the post office with the mail, I passed a man carrying a brick, with his car keys dangling from his mouth. As he mumbled a friendly 'Hello', the keys fell from his mouth and landed – conveniently – on the brick.

At 2.30 p.m. an elderly man came in with a box of military history books to sell, including several on the KOSB (King's Own Scottish Borderers, the infantry regiment that – despite Galloway not being a border county – Gallovidian men traditionally joined). Agreed a price of £120 for them.

Till total £46
4 customers

THURSDAY, 4 DECEMBER

Online orders: 3
Books found: 3

Callum arrived at 10 a.m. to start work on insulating the wall. Spent much of the day boxing up books and dismantling the shelves on the wall he's going to be working on.

Till total £48
5 customers

FRIDAY, 5 DECEMBER

Online orders: 1
Books found: 1

Nicky in. She arrived early and visibly excited; 'Oh, have I got a treat for you!' This 'treat' was supposed to be some sort of compensation for the cinnamon swirl that she had licked the icing off last Friday morning. She produced a box that was covered in 'reduced' stickers and contained a Peppa Pig cake.

Callum was in all day, working on insulating the wall.

Once I'd set Nicky a few jobs (which she nodded enthusiastically about and then decided not to do), I left for a book deal in Sorbie – six miles from Wigtown – at 11 a.m. It was the collection of one of my father's friends, Basil, who died earlier in the year. His nephew was dealing with the estate. There weren't many interesting books, and most of them were engineering textbooks, but I took a couple of boxes and wrote him a cheque for £100.

When I left Bristol to return to Scotland in 2001, death was something with which I was relatively unfamiliar, other than the loss of elderly grandparents and great-aunts. Perhaps I am fortunate never to have lost a close friend. Rural life, though, throws you into contact with people of all ages and backgrounds in a way that it is easy to avoid in a city. Back when I bought the shop in 2001, customers would often comment that I appeared 'very young for a bookseller', and perhaps I was. It is five years since I last heard that said, and the number of funerals I attend increases year by year. Many of my parents' friends have died in this past year. My mother recently told me, 'Your father and I are in the minefield now.'

After work I went for a pint with Callum. We invited Nicky along, but she said she wanted to stay in, so I lit the fire for her and bought some craft beers for her from the co-op (nothing with a bird in its name this time). When I came back at about 8 p.m., she was sitting in front of the fire sewing together a stuffed toy cow which apparently she has been working on for over twenty years. It bore no resemblance to a cow.

Several customers this week have come into the shop and complained that they had forgotten to bring their reading glasses. This is far from uncommon. When I mentioned it to Nicky, she pointed out that she too frequently does it.

Till total £22
2 customers

SATURDAY, 6 DECEMBER

Online orders: 2
Books found: 2

At 8 a.m. I heard Nicky making her breakfast, so I had a lie-in and she opened up. I was woken shortly afterwards by the sound of Callum's hammer drill battering away at the wall downstairs. I spent much of the afternoon running a speaker cable from the stereo, which we have now moved to the front of the shop, out of the reach of children, who seem incapable of passing it without tinkering with it – usually increasing the volume.

Till total £72.29
9 customers

MONDAY, 8 DECEMBER

Online orders: 9
Books found: 8

The shop was extremely quiet all day, the first customer appearing at 11.30 a.m. and asking, 'Where do you keep your books on marketing and financial strategy?' Someone is in for an exciting Christmas present.

As I was sorting through the mail, I found a letter from the council onto which Nicky had executed a very crude sketch of a round face with glasses and curly hair – clearly supposed to be me. When I presented her with it and asked, 'Nicky, what's this?', she replied, 'That? It's a mirror.'

Till total £78.44
6 customers

TUESDAY, 9 DECEMBER

Online orders: 2
Books found: 1

Anna telephoned to say that she isn't going to work on the film that she has been developing with her friend in America because she thinks the budget is too small, so she's booked a flight back to London and is arriving in Dumfries on Thursday.

One of today's customers, an old man, shuffled towards the counter clutching a book with a look of excitement on his face. 'How much do you want for this?' It was a Latin school textbook, and he hurriedly opened it and pointed to the name written in fountain pen on the endpaper, 'It belonged to my father.' The book was £4.50, but I told him that he could have it for free. I don't recall how I came by the book, but he was so delighted to have found it that it seemed like the right thing to do. He was here on holiday from Kent, so it may have come from a large collection I bought from a house outside Canterbury several years ago.

Till total £80
9 customers

WEDNESDAY, 10 DECEMBER

Online orders: 1
Books found: 0

Nicky came in today so that I could get away to look at a library near Stirling, on the eastern shore of Loch Lomond. The house was in a stunning glen, and the road was lined with ancient broadleaf woodland and dotted with grand Victorian villas, of which this was one. It belonged to a couple who were about the same age as my parents, and was full of fine furniture and art. They were congenial and friendly, and kept me fuelled with tea and biscuits as I worked my way through the thousand or so books in the various rooms. Their sons had been to a boarding-school in Perthshire, and one of them was my age, so undoubtedly our paths would have crossed at some point, probably a rugby match. As with so many book deals, they were selling the house and looking for somewhere smaller, on this occasion a flat in the West End of Glasgow.

The book collection was mixed but contained some interesting antiquarian material, including a first edition of Barnard's *The Whisky Distilleries of the United Kingdom*, published in 1887. This is the only copy of the first edition I have ever seen. There was a good collection of other books on whisky, including a couple of antiquarian titles. When we were chatting, it emerged that he had worked in the whisky industry before retiring, and we knew a few of the same people in the distilling business. After some civilised negotiations we agreed a price of £1,200 for ten boxes of books.

The drive home was horrendous. I made the mistake of taking the hill road: twenty miles of single-track. It was covered in snow, raining, and the wind was howling. I met a few fully loaded forestry lorries; then, as I climbed higher, the rain turned to snow, the mountainous landscape occasionally illuminated by sheets of lightning. Made it back at about 6 p.m.

Till total £85.98
7 customers

THURSDAY, 11 DECEMBER

Online orders: 3
Books found: 3

One of the orders today was for a book called *A Drug Taker's Notes*. When I took the orders over to Wilma, there was no sign of William. I asked Wilma where he was, to which she conspiratorially replied, 'He's having his nap', with a wicked smile on her face. I don't think any amount of sleep would be enough to put him in a good mood.

After I locked up I drove to Dumfries to pick Anna up from the railway station.

Till total £27
5 customers

FRIDAY, 12 DECEMBER

Online orders: 1
Books found: 0

Nicky arrived in her black ski suit as usual, with a pasty from the Morrisons skip. It bore more resemblance to a giant scab than to an edible treat. 'Eh, it's delicious. Go on, have a bit.' It was revolting.

Foodie Friday has become a low point in the week, particularly since the cinnamon roll incident.

Today was particularly slow in the shop, and bitterly cold. Nicky's Facebook post:

> Dear friends, Nicky here! When I arrived at work this morning my emotions were all over the place on spying a red light glowing by the counter … was that a heater? Could I remove my Snuggies?
>
> Yes and No. It was a heater with ONLY the light turned on. Snuggies will be in place until April.
>
> Oh, most distressing news in this week's *Free Press* – a coin was stolen from a vehicle parked on a farm. What is the world coming to?
>
> Don't tell him I was here.

Nicky brought in five pairs of glasses that she had bought at the pound shop in Bathgate, for customers who forget their own.

Someone from a lowland distillery heard that we'd acquired the whisky book collection and came to the shop. He offered me £600 for the Barnard, which I gladly took, as it means I am half-way to recouping my investment within a few days. Had it been in better condition, I could probably have doubled that price.

Callum finished work on insulating the wall. Now we need to find someone to plaster it before we can put up new shelves in time for Christmas.

Till total £79.50
3 customers

SATURDAY, 13 DECEMBER

Online orders: 3
Books found: 2

By 9.22 a.m. I had dealt with today's orders, but there was still no sign of Nicky. At 10 a.m. I received a text message from her: 'Am in a ditch near the Doon of May. Waiting on a tractor to pull me out.' She managed to hitch in from the ditch. The Doon is a piece of land near the pretty village of Elrig. It is owned by a man called Jeff, and he runs it as a sort of commune. Nicky eventually appeared at 10.45 a.m.

In the afternoon my father appeared to ask me to print something off for a meeting he has on Wednesday. He and my mother can navigate their way around their iPads, but beyond that family assistance is required for anything relating to computers. The discussion in the shop revolved around what time 'the afternoon' officially begins. I said noon. Anna said 11 a.m. My father said, 'Not until I've finished my lunch.'

Till total £121.79
10 customers

MONDAY, 15 DECEMBER

Online orders: 2
Books found: 1

As I was sorting through some boxes – possibly from one of the ministers' collections – I came across two books that you would not expect to find in the same box: a copy of *Mein Kampf* and an olivewood Bible from Jerusalem.

Coming across a copy of *Mein Kampf* can place you in a tricky position, morally. The copy we have is worth about £60, and a lot of dealers understandably will not touch it, but there is demand for it – not huge, but sufficient to know that this one will go within a month. The question you never know the answer to is into whose hands it will end up falling – some far-right lunatic, or a historian who is debunking Holocaust-deniers. The market for *Mein Kampf* will change next year in any case, once the copyright expires in Germany.

Till total £149.50
11 customers

TUESDAY, 16 DECEMBER

Online orders: 1
Books found: 1

Nicky came in as I had an appointment to see the back specialist in
Dumfries Infirmary at 11 a.m. I've been referred to the MRI unit
for a scan. While I was in Dumfries, I took the opportunity to look
at some books belonging to an elderly woman whose husband died
in May. She was in a tiny flat conveniently close to the hospital. The
books were all about fishing, and some of them were reasonably
rare. We agreed a price of £250 for four boxes, and when I told her
I was a keen fly fisherman, she insisted on giving me all of his old
fly boxes. As I was going through the shelves, I noticed that on a
lot of the tables and shelves photograph frames had been lain face
down. I turned a few of them over out of curiosity. They were all
of the same person, presumably her husband. Perhaps she couldn't
face being reminded of him.

More Facebook activity from Nicky:

> Dear friends, Nicky here!
> Some of you may not be aware of how caring & generous
> Shaun is. When I finally arrived on the Black, Black Ice day,
> vanless, he allowed me to flatten a cardboard box & lay it,
> DOUBLE THICKNESS, on the floor under the worktop, to
> keep out some of the winter draughts. How kind is that!
> And with the red light glowing on the heater (even minus
> any heat), it feels so cosy. He's lovely!

I have been struggling to find a plasterer to finish the newly
insulated wall, and Christmas looms ever closer.

Till total £58.49
8 customers

WEDNESDAY, 17 DECEMBER

Online orders: 3
Books found: 3

One customer – who had been in for about two hours, and had been the only person in the shop during that entire time – said, 'This must be your busy time of year, then, the run-up to Christmas.' There was literally nobody else in the shop for the entire time he was there. Quite what he imagined the shop was like for the rest of the year I have no idea.

Finished *The Restraint of Beasts*.

Till total £103.09
8 customers

THURSDAY, 18 DECEMBER

Online orders: 2
Books found: 2

At 10 a.m. the first customer came through the door: 'I'm not really interested in books' followed by 'Let me tell you what I think about nuclear power.' By 10.30 a.m. the will to live was but a distant memory.

When I took the orders over to Wilma, William was regaling a clearly unwilling customer with a joke of such colossal political incorrectness that, if there was a Beaufort scale of these things, it would have been of a magnitude so great that a new scale would have had to be created. I asked Wilma if she could send the postman over tomorrow to pick up the sacks when he does his end-of-day collection.

The fishing books from the Dumfries deal, while not exactly flying off the shelves, are selling notably faster than anything else. This is a common phenomenon, even in a shop of this relatively large size: it is the fresh stock that always moves the fastest. I suppose there is a sense to it, inasmuch as a book that has been on the shelves for a year and has not sold is probably overpriced or lacks any sort of market. It doesn't feel like that, though; it is almost as though the stock that has just come in actually looks fresher, and the books that have been sitting on the shelves for ages have acquired a certain staleness, rendering them unsellable.

As I was sorting through the boxes of books from Loch Lomond, I found another Sorley MacLean pamphlet signed by Seamus Heaney. The total print run was fifty; I now have two of them. They should make £100 each. Like the Walter Scott signature and the Florence Nightingale inscribed book, there is something that makes you feel connected to those people when you handle material like this. Perhaps the more interesting mystery is that you never know who has handled all the unsigned, un-inscribed books that come into the shop, and what their secret history has been.

We received another email from the Bay Bookshop in Colwyn Bay, Wales. They are closing the shop soon and want to know if we would like to buy the stock. They clearly haven't had any luck selling it elsewhere. I've asked them to email me some photographs.

Till total £184.49
7 customers

FRIDAY, 19 DECEMBER

Online orders: 1
Books found: 1

Colwyn Bay replied with some photos of what looks like reasonable stock of 20,000 books. Apparently they have had an offer that is well below what they are looking for. I suspect that my offer would be in the same region, so I am not going to bother. Very few people now will take on a deal of that size, so you can pretty much name your price. I suspect they are going to struggle to shift them.

The shop was as quiet and cold as the grave, speaking of which, I must ask Nicky if any of our regulars has died recently.

I was sorting through boxes of books when I spotted a copy of Petronius' *Satyricon*. Started flicking through it and I think I'll attempt to read it.

The postman picked up the Random Book Club mail sacks at 3.30 p.m.

Nicky is staying tonight and will be working tomorrow, so that means I will have a bit more freedom to do such exciting things as go to the bank, then to the sawmill to pick up timber for new shelves, and even clean the van.

Till total £122
8 customers

SATURDAY, 20 DECEMBER

Online orders: 5
Books found: 5

Nicky in. While I drove to nearby Penkiln sawmill to collect the timber for the new shelves to go over the newly insulated wall, she hijacked the Facebook page again.

> Dear friends, Nicky here!
> WOW, did we upset the neighbours last night with our 'End of Year' Book Shop mash-up of hip-hop & swing dance moves then some hard drugs (2 ibuprofen each!) knowing that the elderly staff members wouldn't be able to walk today. That's the way we roll. Yeah.

I told Nicky that I couldn't find a plasterer to finish the wall Callum has insulated, and that I want the job done before Christmas. She said 'leave it to me' and walked out of the shop. Five minutes later she was back with someone called Mark, who looked at the job and told me that he can do it tomorrow. She had gone to the bus stop and asked the people in the queue 'Is anyone here a plasterer?' and he had said yes.

Nicky has found a place in Glasgow that will take our reject stock and recycle it, Smurfit Kappa (Cash for Clothes recently told us that they're not operating in Galloway any more). They will pay us £40 a ton for it, which should cover the fuel costs of getting there so I'll head up in the New Year with a van load.

Till total £82
9 customers

SUNDAY 21 DECEMBER

Mark the plasterer came in at about 8.30 a.m. and plastered the wall.

MONDAY, 22 DECEMBER

Online orders: 3
Books found: 2

All the books that were on the shelves we removed to insulate the wall were boxed and put in front of a section that NOBODY ever asks for – geology. They have been there since Callum began working on insulating the wall. Today's first customer, a man with a crutch and a limp, appeared and asked, 'Where's the geology section?'

Sandy the tattooed pagan came in to wish me a happy winter solstice for yesterday.

I spent the evening building shelves and putting the boxed books back on them.

Colwyn Bay Bookshop has put its stock on eBay with a price

of £20,000. There is no way it will sell for that much. They will be doing well if they can realise £5,000.

Till total £181.50
13 customers

TUESDAY, 23 DECEMBER

Online orders: 4
Books found: 4

This morning a customer returned a book that we had posted out last week, with a note saying, 'Please refund as book looks second hand, not new as expected.' The book in question was John MacCormick's *The Flag in the Wind*, and the cover is designed to look deliberately distressed and aged. It was brand new.

Between Christmas and the first Monday of New Year the shop opens at 10 a.m. rather than 9 a.m., so I put a sign in the shop window.

What a feeble effort I make with Christmas decorations in the shop. They went up today and consisted of a few branches of holly, donated by Bev, and some ivy cut from a local farmer's driveway, illuminated by some cheap fairy lights. I decorated each window and a bit in the hall.

Anna and I drove up to Edinburgh to spend Christmas at my sister Lulu's house. I left a note for Nicky (who doesn't celebrate Christmas) asking her to keep the shop tidy and feed the cat.

Till total £140.10
13 customers

WEDNESDAY, 24 DECEMBER

Online orders: 6
Books found: 5

Nicky in charge of the bookshop over the festive season.

THURSDAY, 25 DECEMBER

Christmas Day. Closed.

FRIDAY, 26 DECEMBER

Boxing Day. Closed.
    Anna and I drove home from Edinburgh.

SATURDAY, 27 DECEMBER

Online orders: 3
Books found: 3

Nicky was in today. Apparently she had been waiting patiently outside since 9 a.m. – I had forgotten to tell her that the shop opens at 10 a.m. during the holidays. She was furious. One of the orders today was for a book called *Cuckoo Problems*.

I spent much of the day ploughing through piles of emails offering to improve traffic to my web site, enlarge my penis, and lend me money. The business doesn't have the financial where-withal to do any of them, sadly. Among all the spam were four new Random Book Club subscriptions, which would suggest that people have been giving them as Christmas presents.

Disappointingly quiet day. Perhaps visitors to the area think we're not open.

Till total £140.20
14 customers

MONDAY, 29 DECEMBER

Online orders: 2
Books found: 2

Cold, frosty, sunny day. There was ice on the inside of the kitchen windows when I made breakfast. Opened the shop at 10 a.m. The treat of an extra hour in bed between Christmas and New Year is a luxury. When I checked the emails, I found one from Nicky: 'Are you working today? Hahahahahaha!'

The shop was quiet until about 11.30 a.m., when a few people began to trickle in. After lunch a teenage girl – who had been sitting by the fire reading for an hour – brought three Agatha Christie paperbacks to the counter; the total came to £8. She offered me a limp fiver and said, 'Can I have them for £5?' I refused, telling her that the postage on Amazon alone would come to £7.40. She wandered off muttering about getting them from the library. Good luck with that: Wigtown library is full of computers and DVDs and not a lot of books.

By 4.30 p.m. I was considering closing early, but nine people arrived and wandered around picking up books, so I stayed open until 5.30. They spent £60.

I still haven't submitted the application for the James Patterson grant, so I frantically checked his web site and found that the deadline is 15 January 2015.

Struggling slightly with *Satyricon*, but largely because of the gaps rather than the prose. Far more entertaining than I imagined.

Till total £323.97
25 customers

TUESDAY, 30 DECEMBER

Online orders: 1
Books found: 0

Busy day in the shop, with families visiting grandparents and couples escaping from their parents. No large sales, but steady all day.

Till total £401.33
30 customers

WEDNESDAY, 31 DECEMBER

Online orders: 3
Books found: 2

The shop was busy right through the day. By lunchtime nobody had been rude or asked for a discount. The dream-like tranquillity was finally shattered by Peter Bestel, who came into the shop to tell me that a dog had shat on the doorstep. Peter is a friend whose daughter Zoe is trying to carve out a career as a singer/songwriter. She is extremely talented, and Anna and I made a video for her a few years ago. Peter is the brains behind the Random Book Club web site, and is always there with technical advice whenever I need it. Which is most of the time.

Shortly after I had removed the dog shit with a spade, a family of five came into the shop. The children stamped their muddy boots near the door, but inside the shop rather than outside. They all left without even looking at a book between them.

Anna and I drove down to the Isle of Whithorn to stay with friends for Hogmanay.

Till total £457.50
37 customers

JANUARY

A bookseller has to tell lies about books, and that gives him a distaste
for them; still worse is the fact that he is constantly dusting them and
hauling them to and fro. There was a time when I really did love
books – loved the sight and smell and feel of them, I mean, at least if
they were fifty or more years old. Nothing pleased me quite so much
as to buy a job lot of them for a shilling at a country auction.

George Orwell, 'Bookshop Memories'

On this part of his essay, I have to concede that I have some sympathy
with Orwell. While I still love books, they no longer have the
mystique that they once had – with the exception of antiquarian
books illustrated with hand-coloured copperplate engravings or
woodcuts. Once I had in my possession *Lilies*, eight hand-coloured
bound plates from Thornton's *Temple of Flora*. I doubt whether I
shall ever see so beautiful a book again. It was in an elderly widow's
house in Ayrshire. I had gone through the books she was selling – a
thousand or so – and found very little of value or even of interest
until when, just as I was about to leave, I spotted the book leaning
against a table leg in the dining room. I asked if she would mind
if I had a look at it, as I had never seen a copy before. When I told
her what it was worth, she asked me if I could sell it for her (I
confessed that at the time buying it was beyond my means), so I
took it home, had some minor repairs done to it by a local binder
and consigned it to Lyon & Turnbull's Edinburgh saleroom, where
it realised somewhere in the region of £8,000.

Even the octavo set of Audubon's *Birds of America* that briefly
fell into my possession (one of the holy grails for any bookseller) could not come close to that. Such things will never lose
their appeal. And while there is always the thrill of the chase as
I approach a house whose library I might buy, and have not yet
seen, I read little compared with my life before I bought the shop,
unless I am travelling by train or plane. In those journeys I am
free from the distractions that punctuate my daily life and can
immerse myself completely in a book. When I read James Hogg's
The Private Memoirs and Confessions of a Justified Sinner, which I
started and finished on a train journey to London to see Anna,

I clearly remember emerging from Hogg's extraordinary world, blinking and stunned into Euston station – more disorientated by the place than ever.

During a negotiation over the price of a private library with a seller, the collection assumes the appearance of a glittering prize. The moment that a price is agreed, hands are shaken and the cheque has left my hand, the books instead become a great weight which I have to box up, load into the van, unload and then check, list online, price up and put on the shelves before I will see a penny of my investment returning. The distaste to which Orwell refers happens the moment the books enter your possession – they suddenly become 'work' – but that unease is more than matched by the extraordinary pleasure afforded by the rare and exquisite joy of handling a book like Thornton's *Lilies*.

THURSDAY, 1 JANUARY

Online orders: 3
Books found: 3

Closed due to hangover.

FRIDAY, 2 JANUARY

Online orders: 7
Books found: 4

Nicky turned up wearing her black ski suit.

One of the orders we found today was for a book called *The Universal Singular*. Nicky tidied it up before she sent it out because the top edge was slightly dusty.

Colwyn Bay Bookshop's stock failed to meet the reserve on eBay. They have re-listed them at £14,500, with a note saying 'THIS

HAS TO BE THE FINAL REDUCTION'. I am quite sure they will not realise that figure. The mega-listers are paying public libraries a fraction of that, roughly 15p per kilogram. The Colwyn Bay collection is working out at roughly £1.20 per kilogram. None of the big dealers will touch it at that price.

Anna persuaded me to take her to Glasgow to see the film of her favourite book, *Into the Woods*, which has been turned into a Disney musical. This is my idea of hell: I dislike musicals and I'm no fan of Disney, so the combination of the two will unquestionably result in a film that is the cinematic equivalent of a week in the waterboarding wing of Guantánamo Bay. But we are going next Friday.

The young man with the beard who had been in on 3 November wanting to dispose of 2,000 books from a farmhouse near Newton Stewart came back in with his girlfriend and introduced himself as Ewan and his girlfriend as Sarah. He asked if I could look at the books tomorrow.

Nicky stayed the night and we drank a large scoop of beer between us.

Till total £145
15 customers

SATURDAY, 3 JANUARY

Online orders: 3
Books found: 3

Nicky opened the shop at 10 a.m. She was up and about and clearly not feeling the best, but not bad enough to stop her from hijacking the shop's Facebook page and posting the following message:

Good People of 2014

1. The Ivy Leaf chippy (Stranraer) – kept a fiver for me when I dropped it; the best & most honest in Scotland.

2. Customer who ordered a book in March 2014, we found it 2 weeks ago, did he still want it? 'yes please' & paid MORE than we asked.
3. Customer on hearing the price of a ring was £3.50, yells 'HOW MUCH?' – it IS silver, we reassure her – 'I expected it to be at least £35.00.'
Heartwarming!

Anna and I drove to the farmhouse near Newton Stewart to pick up the 2,000 books. It was a glorious day, and the house and farm buildings were ancient and beautiful. The books were in the spare bedroom of the dairy cottage. While we were chatting to Ewan, it transpired that his American girlfriend was being forced to leave by the immigration authorities in an uncannily similar version of Anna's story. Anna had been deported for unwittingly entering the country more times than was permitted without a resident's visa back in 2010. It took a Herculean effort and a significant amount of money before she was allowed back into Scotland – a country that needs all the well-educated, intelligent, hard-working people who want to live here that we can take in. Odd, also, that he is called Ewan, the name I chose for myself in Anna's book. When we were loading the books into the van, it emerged that the people who live in the dairy cottage are Ewan's brother Will and his girlfriend Emma. Emma worked in the shop for a summer about five years ago and is now a doctor in Dumfries.

The books were boxed, so, rather than go through them, I took them away and we agreed that I would sort through them later. It took two trips in the van to shift them, but thankfully there were a few of us so it didn't take too long.

There was a piece in today's *Guardian* about living in Wigtown called 'Let's move to Wigtown and the Machars peninsula'. It was subtitled 'A little backwater, in the best sense of the word' and included in the text was the following sentence: 'There is always a friendly welcome wherever you go.' The shop's Facebook page was bombarded by comments like 'They clearly haven't been in your shop' and 'Obviously they haven't met you.'

Anna and I took down the Christmas decorations in the shop after we had unloaded the boxes of books from the van. Hardly a great ordeal, considering how pathetic my efforts to celebrate Christmas were. Being Jewish, Anna was probably the only person in Wigtown less interested in Christmas than I was. Apart from Nicky.

Till total £63.98
12 customers

MONDAY, 5 JANUARY

Online orders: 4
Books found: 4

Opened the shop at 9 a.m. By 2 p.m. the door had been opened just three times: first by Kate, the postie; second by my father, delivering a newspaper; and third by the howling wind about five minutes after my father, who hadn't shut the door properly.

As I was picking the orders, I found Captain staring despondently out of the window. Two weeks after the shortest day is a depressing time, whether you are a cat or a bookseller.

I spent much of the day going through the boxes of books from the farmhouse, which were almost without exception disappointing.

Peter Bestel came round in the afternoon to discuss technical problems with the Random Book Club web site. Despite getting thirty-two new subscribers in December on the back of zero advertising, I have been putting off marketing it because the database management system we set up in 2013 isn't best suited to dealing with the complications thrown up by people giving a subscription as a gift, or not renewing etc., so until we sort these problems out I don't intend to seek out new members.

By 3 p.m. I was giving up hope of having even one sale when the Robinsons, a large local farming family, came in and bought some books. Ken, who had recently married into the clan, found a book about St Kilda that he had been waiting for me to reduce in price. I had spotted him looking at it a few times, so after his last visit I raised the price from £40 to £45. He wasn't very pleased but bought it anyway. I reduced it back to £40.

Till total £50
2 customers

TUESDAY, 6 JANUARY

Online orders: 1
Books found: 0

In today's Amazon messages was one complaining about *The Universal Singular*, a book that we had an order for a week or so ago: 'The edges (especially the upper one) is covered with a thick layer of mould – which is a serious health risk to handle the book. It is now sealed and had to be removed out of the building.'

I sent an unnecessarily sarcastic reply that I would arrange for someone in an ebola suit to come and collect it from her, since she considered it such a threat to her health.

Till total £70.47
7 customers

WEDNESDAY, 7 JANUARY

Online orders: 3
Books found: 2

Wild, wet and windy day.

Another very quiet day. Three people came in after lunch. They were visiting from Rutland Water, where they are running an osprey project. They wanted to see what we have done with our (formerly) resident pair of ospreys. One of them bought a reprint of *Bradshaw's Rail Times 1895*.

At 4 p.m. Tracy dropped in to say hello. She is now working in a pub in Newton Stewart.

A young couple came in at 3.55 p.m. and spent an hour and a half sitting by the fire reading things they had pulled off the shelves. At 5.25 p.m. I told them that the shop was closed. They left without buying anything and abandoned the huge pile of books by the fire.

Submitted the grant application to James Patterson's web site. It looks pretty good, and I am quietly confident, which is almost a guarantee that it won't be successful.

Till total £46.99
6 customers

THURSDAY, 8 JANUARY

Online orders: 3
Books found: 3

Further exciting developments in the saga of the mouldy copy of *The Universal Singular.*

Here is her reply to my sarcastic request for her address so that I could send someone in an ebola suit to collect it:

The address is:
Satellite 13RTX77 – X11
Venus orbit 3
Milky Way

I spent the first half hour re-shelving the piles of books that the couple who sat by the fire yesterday had built up.

Depressing news today was that last year global revenue from digital downloads of music overtook CD sales. As music, books and films are probably the three media that can most easily and cheaply be digitised, it seems as though it can only be a matter of time before our trade goes the same way, although it is reassuring that large numbers of people who visit the shop tell me that they much prefer the physical pleasure of reading a book, and dislike Kindles. The Kindle that I shot and mounted on a shield is, without question, the most photographed object in the shop.

Anna reminded me that I promised to take her to see *Into the Woods* in Glasgow tomorrow. She is incredibly excited about it. I am dreading it.

Till total £36.49
10 customers

FRIDAY, 9 JANUARY

Online orders: 1
Books found: 1

Nicky in, wearing her black ski suit as usual. After lunch she set to work on processing the remainder of the books from the farmhouse. She was far from impressed with the contents, which were mostly ex-library, many in Arabic, and a large number of autobiographies of vapid celebrities. She estimated that she was keeping one in thirty. I am not sure what to tell Ewan.

Anna has decided that we should produce a bookshop music video version of 'Rappers' Delight' but rewrite the lyrics to make it 'Readers' Delight' so we spent much of the morning doing that.

After saying goodbye to Nicky, Anna and I drove to Glasgow to watch *Into the Woods*. My expectations were extremely low, yet even they were not met. It was diabolical, and Anna was so upset that she suggested we leave early. Home at about 9 p.m. to find Nicky still in her ski suit, drinking my beer.

Till total £41.99
5 customers

SATURDAY, 10 JANUARY

Online orders: 2
Books found: 2

Nicky opened the shop.

In the morning I went to The Picture Shop in Wigtown to see about framing a print I had bought at auction last year. I was shocked to find Jessie, the owner, in her chair, looking very ill. She is keen to go to hospital, as she says she can no longer look after herself. Anna was worried and went to tell the doctor that he ought to visit her. Jessie is in her eighties, but works every day in her shop. She is the only person still alive to have been born in a house in the Mull of Galloway – the peninsula west of the Machars – before the hospital opened in Stranraer and the maternity unit was set up.

Anna, Nicky and I spent much of the day rehearsing our lyrics for 'Readers' Delight'. The Bestels came over for supper, and we worked out a loose choreography. The plan is to film it next Friday. Nicky is MC Spanner.

In the afternoon a customer dropped off two boxes of books, among which was a copy of *Chattering*, by Louise Stern. Louise came to the book festival in 2011 and was utterly wonderful. She is deaf and doesn't speak. For most of the time when she was in Wigtown she had a signing interpreter, but in his absence she communicated by scribbling on bits of paper. The day after her event she told me that she wanted to go for a swim in the sea, so I took her to Monreith and we braved the October waters. The evening she first arrived in Wigtown she turned up in the Writers' Retreat at about 10 p.m. There were quite a few of us there, and a lot of wine had been drunk. Her arrival brought with it a slight sobering of the atmosphere, purely because very few of us had encountered anyone who was deaf and didn't speak. She sensed the tension and suggested that we each take it in turns to ask one another a question. She pointed at me, and Oliver (her interpreter) signed my nervously pedestrian question 'Did you have a good journey here?' to her. She replied, 'Yes, thank you. My turn. When did you lose your virginity?', at which point the atmosphere instantly turned back to the bawdy ribaldry it had been before her arrival.

Later that night at about 2 a.m., having drunk a fair bit, she attempted to return to her accommodation, but having no idea where it was (other than a key with the number 3 on it), she wandered around until she found a house with the same number on the door. She tried the key but it didn't work, so she banged on the door until a bleary-eyed man in a string vest appeared and asked what she wanted. She made some sounds and started waving her arms. He swore at her and slammed the door in her face. Thankfully, she had been the last person to leave the Writers' Retreat and hadn't locked the door behind her, so she was able to get back into the house and make some sort of a bed for herself on a sofa. At 7 a.m. the following day when Janette (who cleans the Retreat during the festival) turned up to tidy the room; she spotted the sleeping Louise on the sofa and tiptoed around her, silently clearing up. At 8 a.m. Twigger came down from his room. On seeing Janette, he bellowed 'Morning Janette', at which point Janette put her index finger to her mouth and shushed him, pointing to the recumbent Louise. Twigger looked at her and said, 'Don't worry, Janette, she's deaf. Look.' He then walked over to Louise and shouted 'Wake up' right next to her face. There was, of course, no reaction whatsoever, so Janette got the hoover out and began the task of clearing up the carnage from the previous night while Louise slept silently on.

Till total £149
9 customers

MONDAY, 12 JANUARY

Online orders: 4
Books found: 4

The printer ran out of ink after printing off two orders, so I replaced it with a non-proprietary cartridge that resulted in the computer freezing with a message from HP that the machine will only work with branded cartridges. I've ordered two more, but this means that these orders won't go out until Wednesday, so will probably result in negative feedback.

The 'mouldy' book was returned in today's post. It is not mouldy at all. I emailed the purchaser to thank her for returning it and told her that 'mould is in the eye of the beholder' and asked her what life on Venus was like.

Anna went to The Picture Shop to check up on Jessie and returned with the news that she is now in hospital in Newton Stewart. We will go and visit her on Wednesday.

I carried on trawling through Ewan's books. It is such a strange mix that I felt compelled to ask him where they came from.

The mouldy book customer replied to my email:

Not too bad, but I did prefer living on the other planet, which unfortunately is gone now.

Here, we never see stars, days stretch for ages. The screensaver over our heads is orange red, disguising, and it does not change much ... Something possibly went wrong with her Highness Ithess who is in charge here.

I have to go now; using computers is strictly forbidden outside of the Temple.

The Bookshop Band (Ben and Beth) have taken on the residency of The Open Book as its first proprietors. Anna, Eliot and Finn took the idea on and have set it up, so we had them over for supper, along with our good friend Richard. He and I grew up in Galloway and have been friends since childhood. He is an actor, based in London. The last time I saw him he was in a production of *The Tempest* directed by Sam Mendes in New York.

Till total £61.50
4 customers

TUESDAY, 13 JANUARY

Online orders: 2
Books found: 1

Flo came in to cover the shop so that Anna and I could attend the auction in Dumfries. I bought another commode and a stuffed squirrel. Anna bought a bay lot (essentially the equivalent of a box full of junk) for £3, the minimum bid in the saleroom. Whenever the price drops to this, her hand automatically shoots up in what appears to be an involuntary reflex. Lord knows what rubbish she has bought this time.

It snowed all the way back from the auction; very cold afternoon. On returning to the shop I discovered that four boxes of books had been dropped off by Samye Ling.

Till total £51
4 customers

WEDNESDAY, 14 JANUARY

Online orders: 5
Books found: 4

Before I opened the shop, I dropped off the van at the garage for a service. I had forgotten about it, so it meant we had no vehicle and couldn't visit Jessie. When I told Vincent that Jessie was in hospital, he assured me that he would service the van as quickly as possible.

The Shearings coach tour turned up at about 11 a.m. Normally a swarm of miserly pensioners shuffles from the bus and invades the shop. They never buy anything, grab everything that's free and complain about the prices, but today the only one who came in was a young woman who was polite and interesting and even bought some books. I asked her if they had kidnapped her. She looked blankly back at me, then slowly backed towards the door.

In the afternoon a customer spent about an hour wandering

around the shop. He finally came to the counter and said, 'I never buy second-hand books. You don't know who else has touched them, or where they've been.' Apart from being an irritating thing to say to a second-hand bookseller, who knows whose hands have touched the books in the shop? Doubtless everyone from ministers to murderers. For many that secret history of provenance is a source of excitement which fires their imagination. A friend and I once discussed annotations and marginalia in books. Again, they are a divisive issue. We occasionally have Amazon orders returned because the recipient has discovered notes in a book, scribbled by previous readers, which we had not spotted. To me these things do not detract but are captivating additions – a glimpse into the mind of another person who has read the same book.

Till total £77.80
8 customers

THURSDAY, 15 JANUARY

Online orders: 4
Books found: 2

Wild and windy again today, but on a positive note, the gutter didn't leak into the house.

The first customer of the day asked 'Who wrote *To Kill a Mockingbird*?' I told her it was Harper Lee, to which she replied, 'Are you sure it wasn't J. D. Salinger?'

At 3 p.m. the telephone rang. It was a journalist at *The Observer* who wanted to discuss the proposed wind farm.

I shut the shop at 3.30 p.m. and drove with Anna to Newton Stewart to visit Jessie in the hospital. She was in excellent spirits and we got back at 4 p.m. so I opened for the last hour. There were no customers.

Till total £30
3 customers

FRIDAY, 16 JANUARY

Online orders: 4
Books found: 4

It was snowing when I opened the shop. Nicky was twenty minutes late as a consequence. She took one look at the commode that I had bought on Tuesday and said, 'That thing'll never sell.'

We picked the orders then walked through our positions for 'Readers' Delight'. Peter, his wife, Heather, and their daughter Zoe arrived at 2.30 p.m. and we filmed it. It took three takes before we managed to get a completely perfect version. There will be no edits, at Anna's insistence. Poor Peter, who was filming for us, had to walk backwards for the entire time.

Matthew (regular book dealer from London) came to the shop while we were filming and looked nonplussed. He spent £300.

The accountant telephoned to tell me that I haven't signed and returned my tax return for last year, so I frantically scrambled around my chaotic filing system until I found the relevant paperwork, signed it and posted it back to him.

Nicky stayed the night and regaled us with wondrous tales of some of the treasures she has unearthed both metal-detecting and in the Morrisons skip.

Till total £313
3 customers

SATURDAY, 17 JANUARY

Online orders: 2
Books found: 2

Nicky opened the shop. I was putting books on the shelves when a customer accosted me with a book and asked how much it was. I told him it was £3.50. He looked at me, then pointed at Nicky, who was wearing her ski suit and brushing her teeth behind the counter, and said, 'I'll pay your wife, shall I?' Nicky dropped her toothbrush in horror, and I dropped the book I was holding at the same time.

I left Nicky packing the random books for this month's mailing, and Anna and I went for a walk in the morning before the snow melted and the light and landscape changed. When we returned an hour later, Nicky hadn't even started on the boxes of random books, but she had hijacked the shop Facebook page again and posted the following message:

> Craigard Gallery have just delivered home-made, fruit-laden Chelsea buns (the size of a medium turnip) drenched in cream cheese & cinnamon! That's what OUR neighbours are like – what about YOURS?

Finished *Satyricon* and went to bed at midnight.

Till total £44.50
8 customers

MONDAY, 19 JANUARY

Online orders: 3
Books found: 2

Awoke to a message on my telephone from Callum telling me that I was quoted in *The Observer* yesterday in a piece about the proposed wind farm on the other side of the bay, which the developer – for reasons best known to themselves, no doubt – have decided to call California Farm. Shortly afterwards, the person on whose land it is to be built, and who stands to benefit most financially, appeared in the shop to discuss my objections. He began by telling me, 'I'm not here to try to change your mind', then spent the next three hours trying to change my mind. Anna was very impressive dealing with him, asking him how much he was going to be paid for allowing them to be built on his land (over three times what the rest of the community will receive every year) and whether he would be able to see them from any of the properties on his estate. He looked at the floor and sheepishly answered that they would not be visible from any of the numerous properties he owns.

Anna's love of Galloway is passionate and deep, and she is determined both to market the region to the world and to protect it from anything that she perceives might prove detrimental to it, particularly to the tourist industry, on which so much of the local economy depends.

Today we had another order for a book that Nicky listed recently in her new astronomy/physics shelf. As with the last one, it wasn't there. When I dropped off the orders with Wilma in the post office at 10 a.m., I asked if she would be good enough to send the postman over to collect the random books later. William was in the middle of berating her for some minor misdemeanour when I arrived.

The commode sold at 11 a.m. Nicky will be furious.

I seem to have acquired a virus, doubtless picked up from a customer, and I passed the day coughing, sneezing, hugging the radiator and shivering. It is always seen as the curse of the teacher, being exposed to germy children and constantly being ill, but it applies equally to anyone who works in a shop. Customers enjoy sharing their ailments with us.

After lunch I telephoned Smurfit Kappa, who seem quite happy for me to drop off a van load of dead stock for recycling any time, so I'll go next week when I have sorted through the last of the 2,000 boxes from the farmhouse, most of which are only good for recycling.

Posted 'Readers' Delight' video on Facebook at 3 p.m.

Till total £99.99
7 customers

TUESDAY, 20 JANUARY

Online orders: 3
Books found: 2

Email from my cousin who lives in Greece to let me know that the shop was featured in a Greek book blog. Once, shortly after I had bought the shop, a Northern Irishman accosted me as I was putting books out and asked, 'Do you have a copy of the Greek New Testament?' When I told him that I didn't have a copy in stock, he replied, 'No self-respecting bookshop could fail to have a Greek New Testament.' I muttered something about him being welcome to his opinion and carried on about my business. When he left, armed with a few books on Calvinism, he had the decency to apologise and compliment me on the shop's stock, particularly the theology section.

The old ladies appeared at 1 p.m. for their art class.

The postman picked up the five sacks of random books at 4 p.m.

Till total £22.50
4 customers

WEDNESDAY, 21 JANUARY

Online orders: 1
Books found: 1

At lunchtime I received a telephone call from another bookshop interested in one of our books. The Monsoon software we use to manage our online stock is reasonably widely used in online book-selling, so I assumed that she would have heard of it. Monsoon froze while I was trying to find information about the book and still on the telephone, so I apologised and explained that we were having a problem with Monsoon. She replied, 'What? Really? You've had a monsoon? Oh, I am sorry to hear that.'

Picked up a copy of Auden's *Collected Works* and flicked through to 'As I Walked Out One Evening', one of my favourite poems. I have resolved to learn it by the end of the month.

Till total £57.97
4 customers

THURSDAY, 22 JANUARY

Online orders: 1
Books found: 1

The order this morning was for a Second World War book. As I was going through the shelves looking for it, I came across *Colonial Campaigns of the Nineteenth Century* and *Saddam's War*, as well as *The Armies of Wellington*, all in the Second World War section. They were clearly put there by Nicky. When I mention it to her tomorrow, I can guarantee that her explanation will be, 'Well, there wasnae any space in the military section, and it's all about fighting. Customers will understand.'

At 2 p.m. a customer walked in and demanded a copy of Barnard's *The Whisky Distilleries of the United Kingdom*. This is a title that was reprinted in 2008 by Birlinn, and of which I bought several copies (I had a first edition from the Loch Lomond deal back in December). I told the customer we had five copies, upon hearing which he turned on his heel, said 'Hmph' and left.

The thermal curtains and poles I ordered last week arrived, so I spent much of the day putting them up in the draughty corners of the shop in the hope that at night they will trap some of what little heat there is.

It snowed from about 3 p.m. onwards, which inevitably means that people are less inclined to travel and that there are fewer customers.

At 4.30 p.m. a friend from the other side of Wigtown Bay called around. He had heard that we were not too happy with the idea of the wind farm. He lives right in the middle of the proposed site and estimates that if it goes ahead it will reduce the value of his house to almost nothing.

Ewan replied to my email about the 2,000 books from the farmhouse. He is not expecting anything for them, which is a relief. He told me that they came from a cousin's father, who had come to London from Pakistan when he was young, then cut all ties with everyone he knew. His existence was only discovered by his family when the authorities informed them of his death.

Till total £40.50
5 customers

FRIDAY, 23 JANUARY

Online orders: 1
Books found: 1

Heavy rain and freezing cold all day today. Nicky arrived at 9.15 a.m., as usual. I was vaguely jealous of her Canadian ski suit. She told me that she has been ill all week with a fever, and by Wednesday she was hallucinating: 'Aye, it was great. Just like the old days.' The first thing she did was to enthuse sarcastically about the new thermal curtains I have hung throughout the shop – 'Oh, aye, they're lovely. They look like they're from a Barratt show home in a suburb of Swindon. Ya tube.'

Fortunately her illness prevented her from raiding the Morrisons skip, so there was no Foodie Friday this week.

Mr Deacon came in and bought a copy of Lucy Inglis's *Georgian London* which we had in a window display. His left arm was in plaster, but I didn't ask why, and he offered no explanation.

A woman in China emailed this morning. She blogs about books and has seen 'Readers' Delight'. She asked for permission to share it on the Chinese equivalent of YouTube, so I told her that I would be more than happy if she did. She seems to be the Chinese Jen Campbell, travelling around bookshops and writing about them. I have invited her to come and stay here.

When I gave Nicky the paperwork for the orders that I couldn't find during the week, she immediately blamed Bethan – who hasn't worked here since September – for putting the books on the wrong shelves.

Anna and I went to visit Jessie in hospital again. She looks much better and had a stream of visitors. Her latest news is that Chris, her husband, has been admitted to Dumfries Infirmary with a heart attack. The poor man's mother died a couple of days ago, aged 106.

Nicky decided to go home rather than stay overnight, because she wasn't feeling well.

Till total £118.95
8 customers

SATURDAY, 24 JANUARY

Online orders: 3
Books found: 2

The sun was shining when I opened the shop, but by 11 a.m. it was grey. Nicky almost arrived on time. She spent the day complaining about having had the flu during the week and stealing my pain-killers and cough medicine.

Till total £447.05
15 customers

MONDAY, 26 JANUARY

Online orders: 6
Books found: 5

Sandy the tattooed pagan came in at 2 p.m., stayed until 4 p.m. and bought a few books on Scottish folklore. While he was browsing, the depressed Welsh woman telephoned. This time she had found a copy of *Ciceronis Opera* from 1642 that we were selling online, so I couldn't pretend that our stock was devoid of anything in her field. She asked if she could pay for it with a credit card over the telephone, and when I asked for her name and address she replied, 'Dafydd Williams'. So, it was a depressed Welsh man all along.

The Open Book is being run this week by a woman from the Isle of Lewis called Ishi. She is thinking of opening a bookshop there and is here to test the water. Mac TV are going to be filming her during the week as part of a documentary for BBC Alba. She came over for supper. It turns out that she has been running tourists trails in Africa for two years, during which she recently contracted typhoid. She is past the period when it is still contagious, but Anna – ever paranoid about her health – visibly recoiled when Ishi announced this.

Till total £12.99
5 customers

TUESDAY, 27 JANUARY

Online orders:
Books found:

Nicky was in, fashionably late as usual.

Monsoon decided to do an upgrade, and now we can't open it, so I have no idea if we had any orders today or not.

Art class was on this afternoon, so I lit the fire at noon, only to be given a lecture by one of the ladies about how much hotter her wood burning stove is than mine. This week the class is learning portraiture and had a very pretty model. When I was attending the class several years ago, the model for our portraiture lesson was an eighty-year-old man who died while we were painting him.

Nicky took a telephone call from a customer who asked, 'What side of the street are you on?' – a question that clearly depends on which direction you are approaching from. He drove to the shop with a car load of books to sell. Nicky rejected them all.

Heavy snow forecast for tomorrow.

Till total £110
5 customers

WEDNESDAY 28 JANUARY

Online orders: 7
Books found: 6

Monsoon was working again this morning, so today we had two days' worth of orders to deal with.

Till total £90.50
5 customers

THURSDAY, 29 JANUARY

Online orders: 6
Books found: 5

Nicky was in today, and was her usual chirpy self.

Just before lunch a customer came in. Within moments of her

arrival Nicky and I were gasping for air. She must have doused herself thoroughly in a perfume so utterly and horribly choking that I can only assume that it was developed in a chemical weapons laboratory by a particularly sadistic scientist during the Cold War.

Very quiet day in the shop, so even the toxic chemical woman was greeted with feigned enthusiasm. It snowed from about 3 p.m. onwards.

Till total £32

3 customers

FRIDAY, 30 JANUARY

Online orders: 6

Books found: 5

Nicky was back in again. Following her illness, she appears to have forgotten about Foodie Friday, much to my relief.

While I was looking for a book – one of today's orders – I discovered a copy of Rudyard Kipling's *Barrack-Room Ballads* in the Scottish poetry section, *The Rubaiyat of Omar Khayyam* in the history section and *Journal of the Waterloo Campaigns* in the First World War section. I have given up trying to understand how Nicky's mind works.

The worst customer today was a balding man with a yellow ponytail who spent an hour breathing heavily in the erotica section, and thumbed his way through nearly everything with illustrations. He left without buying anything. In fact, I wonder whether it was a good thing that he left empty-handed, thus sparing me any sort of social interaction with him.

Till total £107

7 customers

SATURDAY, 31 JANUARY

Online orders: 5
Books found: 5

Nicky was in again: that makes three days in a row. I was ready to
be sectioned by closing time.

Managed to recite 'As I Walked Out One Evening' to myself.

Till total £383
12 customers

FEBRUARY

The combines can never squeeze the small independent bookseller out of existence as they have squeezed the grocer and the milkman. But the hours of work are very long – I was only a part-time employee, but my employer put in a seventy-hour week, apart from constant expeditions out of hours to buy books – and it is an unhealthy life. As a rule a bookshop is horribly cold in winter, because if it is too warm the windows get misted over, and a bookseller lives on his windows. And books give off more and nastier dust than any other class of objects yet invented, and the top of a book is the place where every bluebottle prefers to die.

George Orwell, 'Bookshop Memories'

The 'combines' of which Orwell speaks did indeed come to squeeze the small independent booksellers almost out of existence: Ottakar's, Waterstones and Dillons tried to do precisely that. Now two of those three have been squeezed out of existence themselves, and the last man standing, Waterstones, faces a perilous future thanks to that combine-of-combines, Amazon. Waterstones has attempted to become a bedfellow with 'the everything store' by selling Kindles in its shops, but when you sup with the devil you need a long spoon, and no spoon – not even the longest available in the Amazon 'Kitchen and Home' department – is, I suspect, quite long enough to prevent Waterstones from getting a little too close to Amazon for its own good.

There is no doubt, though, that bookshops – mine in any case – can be bitterly cold places in winter. Mine, not because of the risk of the windows misting up, but rather because it is a vast, doorless place with little insulation and draughts that whistle through it like the spirits of dead writers. Winter trade is too sparse to allow for anything more than a couple of hours a day with the heating on.

MONDAY, 2 FEBRUARY

Online orders: 7
Books found: 5

Mac TV telephoned to organise the film shoot for Wednesday. I spoke to Ishi and arranged to meet her here at the shop at 2 p.m. on Wednesday to have a conversation about what the reality of running a second-hand bookshop is like.

Telephone call this morning:

> Caller: 'Hello! Hello! I think I have got the wrong number, is that Allison Motors?'
> Me: 'You have got the wrong number, this is The Book Shop.'
> Caller: 'Never mind, you might be able to help. Have you got an alternator for a Vauxhall Nova?'

It was dark outside when I locked up, but the days are getting noticeably longer now.

Till total £32.50
5 customers

TUESDAY, 3 FEBRUARY

Online orders: 2
Books found: 1

One of this morning's orders was for *British Trees: A Guide for Everyman*. According to Nicky's locator code, this is filed under Scottish poetry.

After lunch I drove to Newton Stewart for a meeting with the accountant. He surprised me by telling me that – after a few precarious years – this set of accounts is looking considerably healthier. It certainly feels like I am working harder than I did when I bought the business fourteen years ago, but I suppose now more time is spent listing books on the computer, and competition online is fierce, whereas back then, that side of the business was relatively small in comparison. Still, whatever is required to keep the ship afloat will be done. This life is infinitely preferable to working for someone else.

A very irritating man with a greasy moustache bought a set of Victorian leather-bound *Waverley* novels for £110. When I gave him a £20 discount, he replied, 'Is that all?'

Putting books out in the Scottish paperbacks section this afternoon, I spotted a copy of Robin Jenkins's *The Cone Gatherers*. Started reading it after supper.

Till total £141
5 customers

WEDNESDAY, 4 FEBRUARY 2015

Online orders: 5
Books found: 4

Nicky came in so that I could head up to Edinburgh to look at a private library in the afternoon.

We failed to locate a book about medieval Gothic art that Nicky had listed as being in the India section.

In the afternoon the film crew arrived and we filmed part of the documentary that Ishi is presenting. The shop was funereally silent all day until the moment the crew started filming, at which point customers suddenly started flooding in, asking questions and tripping over cables. One tall, elderly man in a crumpled black suit made a particular nuisance of himself before settling down in front of the fire. As I passed him to put a book in the poetry section, I noticed that he had removed his false teeth and put them on top of a copy of Tony Blair's autobiography which had been left on the table.

While we were filming, I spotted Nicky grubbing around

in a box of books that I had earmarked for the recycling plant in Glasgow. She and I had a discussion about death. Nicky: 'If I die before Armageddon, my pal George is going to make me a coffin out of an old pallet, put me in the back of my van and dump me in the woods somewhere.' I told her that I want a Viking ship burial, to which she responded, 'Ye cannae do that. The only way around it is to have a Romany funeral. You'll have to build yourself a caravan and set fire to it. Oh, wait, you'll be dead. You'll have to get someone else to set fire to it.'

When the old man in the crumpled suit came to the counter to pay for the copy of Dostoevsky's *The Idiot*, I discreetly pointed out that his fly was open. He glanced down – as if for confirmation of this – then looked back at me and said, 'A dead bird can't fall out of its nest', and left the shop, fly still agape.

Mr Deacon came in at 4 p.m. to order a book, *The Princes in the Tower* by Alison Weir. His arm is no longer in plaster. Today's exchange was typically brief and pragmatic until I had a coughing fit as he was on the point of leaving. He said, 'You have my sympathy, I am ill too.' Curious to find out what his ailment was, I took the unprecedented step of inquiring, to which he replied, 'Alzheimer's. Can't remember words very well these days.' Following this rather sad revelation we had the first conversation about his life that we have ever had, other than the announcement that the companions he once brought to the shop were his daughters. He had been a barrister and was finding his inability to find the correct words deeply frustrating.

I left the shop at 4.30 p.m. to go to Edinburgh. As the door swung shut behind me, I turned around to see Nicky sellotaping another of her home-made labels onto the edge of a shelf. It appears that 'Home Front Novels' have made an unwelcome return.

Till total £18.50
4 customers

EPILOGUE

The diary was written in 2014, and today is 1 November 2016: fifteen years to the day since I bought the shop. Since I completed the first draft of the diary, almost two years have elapsed, and a few things have changed.

The distillery has recently re-opened, and an Australian businessman is overhauling it with a view to significantly increasing production.

The Box of Frogs (the shop next door) changed hands a year ago and is now Curly Tale Books, run by Jayne (Flo's mother).

The Wigtown Ploughman has changed hands and is now Craft Hotel.

Captain has continued to put on weight, and customers rarely fail to comment on his size.

In 2015 Waterstones stopped selling Kindles, following poor sales and a resurgence in print book sales.

The Open Book continues to attract visitors and runs under the umbrella of the Wigtown Festival Company. It has surpassed everyone's most optimistic expectations in the success that it has proved to be. Residents have come from as far afield as Canada, the Americas (both North and South), France, Spain, Italy, New Zealand and Taiwan. Many of them have returned for holidays in Wigtown and the area, and, with a couple of exceptions, they have all adored it. It is fully booked for the next eighteen months.

Nicky has found another job, closer to her hovel, and now works in the Keystore in Glenluce selling lottery tickets, cigarettes and cheap cider.

Laurie is a chocolatier and lives in Glasgow.

Katie has finished medical school and is working as a doctor in Falkirk hospital.

Flo is charming her way through Edinburgh University.

Eliot continues to do an excellent job of programming the Wigtown Book Festival, which grows year on year.

Jessie from The Picture Shop sadly died a few days after the end of the diary.

I have only seen Mr Deacon once since he told me about his

Alzheimer's. He had undergone a significant decline, and clearly didn't recognise me.

Anna and I have gone our separate ways, but remain good friends.

The shop is still open.